THE
REYNOLDS
CAMPAIGN
ON POWDER RIVER

THE REYNOLDS CAMPAIGN ON POWDER RIVER

By J. W. Vaughn

UNIVERSITY OF OKLAHOMA PRESS
Norman

By J. W. Vaughn
With Crook at the Rosebud (Harrisburg, Pennsylvania, 1956)
The Reynolds Campaign on Powder River (Norman, 1961)

Library of Congress Catalog Card Number: 61-15149

Copyright 1961 by the University of Oklahoma Press,
Publishing Division of the University.
Composed and printed at Norman, Oklahoma, U.S.A.,
by the University of Oklahoma Press. First edition.

Dedicated to my sister Rebecca

INTRODUCTION

WHEN the Civil War commenced, all available troops were diverted to the East, leaving only skeleton forces to guard the western frontier. The Sioux and Cheyenne Indians, taking advantage of the situation, increased their raids upon emigrant trains and the border settlements. In retaliation, a large force under Brigadier General Alfred Sully attacked villages of Teton Sioux at Killdeer Mountain, in July, 1864, and, after a battle lasting three days, inflicted severe losses upon the Indians, compelling them to move farther west. In the following November, volunteer troops under Colonel Chivington destroyed a village of Southern Cheyennes at Sand Creek, in eastern Colorado, killing many warriors, women, and children. The survivors and other bands moved northward and joined the camps of the Northern Cheyennes and Sioux in the Powder River country. In the spring, the combined tribes declared war against the white man. After many attacks on the border stations by small war parties, the warriors from the big encampment fought the soldiers at Platte Bridge Station in July, 1865, suffering severe losses. The Indians split up, most of them returning to their home lodges in the north, while small war parties continued the harassment of border settlements and emigrant trains on the Oregon Trail.

When the army established Fort Reno, Fort Phil Kearny, and Fort C. F. Smith in 1866 along the Bozeman Trail which ran northward into Montana, the hostile Indians resented this intrusion into their territory, and made continuous war upon the forts. After several years of border warfare, highlighted by the Fetterman Massacre and the Wagon Box Fight, near Fort Phil Kearny, the treaty of 1868 was entered into at Fort Laramie. The government agreed to abandon the Bozeman Trail forts while permitting the Indians to retain their territory north of the North Platte River, including the Black Hills. The Indians could either live on the reservations, supported by the government, or continue their roving existence, living upon the game they found. The treaty worked out fairly well. Although the government failed to provide adequate subsistence for Indians on the reservations, and several Indian bands were punished for depredations committed by their young warriors, hostilities had temporarily ended. The Southern Cheyenne village of Black Kettle was destroyed in November, 1868, at the Washita River in Oklahoma, while on July 11, 1869, a Cheyenne village was attacked at Summit Springs in Colorado. Several expeditions were sent by the army into the Yellowstone country, which naturally provoked a number of skirmishes with the resident Sioux Indians.

The uncertain peace continued until the expedition of General Custer discovered gold in the Black Hills, the sacred territory of the Sioux, in the summer of 1874. Since the resulting gold rush was a violation of the treaty rights of the Indians, the government, through the Allison commission, attempted to buy the Black Hills. On the failure of this attempt, the Indian Bureau ordered the tribes back to the reservations, apparently on the theory that, while there, the Indians would be easier to deal with and would be unable to protect their property. When they failed to return by the deadline, January 31, 1876, the Indian Bureau, in response to public opinion, turned the matter over to the army.

As the hostile warriors were believed to number only from 500 to 800, it was thought that a winter campaign against them would be successful, since the Indian ponies would be weak from lack of forage. General George Crook, who shared this opinion, was ordered to lead an expedition northward from Fort Fetterman to compel the hostiles to return to the reservations. On March 1, he

Introduction

set out with a force of ten companies of cavalry and two companies of infantry, a total of 883 men. After a long march in very cold weather and over rugged terrain, a portion of the column under Colonel Joseph J. Reynolds surprised a village of Cheyenne Indians on Powder River in southern Montana on March 17. The soldiers, who thought they had struck the village of the great Oglala chief, Crazy Horse, burned the tipis and captured the pony herd; but after a fight lasting five hours were driven back. The Indians recaptured most of their ponies, and Crook marched back to Fort Fetterman.

This engagement, like the Killdeer and Sand Creek battles of 1864, started a new cycle of conflict in which column after column was thrown against the Indians, resulting in the bloody fields of the Rosebud, Little Big Horn, Slim Buttes, Dull Knife village, Wolf Mountain, and many lesser encounters. By 1879 the Sioux and Cheyennes were completely subjugated and had been herded onto the reservations. A few friendly Indians signed a new treaty giving the Black Hills to the government without compensation, bringing the war cycle to a close.

This is the story of the expedition of General Crook into the frozen north and the attack on the Cheyenne village by Colonel Reynolds. The little drama was enacted against the backdrop of the frenzied gold rush to the Black Hills. Although an obscure episode, lacking the glamour and popular appeal of the Rosebud and Little Big Horn battles, it was one of the most important events in western history. While marking the decision of the government, in response to popular clamor, to force a final showdown with the hostile Indians, it was the beginning of the end for those bands who opposed the surging tide of white civilization. Because the results of the campaign were indecisive, the high command, which held all Indians in contempt, blamed Reynolds for failing to drive these back onto the reservations. The ensuing controversy resulted in court-martial proceedings which set comrade against comrade while lifelong friendships were forgotten. It might be said that if the soldiers had fought as hard against the enemy as they later fought among themselves, they would have won a sweeping victory.

The details of the fighting at the village have been obscured by conflicting reports and the passage of the years.

In the summer of 1957, I first visited the site of the engagement on historic Powder River, surrounded by the rugged grandeur of many-colored mountains and buttes dotted with pine trees. This is the heart of the Indian country; and anyone who has seen the wild beauty of the Tongue, the Rosebud, and the Powder will understand why the Indians fought to remain there. Deciding to reconstruct the battle, I obtained all known accounts and a microfilm copy of the court-martial records from the National Archives. Armed with the sketch maps of Captain Mills and Captain Noyes and an aerial photograph of the area, I returned to the field many times and made a complete coverage with a metal detector, finding cartridge cases, bullets, and other debris marking battle positions. I also consulted persons having knowledge of the affair.

From all the information obtained, a highly detailed and completely factual account of the action has been compiled. Where the evidence is conflicting, an opinion is expressed as to which is correct. Graphic statements of eyewitnesses are quoted throughout, and their expressions and phraseology are used wherever possible to recapture their thought and mood. Although the battle is described at length from the point of view of the soldiers, the Indian side of the engagement is included in Chapter VII, and is shorter only because of lack of material. It is hoped that both the soldiers' and Indians' points of view have been presented with a sympathetic understanding of each.

I am indebted to the General Services Administration in the National Archives for furnishing microfilm of the court-martial records, to the Nebraska State Historical Society for supplying a microfilm copy of the Ricker *Interviews,* and to the Library of the United States Military Academy for permitting the use of material from the diary of Lieutenant John G. Bourke.

Charles D. Roberts, brigadier general U. S. Army, retired, of Chevy Chase, Maryland, a friend of General Crook in his youth, has read the manuscript and made valuable suggestions. Mari Sandoz, of New York City, has graciously contributed material

Introduction

bearing upon the identity of the Indians in the village. Our friends, Slim Frandsen and Lucille Frandsen, of Moorehead, Montana, provided my wife and me with suitable quarters and creature comforts during our visits to the field and guided us on trips about the area. To all others who have aided this project, and their numbers are legion, I am truly grateful.

J. W. Vaughn

Windsor, Colorado
July 17, 1961

CONTENTS

			page	vii
		INTRODUCTION		vii
Chapter	1	GOLD IN THE BLACK HILLS		3
	2	CONCENTRATION AT FORT FETTERMAN		20
	3	THE MARCH TO POWDER RIVER		43
	4	THE ATTACK ON THE VILLAGE		68
	5	BURNING THE TIPIS		90
	6	THE PONY HERD		110
	7	IN THE INDIAN CAMP		123
	8	THE RETREAT TO LODGEPOLE CREEK		136
	9	THE RETURN TO FORT FETTERMAN		148
	10	THE COURT-MARTIAL PROCEEDINGS		166
Appendix	A	NAMES OF TROOPS IN THE CAMPAIGN		191
	B	OFFICIAL REPORTS OF THE BATTLE		200
		BIBLIOGRAPHY		231
		INDEX		233

ILLUSTRATIONS

General Crook's headquarters at Fort Fetterman	*facing page* 16
The camp near Fort Fetterman	16
Scouting Party	17
Colonel Joseph J. Reynolds	48
Major T. H. Stanton	48
Frand Grouard	49
John Shangreau	49
Little Wolf	80
White Bull	81
Captain Anson Mills	112
Captain Henry E. Noyes	112
Looking north from Rawolle's ridge	113
Campsite near the mouth of Lodgepole Creek	113
Away the Led Horses	144
Charge	145
Captain James Egan with Company K	176
Sketch map of the battle area	177

MAP

The Powder River Battlefield	*page* 71

THE REYNOLDS CAMPAIGN
ON POWDER RIVER

Chapter 1 GOLD IN THE BLACK HILLS

"BLACK HILLS or Bust!" Gold-mad miners and prospectors hurried over the trails leading to the new promised land in the Sioux country. Gold "from the grass roots down" had been discovered in July, 1874, by the expedition led by General George A. Custer. That the importance of the discovery had been minimized by the War Department had failed to dampen the enthusiasm of a people still suffering from the panic of 1873.

The Black Hills were the sacred medicine ground of the Sioux nation, set aside for them by the treaty of 1868. An uneasy peace had followed which was violated on both sides, by the Indians in occasionally making raids on the border settlements and by the government in failing to provide the Indians at the agencies with sufficient food. The invasion of this sacred territory was a glaring violation, and the War Department made a halfhearted effort to turn back those who were traveling the "Thieves' Road." General George Crook was transferred from Arizona to prevent these incursions, but adventurers who had been turned back at one point by the military would re-enter by a more secluded route. The hills were soon alive with the sound of men, and returning parties reported that hidden treasure lay wrapped in the folds of the mountains. All attempts to enforce the treaty were abortive. The Sioux retaliated by bloody attacks upon the trespassers, and although many were killed or driven out, the procession continued.

Public opinion became so strong in favor of the settlement of the Black Hills that it was determined to buy the land from the Sioux; for that purpose a peace commission of thirteen members was appointed in June, 1875, headed by Senator William B. Allison, of Iowa. A council meeting with the Indians was set for the fall of 1875 at Red Cloud Agency in the northwest corner of Nebraska, and runners were sent forth to all the bands of Sioux, including the affiliated tribes of the Northern Cheyennes and Arapahoes, notifying them to send their representatives to the council. Some obeyed the summons, some quietly disregarded it, and one band, a small one, under Sitting Bull, flatly refused compliance. When the message reached him early in the summer of 1875, directing him to come in to Red Cloud Agency, this was the reply that Louis Richaud, the French-Indian messenger, received:

"Are you the Great God that made me, or was it the Great God that made me who sent you? If he asks me to come see him, I will go, but the Big Chief of the white men must come see me. I will not go to the reservation. I have no land to sell. There is plenty of game here for us. We have enough ammunition. We don't want any white men here."

Sitting Bull delivered the above in his haughtiest manner, but Crazy Horse had nothing to say. Crazy Horse was the general, the fighter; Sitting Bull was a Medicine Man and a fine talker, and rarely let pass an opportunity for saying something.[1]

In September the commissioners came to Cheyenne and, after remaining a day or two, started for the Red Cloud Agency.

A good joke happened in connection with the departure of these commissioners. After travelling many miles toward the north they were met by a cowboy who was coming toward Cheyenne, who heard one of the commissioners tell one of the others that he had lost a little book somewhere on the road after starting from Cheyenne. The cowboy who somehow learned who they were concluded to look for that little book as he was going in to Cheyenne over the same road. Before he had ridden two miles he discovered the book lying in the middle of the road. Getting off his horse he picked it up. The book proved to be Fenimore Cooper's *"Last of the Mohicans,"* and the supposition was that the illustrious

[1] John G. Bourke, *On the Border with Crook*, 245.

"Indian Commissioner" was posting himself up on the character of the average North American Indian, and an inquisitive individual eventually ascertained where he purchased the book in Cheyenne.[2]

The Indians refused to enter Fort Robinson, declaring they would make no treaty under duress, so it was agreed that the council would be held in a grove on White River eight miles northeast of the post, on September 20. The commissioners proceeded to the appointed place escorted by a troop of the Third Cavalry under Captain Anson Mills,[3] and a white horse troop of the Second Cavalry under Captain James Egan.[4]

At the designated time a horde of savages, 30,000, of all ages, sex and conditions, gathered at the council grounds. They had come from

---

[2] C. G. Coutant, *History of Wyoming*, chap. 20, reprinted in *Annals of Wyoming*, Vol. XIV (January, 1942), 66. Quotations from *Annals of Wyoming* and *Historical Collections of Wyoming* are used with the permission and courtesy of the Wyoming State Archives and Historical Department.

[3] Captain Anson Mills was a Texan who had served in the U. S. infantry during the Civil War. He had been brevetted captain on December 31, 1862, for bravery in the battle of Murfreesboro, Tennessee; major on September 1, 1864, for bravery at Chickamauga and the Atlanta campaign; and lieutenant colonel on December 16, 1864, for gallantry at the battle of Nashville, Tennessee. In later years he rose to the rank of a general officer and traveled extensively. He became famous for designing for use in the first world war many articles of military equipment which bore his name.

Captain Mills was a handsome man with black hair, black eyes, and mustache and goatee worn in the style of the period. In his speech he was very abrupt and nervous. Being excitable and ever ready to criticize and offer advice, he must have been found very trying by his superiors.

Data on commissioned officers in this work are taken from the *Army and Navy Register;* the *Army and Navy Journal; Annuals* of the Association of West Point Graduates; and Heitman's, *Historical Register and Dictionary of the U. S. Army*. The bimonthly company muster rolls furnish information on the enlisted men.

[4] Captain James Egan was an old veteran who served under Crook at the Reynolds fight as captain of Company K, the white horse troop of the Second Cavalry. "Teddy" Egan commenced his military career as a private in Company H of the Second Cavalry in 1856. In March, 1860, he was transferred to Company E of the First Cavalry, where he served as private, corporal, and sergeant until August, 1863, when he was commissioned a second lieutenant in the Second Cavalry. He was brevetted for gallant service in the battle of Cold Harbor, Virginia, and commissioned a first lieutenant in October, 1864. After receiving his captain's commission in February, 1868, he served on the frontier, where he engaged in many Indian skirmishes. He retired on May 9, 1879, and died April 14, 1883, as the result of old wounds and many years of exposure in the service of his country.

the sterile borders of the Missouri River, from the rocky slopes of Wyoming, from the table lands of Montana, and from the inhospitable and barren regions of Dakota—warriors, orators and diplomats of an uncouth nation, adorned by all the gew-gaw finery of barbarian apparel. Never again will be assembled such a concourse of red men, as earnest and performing as important an act, fraught with such far reaching consequences to a doomed race, as when representatives of this Government, in council, put forth learning, power, craft and cunning to cloak the greed for gold. . . .

The hills around the limpid stream were covered with herds of war ponies. The valley of the White River was thronged by masses in holiday attire, wending their way to the Grand Council. Fleet-footed and caparisoned ponies bore to the scene the savage knights, decked in gorgeous war bonnets trailing to the ground, and from whose lances flowed gay-colored pennants. The foam-covered steeds displayed the warriors' horsemanship for the applause and admiration of the paint-embellished maidens. Mingling sounds of mirth and song of battle echoed along the vales and through the pine-crested hills. From the rude stone club, the brutal implement of death, to the magazine rifle, a weapon was not wanting from their armory. The council proceedings were opened by a brief statement from the Commissioners as to the desires of the Government. Chiefs Red Cloud, Spotted Tail, Red Dog, White Antelope and others recited with impassioned eloquence and dramatic gesticulations of the oft-repeated history of their tribes. In words of burning reproach they laid bare the unbroken record of robberies and other wrongs perpetrated upon their people. These leaders told how they had been crowded from place to place, until now their exile from home and country, from the scenes of their youth and the burial places of their kindred, was demanded to satisfy the grasping, restless spirit of the whites. Spotted Tail, of majestic presence, the folds of his blanket draping his massive form, stood before the Commissioners, in the center of the vast multitude, on the uncertain brink of national existence, an ideal Chieftain, a Chief among Warriors. He pleaded his case with fervent voice, clear and soft, that was borne on the free air as a requiem, though swayed by the consciousness of right. His appeal to reason, justice, and humanity was lost upon his pale-faced listeners, for, as made known by an unlettered interpreter's translation, it became a marvel of incoherent speech rendered in execrable English. The speech of Red Dog, the orator of the Sioux Nation, in imagery and beauty of Indian Rhetoric, has perhaps never been excelled by untutored man. He had scarcely finished when an excited commotion was observed among the thousands there assembled. Riding naked to the front on an iron gray horse, and brandishing a grim weapon in air, Little-Big-Man proclaimed: "My heart is bad. I have come from Sitting Bull to kill a white man." Rapidly the ponies disappeared from the hills. Wrinkled squaws and soft-eyed maidens hurried to their camp. As the painted and armed Tartar Cavalry of the Plains seized the contiguous knoll, the martial tones of Captain Egan, Second Cavalry, as valiant a soldier as ever breasted a foe, rang out loud and firm, "Stand to Horse—Mount." Impelled by the command, each trooper, grasping carbine, vaulted into saddle. . . . Happily the impending crisis was averted by the promptitude of Young-Man-Afraid-of-His-Horses espousing the cause of the troops, on which flank he hurriedly arrayed his blanketed braves as support. As a conservator of the peace, he approached Sitting Bull's Emissary, Little-Big-Man, and in unmistakable meaning ordered him to leave the Council grounds on pain of being killed. But Sitting Bull's work was done. The council was at an end, and no treaty was accomplished, for on the morrow the congregated bands began journeying to their rude habitations, many days distant.[5]

The commissioners returned to Cheyenne, where they met President Grant, who, with General John M. Thayer, governor of Wyoming, was returning from a trip to Salt Lake City. Grant was disgusted with the commissioners and intimated as much to them. There was speculation among Cheyenne residents about whether the failure to conclude a treaty with the Sioux was due to the loss of the Fenimore Cooper book which was the standard authority on the Indian character in the East.[6]

After the failure of the Black Hills council, the Commissioner of Indian Affairs abandoned his policy of appeasement towards the Indians and turned the problem over to the military. General Sheridan, who had long urged a policy of force towards them, now believed that they should be attacked and punished during the winter while they were divided into small bands and their ponies

---

[5] J. A. Baldwin, "Surrender of the Black Hills," *Historical Collections of Wyoming for 1897*, 184.

[6] C. G. Coutant, *History of Wyoming*, chap. 20, reprinted in *Annals of Wyoming*, Vol. XIV (January, 1942), 66.

weakened from lack of forage. Plans were formulated for a winter campaign against the Indians, but at the insistence of the Interior Department, the hostiles were to be given one more chance. The various Indian agents were instructed to notify all of the Indians in the unceded territory that they were to come in to the agencies by January 31, 1876, and that if they did not, they would be considered enemies and subject to military action. This message was received at the agencies shortly before Christmas and was sent on to the hostile bands by Indian runners. The winter was severe, and not all the runners sent out to these camps were able to get through the deep snow. Few of them even reached their destination before the end of January, when the time allowed for return to the agencies expired. In January, the agent at Red Cloud reported that his supply of beef and flour would be exhausted before March 1, so some of those already in that agency left to join the hostile camps in the belief that they would have to either hunt or starve. The Indians must have marvelled at the inconsistency of the white man. These summons proved to be a futile gesture, as few of the chiefs took the order seriously.

All during this time the army was preparing for the campaign which was believed to be inevitable, as General Sheridan had no faith in the idealistic policy of the Interior Department. As early as December the various commanders had been alerted and ordered to place their troops in readiness to move on short notice.

On January 18 the Commissioner of Indian Affairs ordered that all sales of arms and ammunition to the Indians be stopped because there had been reports that there had been much trading of hides for arms and ammunition. On February 7 the War Department received authority to take action against the hostile camps and put into execution the plans of General Sheridan. General George Crook would lead a column from Fort Fetterman northward into the Powder River country, Colonel John Gibbon was to lead another force from the Montana forts southeastward down the Yellowstone River, and General Terry was to move westward from Fort Abraham Lincoln. The Indians were believed to be in small scattered bands south of the Yellowstone River in the area of the

Powder, Tongue, and Rosebud rivers, and to number not more than from five to eight hundred warriors in all. The soldiers were to converge upon them from the three directions so that they would be surrounded and unable to run away. The winter was so severe in the Dakotas that General Terry was unable to march until May, but Colonel Gibbon commenced his movement down the Yellowstone in February to prevent the Indians from escaping towards the north.

All through February of 1876 guns, ammunition, wagons, teams, mules, and supplies were assembled at Fort Fetterman, the concentration point for the "Big Horn Expedition," the official designation of the column. Those cavalry units which were in the best fighting trim were ordered out from Fort Laramie and Fort D. A. Russell. Fort Fetterman was situated on a plateau a short distance south of the North Platte River, about ten miles northwest of the present site of Douglas, Wyoming, and a few miles north of the crossing of the old Oregon Trail with the Bozeman Trail. The troops from Fort Laramie marched westward over the Oregon Trail on the south side of the North Platte River, the shortest route. It was not necessary to use the new army bridge, built by Captain Stanton of the U. S. Engineers the year before, near Fort Laramie, because the river was low during the winter and easily crossed at the fords. The route from Fort D. A. Russell near Cheyenne ran north along the old road towards Fort Laramie as far as Bordeaux, where it branched off to the northwest, forming the cutoff to Fort Fetterman.

Among those hurrying to join the expedition was a young man by the name of Robert A. Strahorn,[7] the war correspondent of the

---

[7] Robert Edmund Strahorn was a journeyman printer who came to Denver in 1870 from Sedalia, Missouri, as a newspaper reporter. By 1876 he had already accompanied several expeditions with the soldiers and had been through one skirmish with the Indians. At the time of the Reynolds fight he had black hair and mustache, and was "tall and boyishly slender." He was a personal friend of General Crook and accompanied him as newspaper correspondent on his other 1876 campaigns. In 1877, as a journalist in Denver, he went with various railway surveying parties which led to his engaging in railway promotion and construction. Strahorn accompanied General Crook on many of his hunting expeditions, and they remained fast friends until Crook's death. In 1911 his wife, Carrie A. Strahorn, published a book, *Fifteen*

Denver *Rocky Mountain News*. He had accompanied other Indian expeditions in this capacity and had won a reputation with the troops for his fearlessness in action, and with the public for his vivid and accurate newspaper accounts appearing over the signature of "Alter Ego." His dispatches sent back to his newspaper afford a highly detailed and accurate source of information on this campaign. His first dispatch, dated at Fort Fetterman, Wyoming, February 27, 1876, describes his trip from Cheyenne to join the troops at Fort Fetterman:

Leaving Cheyenne at dawn of the 24th inst. for the purpose of joining Gen. Crook in his northwestern campaign, our small party and escort made a forced march of 54 miles before sunset, and tarried at night at the ranch of Portugee Philips on the Chugwater.... In conversation with Mr. Philips, who is a pioneer in the true sense of the word, he has been in government employ as scout and guide for many years and among other thrilling experiences he was an eye witness of the Phil Kearny massacre.... The Indians, known to be scattered over its vast extent, he said would number at least 18,000 or 20,000, and could muster nearly 4,000 warriors; that they would fight he considered there would be no reasonable doubt, as he witnessed their prowess in that line on more than one occasion when there was not as much to arouse them as at present. Unless the savages were thoroughly demoralized at the first encounter— which could result in the event of their being concentrated—he was of the opinion that it would require more than one campaign to force them to the extreme of suing for peace.

Early on the morning of the 25th we were again on the trail which for 25 miles descended Chugwater valley. Signs of late improvements were noted at many points, plains and valley were covered with well-conditioned stock and our occasional meeting a ranch man suggested a new state of affairs in spite of incursions of Mr Lo. During the forenoon, a superlative bright and pleasant one, we overhauled several pack and transportation trains. The former consisted of over 200 stout mules, laden with supplies for the expedition in charge of a large corps of professional "Packers," and the latter were the usual huge and heavily-laden army

---

Thousand Miles by Stage, wherein she revealed for the first time that during the charge at the Indian village, Strahorn's horse had stampeded and fallen over a precipice, breaking its neck.

wagons with 6 mule teams for motive power. Later in the day a high grassy divide literally covered with cattle was crossed and after fording the main Laramie River, we ascended to where it receives the waters of the North Laramie and made camp. . . . On a fertile "Bench" overlooking our riverside camp, a too venturesome pioneer was scalped only a few months ago and recent advices tell of the successful entry of several plundering bands of Indians within as many weeks just passed. Cattle and horses were carried off in each instance, but thus far this season no loss of human life has occurred. In the course of a little hunt up the valley during the evening of our stay, I came upon the ranch of T. A. Kent, of Cheyenne—the only one for a number of miles up and down the river. Passing through a strong cordon of dogs and finally gaining the single entrance to the little fortress of a cabin, I had an excellent opportunity to see how men live who are in momentary danger of an attack by Indians. Guns of the most approved pattern were more numerous than chairs and all other articles of furniture combined. A window, hardly designed for "transit observations" commanded a wide view of the plain and valley and was flanked on either side by general piles of robes and blankets, where quite undisturbed repose, mayhap, is oftener thought than found—for to be a Rancherio here is to be a man on the constant alert, and on the tiptoe of expectant intrusion, and in perfect preparation to extend the warmest of warm greetings. About noon of the third day out we commenced overtaking the long column of picked cavalry headed by the gallant officer whose hardships and duty we were to share in the very near future. Men they looked and men of the best stamp they are, whom General Crook has detailed for this difficult undertaking. Rank and file are in excellent trim, mounted upon the best horses the Department affords, and everything in their appearance betokened "business," from the start. As we entered camp at the Elkhorn, it was discovered that several companies had already pitched their tents, by the side of that pretty little stream and were comfortably fixed for the night. Before dark six companies had their quarters arranged up and down the creek on either side and these, with their horses, a large pack and transportation train, and the mounted sentries on surrounding bluffs, quickened the quiet neighborhood into a life that it seldom and, perhaps, never will ever again see. Snow commenced falling about the middle of the afternoon and continued through the night. . . .

From officers met at the camp above referred to we had learned that some unruly renegades were having about their own way down along the North Platte, just above Fort Laramie. A few nights ago they cut a valuable cavalry horse out of the band belonging to one of the companies now approaching this fort, and were successful in getting across the river with him almost under the noses of the command. Next day a soldier was sent back to Ft Laramie armed to the teeth and whom it was supposed the bandits would hardly attempt to intercept, in broad daylight, when four or five miles above the Fort he saw two men crossing the river and making their way toward him, but as they did not display any arms, and seemed otherwise peaceable he did not think it was necessary to show signs of distrust by preparing himself for an attack. Upon overtaking him one rode up on one side and one on the other, and the audacious and rascally pair almost instantly whipped out revolvers and presented them at the head of the unfortunate bearer of dispatches, at the same time requesting him to "Git down off that hoss!" He obeyed, as a great many men have done before in such emergencies, and then was relieved of the possession of a splendid new Sharps rifle, revolver, etc., and told to carry another message to the officers at the Fort, to-wit: "Tell them fellers down there that infantry ain't calculated to follow us, and that as General Crook has got all the cavalry we jest politely request them to go to Hell!" The soldier recognized one of the horses ridden by the highwaymen as the one stolen from his command the night before.

We rode in the face of one of the most severe storms of the season until 2 PM today, when we reached this post, considerably in advance of our transportation, having accomplished 170 miles in less than four days. Colonel Stanton, his secretary, Mr. Chase, and your correspondent, were at once requested to report at the quarters of Col. Chambers, Commandant of the Post, where General Crook and Reynolds also have their headquarters. Remaining hours of the day, as well as those of the evening, have been most delightfully spent in the company of officers named, and the accomplished and entertaining hostess, Mrs. Chambers. We find many changes in rank and file have occurred here during our visit of a year ago, some of the most familiar of the officers having been assigned to other posts of duty. But a greater and far more noticeable change is that which marks their new departure to the northwest. Long lines of tents are pitched on the banks of the quiet and peaceful La Prelle nearby; hundreds of men are crowding around the campfires—which tonight lead me in fancy back to Denver's lamplit streets—cleaning their arms, looking up the few necessities that a soldier is allowed to possess, and speculating, as a soldier will, upon the campaign and its results; horses, mules, and pack animals, to the number of a thousand or more, are pawing and neighing a loud refrain to the hum of masters' voices; the fort is flooded with commissary supplies, arms, ammunition, etc., and officers are galloping back and forth with the orders that bring system out of all this din and chaos.

ALTER EGO.

The new commander of the Department of the Platte was Brigadier General George Crook,[8] who had been brought up from Arizona to take charge of this area when it became apparent that there would be trouble with the Sioux. General Crook, a famed cavalry leader, had commanded an army and an army corps during the Civil War, and since that conflict had been successful in leading expeditions against Indians in Oregon, California, Idaho, and Arizona. The Pitt River Indians had sent an arrow through him in 1857, and the Apaches in Arizona, the most impoverished tribe on the continent, had set a high price on his scalp.

General Crook had been appointed to West Point from Ohio and was graduated in the class of 1852. Weighing 170 pounds, he was six feet in height, broad shouldered, and of erect military bearing. He carried an arrowhead in his thigh to the day of his death. While at ease in camp he kept his light, full beard taped up, but when his beard was done up in three or four braids, the soldiers knew he "meant business." He was well known throughout the country for his unkempt personal appearance and disinclination to

[8] Brigadier General George Crook was born near Dayton, Ohio, on September 2, 1828, and died in Chicago, March 21, 1890. He served in the army continuously from his graduation from West Point to 1888, when he attained the rank of major general in the regular army. He was colonel of a volunteer regiment when the Civil War broke out, and took part in many hard-fought battles. He fought with Sheridan and was one of the most trusted lieutenants through all the battles in the Shenandoah Valley and around Richmond. During his service on the frontier the Indians feared yet trusted him. He was a persistent, vigorous fighter, but humane and magnanimous to the vanquished. In later years he gained the confidence of the Indians for his mild and generous treatment of them in peace.

General Crook was married to Mary Tapscott Dailey of Moorefield, Virginia, and maintained his family estate at Crook Crest, Oakland, Maryland. Because he had no children, Crook Crest went to his widow upon his death. Mrs. Crook died in 1895, and her younger sister, Fanny Reade, who had lived with her, inherited the estate. Fanny Reade married Major Matthew Markland, who inherited Crook Crest upon her death in 1905.

wear a uniform. In the field his favorite mount was a small gray mule named "Apache."

Lieutenant John Gregory Bourke[9] had served as aide-de-camp to General Crook for many years. Bourke was graduated from West Point in 1869 (number eleven in a class of thirty-nine), and was appointed to the Third Cavalry. From that time forward, he had his full share of frontier duty and Indian fighting. He had served all through the Civil War and received a medal of honor for gallantry at Stone River while serving as a private in Company E, Fifteenth Pennsylvania Cavalry. Later he declined two brevets—Captain and Major—for gallantry in action against Indians in 1873 and 1876. During the campaigns against the Sioux in 1876, Bourke kept a diary which in later years furnished material for

[9] While Bourke wrote freely about his brother officers, he was very reticent about himself. However, in an entry from his diary of August 12, 1876, we get a glimpse of the real Bourke when he told about meeting an old comrade. He was then only thirty years of age, but he was already a veteran of the Civil War and had had eleven years of Indian fighting. On this date, General Crook was on his famous "Mud March" in pursuit of the elusive Indians in eastern Montana. The men were hungry and disgruntled. They had undergone many hardships without even seeing any Indians. "After dark I heard someone inquire for Lt. Bourke. I announced myself and was asked by the visitor, a rough, burly, shaggy-bearded officer, 'Not Johnny Bourke?' I asserted my claim to that title and felt my hand warmly grasped and shaken by that of Lt. Hamilton, Second Cavalry, who had been a comrade with me during the war. We talked over the past and once more were recruits in camp near Carlisle Barracks—then we made the journey by rail to Louisville, Kentucky, and marched with our regiment from Kentucky to Nashville, Tennessee, and on down to the bloody battlefield of Stone River. Of course we fought that conflict over again and for seven days and nights held Bragg's army at bay. I can't say how much more of the war we would have gone over, but by that time, it was long after midnight, and we agreed to give the rebels a rest. It made me feel old, as well as sad, to encounter one of my old comrades: my chequered life during the past fourteen years passed rapidly in review before my mind. I reflected how thankful I ought to be that I held the position I held with General Crook and I tried to make myself believe it was a grand thing to have my garments saturated with water, my feet cold and wet, my miserable straw hat torn by the breezes, no tent, no blanket, no supper to speak of. This, I said to myself, is heroism and I am a first-class hero; but it wouldn't work. Like Banquo's ghost, the thought would not down that a good hot stove, with plenty of champagne and oysters would be good enough for the likes of me and it was then I made up my mind, if I ever married an heiress, to live for the remainder of my days in a brown stone front and retire from the hero business forever."

Bourke died in Philadelphia on June 8, 1896, at the age of fifty. An early grave was the price he paid for being a "first-class hero." A memorial to Bourke by F. W. Hodge appeared in *The American Anthropologist*, Vol. IX (July, 1896), 245.

Gold in the Black Hills

his book *On the Border With Crook*. These are accurate and dependable accounts of these campaigns as seen from the headquarters tent. Bourke was a lifelong friend and admirer of General Crook, and there was a strong bond of affection between them.

Lieutenant Bourke recorded in his diary that he took the train from Omaha to Cheyenne and then rode to Fort Fetterman by way of Fort Laramie to join the expedition:

Left Omaha Neb. Feb 17 for Cheyenne Wyo. in company with Gen Crook, Col. Stanton, Col. Van Vliet 3rd Cav, and Ben Clarke of Indian Territory whose services Gen Crook has secured as guide, reached Cheyenne 18th and put up at the InterOcean Hotel. During the day and evening the officers stationed at Fort D. A. Russell and Camp Carlin, improved the occasion of calling upon Gen Crook to pay their respects. Found the pack train of the expedition ready to take the field well equipped under the experienced management of Tom Moore. The proposed expedition is to consist of 10 companies of cavalry 5 of the Second and 5 of the Third under the command of Gen J. J. Reynolds Col of the Third Cavalry. . . . It is their intention to move in the lightest marching order possible, leaving everything out not absolutely needed in the way of clothing and mess equipment, and bedding is to be rejected. Saturday the 19th and Sunday the 20th remained in Cheyenne working up the details of the organization. The 2 companies of the 2nd Cavalry got off early Sun. morning. . . . Capt. Nickerson ADC arrived back from the Indian Agency at Red Cloud and Spotted Tail where he had gone to secure guides and trailers from among the half-breeds and also to note passing events. We are now on the eve of the bloodiest Indian war the Government has ever been called upon to wage. The war with a tribe that has waxed fat and insolent on Govt. bounty and has been armed and equipped with the most improved weapons by the commissioners or the carelessness of the Indian agent, of this more hereafter.

In Cheyenne we could see and hear nothing but Black Hills. Every store advertises its inducements as an outfitting agency. Every wagon was charged to convey freight to new pastures. The Q. M. Dept. experiences great difficulties in finding the transportation needed by the Army at the different camps. Everything is bound for the Black Hills. Cheyenne is full of people and the merchants and the saloon keepers are doing a rushing business. Great numbers of new buildings mostly brick have been erected during the past 6 months giving the town a bustle and activity as well as appearance of advancement in favorable contrast with Omaha, Denver and Salt Lake.

5 companies of 3rd Cavalry . . . left for Fort Fetterman Wyo. at 6 o'clock, Monday the 21st. Feb 22 left Cheyenne for Fort Laramie passing through Camp Carlin, 1½ miles from Cheyenne and Fort D. A. Russell 3 miles distant. . . . Stopped the 1st night at Portagese Phillips. . . . Arrived at Fort Laramie in the afternoon of the 23rd. The distance being about 90 miles from Cheyenne. At the Post there was much excitement and bustle attendent upon the departure of Capt Egan and Capt Noyes and Lt. Hall of the 2nd Cavalry whose companies are to join the expedition. Dr Munn who is to be surgeon of the command was occupied in preparing the field medicine chest and other details pertaining to his department. In the evening witnessed a theatrical entertainment given by the ladies and officers of the post the pieces *Faint Heart Neer Won Fair Lady* and *A Regular Fix* were capitally interpreted. The best performers in my opinion Maj. Burt 9th Inf. Miss L. Dewey Miss Lucy Townsend Mr L. T. Bradley and Mr Ford.

From this point and on the road saw many adventurers journeying to the Black Hills their wagons and animals looked new and good as a general thing and the supplies carried ample in quantity however there were many on foot and without adequate sustenance and some begging their way from ranch to ranch along the trail what they hope to gain by going at this time to the Black Hills where the thermometer is reported minus 23 degrees creeks frozen up all placer mining frustrated, is one of those things no one can find out. It is strongly suggestive of the want and misery of the eastern states that so many people should rush upon such slight stimulus toward the new El Dorado. The reason the Cheyenne route is preferred is the new iron bridge across the North Platte River constructed under the supervision of Capt Stanton of the Engineer Corps of USA which gives us secure passage not found on the other trails leading out from Sydney, North Platt and elsewhere. Indications of bad weather approaching are discernable in the sky. Hopes are entertained that if a storm comes up the Sioux may be compelled to keep under shelter and thus give our column a chance to creep undetected into the Yellowstone and Tongue River country where their villages are. General Crook was busy all day the 25th in examining guides and scouts and studying maps of the country in which we are to operate.

Feb 27th arrived at Fort Fetterman last evening in company with Gen Crook Gen Reynolds Lt Drew and Lieut. Morton. Our journey of

Harper's Weekly

General Crook's headquarters at Fort Fetterman.

Signal Corps, U.S. Army

The camp near Fort Fetterman.

Library of Congress

SCOUTING PARTY.
From a painting by Frederic Remington.

two days duration took us over some 80 miles of country barren of vegetation. . . . From time to time a prairie dog protruded his little head above the entrance of his domicile and barked at our cortege passing by. That night the (25th) we camped with Egan's and Noyes' companies of the 2nd Cavalry at the Bull Bend of the North Platte about 32 miles from Fort Laramie in a very pleasant grove of Cottonwood trees. . . . On the 26th we passed the "Twin Springs" a pair of pretty sources of water, then "Horseshoe Creek" (Cave Springs) "Elk Horn Creek" "La Bonte Creek" "Wagon Hound Creek" "Bed Tick Creek" and "Whiskey Gulch." The last is 3 miles from Fort Fetterman and is the place of concealment of all the vile intoxicating drinks smuggled in for the use of the enlisted men of the command. . . .

At Fort Fetterman found Lewis Coates' and Bubb's companies of the 4th Infantry and Dewees of the 2nd Cavalry. This post commanded by Major Alex Chambers of the 4th Infantry is now the most Northern of those protecting our settlements from the incursions of the Sioux, Cheyennes and Arapahoes. At the time of our arrival Black Coal, an Arapahoe Chief of not much prominence, was at the post with his small band. He reported Sitting Bull and the Minniconjous living on the Powder River below old Fort Reno some 100 miles from Fetterman. On the 27th Capt. Peale with Lt. F. U. Robinson, Lt Rawolle and Lt. Sibley all of the 2nd Cavalry arrived with 2 companies of their regiment. Paymaster Stanton also reached the post in the afternoon, bringing with him Mr. Strahorn, Special Correspondent of the *Rocky Mountain News*. My old classmate, D. C. Pearson of the 2nd Cavalry, insisted upon taking care of Lt Morton and myself during our stay at the post. Made the acquaintance of his charming young wife and received during this stay calls from all those stationed at the post, among whom were quite a number of old friends. . . . I may now say without much imprudence that Gen Crook hopes to be able to strike each band of ill-disposed Minneconjous as he may encounter in the Powder, Tongue, and Big Horn Rivers between the old Montana road and the confluence of the above named streams with the Yellowstone.

The old trails followed by Mr. Strahorn and Lieutenant Bourke are still visible.[10] These were military roads constructed in 1867 for the purpose of connecting the newly established Fort D. A.

---

[10] Agnes Wright Spring, *Cheyenne and Black Hills Stage Routes* (Glendale, Arthur H. Clark Company, 1949).

Russell with Fort Fetterman and Fort Laramie. Leaving Fort D. A. Russell [now Fort Francis E. Warren] the old ruts covered with grass run northward nine miles to the Davis ranch, also known as "Nine Mile," where in the early days the buildings were burned by the Indians and never rebuilt. Farther northward the road crosses Lodgepole Creek eighteen miles north of Cheyenne. On the north bank was the Fred Schwartz ranch, which was also burned by Indians and never rebuilt, while along the south bank was a popular camping place. From here the road veers northeastward and crosses Highway 87 about twenty-two miles north of Cheyenne, where one can see the ruts extending northeast towards the crossing at Horse Creek where the old Fagan ranch was located four miles east of the present highway. From Horse Creek the road swerves back to the northwest to Bear Springs on South Bear Creek, which is close by the east side of the highway. Fifty-four miles north of Cheyenne was Portugee Phillips' ranch near the present site of Chugwater, Wyoming. Farther on fourteen miles down the "Chug" was Bordeaux, the ranch home of John Hunton, an early settler who came west after having served as a captain in the Confederate Army. Here the road branched with one fork leading northeast twenty-one miles to Bullocks', also called the "Six Mile Ranch," and then continued another six miles to Fort Laramie. The other branch, followed by Mr. Strahorn, led to the northwest about eighty-four miles to Fort Fetterman. This was the cutoff by which travelers could go directly from Cheyenne to Fort Fetterman without going around by Fort Laramie. These military roads played an important part in the development of the West, every mile having its own bloody history.

The country north of the North Platte River was Indian territory, and that south of the river was sparsely settled with ranches and public resorts along the roads and tributaries at infrequent intervals. Many of the huge ranches had cowboys who herded the owners' cattle, while the resorts were frequented by a floating population of teamsters, bullwhackers, miners, settlers, and public characters.

As troops and supply trains converged upon Fort Fetterman,

John Hunton watched the passing parade from his ranch at Bordeaux. In his diary[11] for Tuesday, February 22, he noted that Captain Peale's Company B, Second Cavalry, passed, while Company E of the Second Cavalry camped at his place that night. Wagons and pack trains were with them and all wanted hay, but there was none to be had. On Wednesday night, February 23, Lieutenant Reynolds and Mr. Moore (boss packer) stayed at Bordeaux. On the next day General Reynolds passed with five companies of the Third Cavalry. On Saturday, the twenty-sixth, Crook and Bourke passed in an ambulance on their way to Fort Laramie.

Hunton contracted to supply baled hay for the troops. On the twenty-eighth he and his neighbors set up a hay press at the Phillips ranch on the Chug.[12] On March 1 wagons came from the fort and hauled away all the hay on hand. Another neighbor, Colon Hunter, had furnished sixty beeves for the expedition. Hunton and his friends baled hay steadily and hauled it to the fort to replenish the supply taken by Crook's column.

[11] *Diary of John Hunton,* ed. by L. G. Flannery, printed in the Lingle (Wyoming) *Guide-Review,* commencing February 3, 1955.
[12] Chugwater Creek was originally called the "Chug." This little stream for many miles is lined by steep cliffs on the east. Formerly the Indians had stampeded buffalo over these cliffs in order to obtain their meat and hides, and told the early settlers that when the buffalo hit the ground many hundred feet below, they would "go chug." From this the stream derived its name.

Chapter 2   CONCENTRATION AT FORT FETTERMAN

FORT FETTERMAN, the springboard for General Crook's expedition against the Sioux, was named after Lieutenant Colonel W. J. Fetterman, of the twenty-seventh Infantry, killed with his whole command by Sioux Indians near Fort Phil Kearny on December 21, 1866. It was built in the summer of 1867 under the supervision of Major William Mc E. Dye, of the fourth Infantry.[1] The fort was arranged and built to garrison five companies of troops and was generally occupied by four companies of infantry and one troop of cavalry, but occasionally there was no cavalry stationed there. At such times infantry details of about twenty men, mounted on mules and such horses as the quartermaster happened to have, were assigned to act as cavalry in emergencies. There were from seventy-five to one hundred citizen employees,

---

[1] "Fort Fetterman contained quarters for 300 enlisted men and the necessary officers; various magazines and storehouses required for preservation of the ammunition, rations and other supplies; a hospital of fifteen beds; stables for fifty horses and a corral for fifty six-mule wagons with the animals; theatre, ice house, granary, root house, blacksmith shop, bake house, saddler's shop, paint shop, laundresses' quarters, sawmill, and a steam engine for pumping water from the North Platte. The buildings had no pretensions to architectural elegance, being a single story each, of adobe, fronted by a veranda; but they served their purpose, were kept in good repair, neatly painted, and in a mild way became a mecca for the first glimpse of which many a weary eye had strained its first glance across the interminable plains between the Laramie and Big Horn River." Bourke, "Mackenzie's Last Fight with the Cheyennes," *Winners of the West* (December 30, 1929), 7.

Other sources used for data on Fort Fetterman are *Annals of Wyoming*, Vol. IV (January, 1927), 358, and the unpublished statement of John Hunton, dated November 20, 1925, in the archives of the University of Wyoming.

Concentration at Fort Fetterman

carpenters, stonemasons, plasterers, and teamsters at the post. Fort Fetterman was of considerable importance because it was the southernmost of four military posts extending from the Montana border southward and because it was nearest the railroad. When Forts Phil Kearny, Reno, and C. F. Smith were abandoned in 1868, pursuant to the treaty with the Indians of that year, Fort Fetterman became the most advanced of all the posts bordering the Sioux territory. It afforded protection for emigrants traveling the Oregon Trail and also those using the Bozeman Trail, which ran northward into Montana. The fort was abandoned as a military post in 1882 when it was no longer needed to protect emigrants from Indian incursions.

During these years the cavalry troops were kept busy chasing bands of marauding Indians that came across on the south side to kill those that were unfortunate enough to be unprotected, to steal a few ponies and perhaps take a few cattle. By the time the news of these outbreaks reached the Fort and the troops had gathered into the field, the Indians were back on the reservations and the troops not allowed to follow.

The scout and guide on these trips was an old half-breed, Joe Monaz [John Hunton claimed his name was Joe Maryavale], who lived in the Fort with his family of squaws, papooses and dogs. The impression prevailed among the military men that Joe never led the troops to a part where there might be danger and eventually Joe disappeared, probably to the reservation.

Here some military genius conceived the bright idea of using Indian scouts and to bring this plan to fruition, ten Arapahoes were induced to swear allegiance to the Government for a year and as a compensation for their services, they were allowed the same pay and allowance as soldiers. The Indians might have rendered some services, had it not been for Capt. A. B. Cain, then in command, who was on intimate terms with John Barleycorn. He insisted that as they were sworn in and drawing pay and allowances, they must appear at Headquarters daily in full military dress, from hat to shoes, for inspection. Of course they soon grew tired of military discipline, so one morning after pay and a bountiful supply of rations, clothes and annuities, they were conspicuous by their absence.

One remained, who stuck manfully to his job of drawing his allowance and his breath, and at the expiration of his services was given his discharge that certified that Little Dog was "a good soldier but a poor scout."[2]

There were no full-scale battles with the Indians around the fort, but two of the soldiers buried in the post cemetery were killed by Indians who used to camp on the north side of the river periodically for the purpose of trading at the fort. These men were crossing the river at night to meet some of the Indian women from the camp in whom they were romantically interested. The resentful Indian braves waylaid and killed the two men. As early as 1869, John Richaud, Jr., a French-Indian at the post, while in a drunken rage, shot and killed a corporal of Captain Egan's company. In the fall of 1875, when roving bands of Sioux were committing depredations, a hostile party killed some soldiers on the parade ground right in the presence of the officers and men of the command, and the Indians pinned one of the soldiers they had killed to the ground with sticks in full sight of the troops. On a hot day in August the mutilated body of wagonmaster George Throstle was brought in and buried in the post cemetery. He had been killed when Indians had attacked and partially burned his wagon train, loaded with supplies for the fort, on the divide north of Elkhorn Creek.

One mile to the north of the post was situated the notorious Hog Ranch, which consisted of a saloon and dance hall and a hotel and restaurant, with a branch road east of the Bozeman Trail running between them. Ruts three and four feet deep are still visible and attest to the popularity of the resort. About one hundred yards to the north on the bank of a small creek was a log cabin where the "soiled angels" from the dance hall lived. Violence and death were commonplace in those days. A cowboy named Phoenix was shot to death while he was tying his horse to the hitching rack at the Hog Ranch. Phoenix and his friend Frank "Pretty Boy" Wallace were young fellows who, having had a few drinks, had bragged about the fort that they were going to "clean out" the Hog Ranch that night. They were overheard by a small boy who ran over and

[2] J. O. Ward, late first sergeant, Company C, Fourth Infantry, *Annals of Wyoming*, Vol. IV (January, 1927), 359.

told the owner of the establishment, Kid Slaymaker. That night when the two men rode up to the Hog Ranch, two of the bartenders, John Lawrence and Jack Sanders, were waiting behind the saloon on the west with shotguns, and killed Phoenix without warning and shot out one of Wallace's eyes.

At the time the post was abandoned, one Red "Arkansas" Capps killed a man, and was hanged in the adobe guard house. Civilians who came and occupied the fort later found Capps still hanging "with his face black and his tongue hanging out a foot."[3]

The sutler's store was the center of the social life of the garrison, and E. Tillottson was the sutler from 1871 to 1880. Bill Hooker, a bullwhacker who worked for John Hunton, and other freighters in the vicinity of the fort described the social distinctions which prevailed on the post:

There were two bars in Tillotson's sutler store—one for officers, the other for white citizens and buck soldiers. The officers didn't care to rub elbows with the bullwhackers and at this distant period it doesn't seem so serious a slight as it did then, for there was a great contrast in appearance between the men who faced the blizzards, forded the streams and ducked the obsidian and flint arrows of the Sioux, to haul flour, bacon, coffee, etc., across the uninhabited plains and mountains to the "jumping-off place," and the well dressed, clean-shaven officers—between Major Kane [Cain], for instance, and Sim Waln or some other bullwhacker, who wore a pair of elkskin breeches, a greasy sombrero, a buckskin shirt and a belt with two revolvers, forty rounds of ammunition and a butcher knife with a ten-inch blade.

While the bullwhacker was surely a picturesque looking character, he was of necessity untidy, whether it suited his fancy or not. On the other hand, the army officer at old Fort Fetterman was as slick and neat as he was the day he left West Point.

The officers were not very friendly with the bullwhackers and while most all the former drank hard liquor—some of them excessively—they watched the bullwhackers who came out of the post sutlers with jealous

[3] The author is indebted to John Henry, Albert Sims, and Henry Bolln, who lived in the vicinity of the fort during the early years, for relating to him these incidents of violence which they had heard directly from the lips of soldiers who had been at the fort during the period.

eyes, so a crooked step—hardly a stagger—meant a trip to the guard house.

There was no semblance of civil law north of Medicine Bow and not much of it there or anywhere else except at Cheyenne and Laramie City. The military was all-powerful. There were none other than the belligerent-looking bullwhacker for an army officer to experiment upon, consequently at least one of the men who whacked bulls for John Hunton, and who innocently crossed a forbidden spot on the parade ground, takes this opportunity to forgive Major Kane [Cain] for the indignity heaped upon him by ordering him thrown into the guardhouse and kept there until several days later on a diet of sour bread and plain water from LaPrelle Creek and which came from a mysterious hand that pushed it in a tin receptacle through a small aperture at the bottom of a heavily barred door....

But beyond glaring at one another for a year or two, there were no clashes between the bullwhackers and the officers or private soldiers. It was too one-sided. The military had the upper hand. Nevertheless, a lot of hatred was engendered by the rough treatment accorded the few citizens who ventured on to the reservation.[4]

In February, 1876, there was much activity about the fort in getting the command ready for the campaign. The wagon train and pack train had to be assembled and then loaded with supplies and forage; food, clothing, and ammunition had to be freighted in and distributed to the men. Neither General Crook nor General Sheridan knew if it was practicable to make this march into the frozen north at this time of year, but every precaution was taken in equipping the soldiers with an adequate supply of food and warm clothing and their animals with forage. The main problem was to provide forage for the mules and horses, as the grass in the valleys and river bottoms would be covered with ice and snow. Consequently the wagons were given up to carrying grain, which was also the principal burden of the pack mules. Whenever good grazing could be found, grain would not be issued. Heavy clothing was furnished the men to protect their feet, knees, wrists, and ears from the cold weather. Their bedding consisted of one canvas

[4] Letter of Bill Hooker, *Annals of Wyoming*, Vol. VII (January, 1931), 418.

wrapper, one plaid heavy blanket, one comforter, one pair of buffalo robes, one large wolf or beaver robe, one rollable mattress, one pillow and case, and one large rubber poncho.

On February 27, Colonel Joseph J. Reynolds,[5] brevet major general, issued general orders announcing the organization of the Big Horn Expedition and assumed command. General Crook had decided to accompany the column only as an observer. Colonel Reynolds, the commander of the Third Cavalry Regiment, recently ordered to join his troops after many years on detached service as head of the Department of Texas, was to take official command and responsibility. He was a gray-haired man of about sixty years of age. He had a genial personality and was well liked throughout the service. He had been appointed to West Point in 1839, from which he was graduated in 1843, a classmate of General Grant. Commissioned a second lieutenant in the Fourth Artillery, he served until his resignation in February, 1857. For many years he was a professor of engineering at Washington University of St. Louis, Missouri, and other colleges. After rejoining the army he served as an assistant professor at West Point. In 1867 he was brevetted brigadier general for gallant service in the battle of Chickamauga, Georgia, and major general for gallant service at the battle of Missionary Ridge, Tennessee. He was transferred to the Third Cavalry in December, 1870, and served as colonel of that regiment until his retirement on June 25, 1877. His son, Bainbridge

---

[5] Colonel Joseph J. Reynolds was born in Kentucky on January 4, 1822, but was appointed to the Military Academy from Indiana. After completing his first assignment, with the Fourth Artillery at Fort Monroe and in Texas, he was, in 1846, assigned to the Third Artillery. He was on frontier duty at Fort Washita, Indian Territory, in 1855–56. After the beginning of the Civil War he rapidly rose in rank from colonel of the Tenth Indiana Volunteers to major general, United States Volunteers. After a brilliant record, he was mustered out on September 1, 1866, being one of the eighteen full major generals in the service who resigned their commissions. Shortly thereafter he accepted the commission of colonel of the Twenty-fifth Infantry, where he served for three years before being transferred to the Third Cavalry. A month before his death he had an attack of paralysis, which culminated in cerebral hemorrhage. He died February 25, 1899, at Washington, D. C., at the age of seventy-seven years.

He left a wife surviving him, two daughters, and three sons, Captain Reynolds

Reynolds, was a second lieutenant in the Third Cavalry in Captain Alexander Moore's[6] company which accompanied the column.

The expedition was divided into six battalions composed and commanded as follows:

First Battalion—Companies M and E, Third Cavalry, Captain Anson Mills commanding.

Second Battalion—Companies A and D, Third Cavalry, Captain William Hawley commanding.

Third Battalion—Companies I and K, Second Cavalry, Captain H. E. Noyes[7] commanding.

Fourth Battalion—Companies A and B, Second Cavalry, Captain T. B. Dewees commanding.

Fifth Battalion—Companies F of Third Cavalry and E of Second Cavalry, Captain Alexander Moore commanding.

Sixth Battalion—Companies C and I of Fourth Infantry, Captain E. M. Coates commanding.

In his official report, Colonel Reynolds stated that his column consisted of 30 commissioned officers; 662 enlisted men; 35 scouts, guides, and herders; 5 pack trains; chief packer and employees, numbering 62; 89 wagon train employes; and 5 ambulance employees; making an aggregrate number of 883 men. Wagons of all

---

of the Twentieth Infantry, Lieutenant Reynolds of the United States Navy, and Lieutenant Bainbridge Reynolds of the Third Cavalry.

[6] Alexander Moore, a native of Ireland, was appointed first lieutenant from Illinois in the Thirteenth Wisconsin Infantry when the Civil War began. He served until November, 1862, as aide-de-camp to General Kearny, when he was appointed captain and aide-de-camp of volunteers. In March, 1865, he was brevetted major and lieutenant colonel of volunteers for gallant and distinguished conduct in the Army of the Potomac prior to Gettysburg, and brevet colonel of volunteers for gallant and highly meritorious conduct in the battle of Gettysburg. In January, 1867, he was appointed captain in the Thirty-eighth Infantry, but later in the year was brevetted major in the regular army in further recognition of his services at Gettysburg. He was assigned to the Third Cavalry on December 15, 1870, and resigned from the service on August 10, 1879.

[7] Captain Henry E. Noyes was born in Maine and was graduated from the Military Academy in the class of 1861. He served with the Second Cavalry all through the Civil War and was brevetted for gallant and meritorious services in the battle of Brandy Station, Virginia, and the capture of Selma, Alabama. He served with General Crook all through the Sioux wars, and on May 31, 1898, was commissioned colonel of the Second Cavalry Regiment during his services in the Spanish-American War. He enjoyed a long and successful career in the army.

kinds including ambulances, numbering 85; public horses, numbering 656 were used; while the public mules, including pack mules and mounts of employees, scouts, and guides, numbered 892. Forty days' rations were to be taken consisting of meat, two-thirds beef on the hoof and one-third bacon, and 200,000 pounds of grain.

Dr. C. E. Munn was the chief medical officer of the expedition and Dr. John Ridgely and Dr. Stevens were named as his assistants. Hospital Steward W. C. Bryan, from Fort Fetterman, completed the medical staff. Four ambulances, wagons, and one supply wagon were distributed in the column under the charge of the medical officers. The medical supplies were later carried on two pack mules.[8]

The cavalrymen were armed with the Model 1873 Springfield single-shot, .45-caliber breech-loading carbine. The infantrymen used the same type of weapon with a longer barrel which was called the "Long Tom." The cartridges for both were of copper with 405-grain bullets, but those used in the rifle were loaded with 70 grains of powder while those used in the carbine had only 55 grains of powder. The cartridges were interchangeable, but the rifle cartridge fired in the carbine caused excessive recoil. The carbine was effective up to 600 yards, while the rifle was accurate for 1,000 yards because of the longer barrel and greater powder content. Both had ejectors which often failed to expel cartridge cases when the action was heavy. After five or six rounds had been fired in rapid succession, the empty cases would stick in the chamber so that the ejector would pull the head of the cartridge off, leaving the rest in the gun. Sometimes it was impossible to get a loaded cartridge all the way into the chamber, and in trying to get it out, the ejector would pull the head off, leaving the bullet, powder, wads, and the rest of the copper case lodged in the chamber. Recognizing this defect, the army furnished one ramrod to every twelve men for the purpose of poking out cartridge fragments stuck in the chambers. Major Reno of the Seventh Cavalry claimed after Custer's defeat at the Little Big Horn that the cartridges stuck in chambers because of faulty ejecting mechanisms in the carbines,

---

[8] All material relating to the medical department of the Expedition has been taken from the official reports of Assistant Surgeon C. E. Munn.

although other experts claimed that this was caused by vertigris forming on the copper cartridges while being carried in cartridge belts with leather loops. The leather absorbed all the moisture from the copper, causing vertigris to form.[9]

The cavalrymen had been issued sabers, but these were left behind at the various army posts because it was believed that experience during the Civil War had proved that sabers were not as effective as pistols. The troopers carried Colt .45 pistols in holsters attached to belts which were held up by leather straps passing over the left shoulder. Leather pouches for cartridges were issued to all the troops, but the men sewed loops on their belts and carried their cartridges in the loops.[10] All the soldiers wore the blue uniform with black campaign hats, but commissioned and noncommissioned cavalry officers wore the yellow facings down the trouser legs. Many of the officers and sergeants owned and used their own favorite guns. Captain Mills carried a shotgun. Every cavalry trooper had an extra set of horseshoes fitted to his horse by the company blacksmith.

Many of the older officers held a brevet rank in the army. Brevets were awarded both in the regular and the volunteer armies. Many officers served in the volunteers while retaining their regular army rank, and were frequently awarded brevets in both services. While brevet rank was chiefly honorary, those brevetted were, for some years, entitled to be addressed by their highest brevet title and, on certain occasions, to wear the uniform of the brevet rank. The President was also empowered for a number of years to assign officers to command in accordance with their brevet rank and very often exercised this authority during the years immediately after the Civil War when the army had been greatly reduced.

Major Thaddeus H. Stanton,[11] an army paymaster, was paying

[9] James S. Hutchins, "The Cavalry Campaign Outfit at the Little Big Horn," *Military Collector and Historian*, Vol. VII, No. 4, 91–101; "Letter of Major Marcus Reno," *Army and Navy Journal*, Vol. XIV (August 19, 1876), 26.

[10] *Ibid;* Hutchins, "7th U. S. Cavalry, 1876," *Military Collector and Historian*, Vol. X, No. 4, 108–10.

[11] Thaddeus H. Stanton was born in Indiana. After serving as a private he was appointed captain of the Nineteenth Iowa Infantry in August, 1862. After serving as paymaster, U. S. Volunteers, he was brevetted lieutenant colonel of volunteers on

the troops at Fort Fetterman shortly before the expedition left when he was appointed chief of scouts by General Crook. Major Stanton had served all during the Civil War, but had had no combat experience except for several small skirmishes. General Crook had been trying to get a newspaper correspondent from the New York *Tribune* to accompany the expedition, as he knew that much would be said about the campaign, and he wanted someone along who would present all the facts of the matter to the country. Editor Whitlaw Reid telegraphed that he could not get anyone to go and that he wanted Major Stanton sent with the column as correspondent to write up the campaign for his newspaper. With General Crook's consent to this arrangement, Stanton reported to Colonel Reynolds the day before the march. During the Indian wars officers often wrote accounts of the campaigns which were published in newspapers under assumed names. The practice was frowned upon by the army, and at the conclusion of the Reynolds court martial, the court reprimanded General Crook for permitting Major Stanton to act as a newspaper correspondent in the campaign.

When General Crook was transferred to the Department of the Platte in 1875, the pack trains were brought up from Arizona and stationed at Camp Carlin, near Cheyenne, Wyoming, under command of Major J. V. Furey. A select number of pack mules and packers were ordered to Fort Fetterman to accompany the column. The pack train in the Big Horn Expedition consisted of five units of eighty roughshod mules each, with each unit assigned to one of the cavalry battalions. The pack train of Mr. Tom McAuliff was assigned to the First Battalion; Mr. Richard (Uncle Dick) Closter's,[12] to the Second Battalion; Mr. Foster's, to the Third Bat-

March, 1865, for gallant services during the war. He was appointed paymaster with the rank of major on January 17, 1867, and served in that capacity until his appointment as paymaster general of the U. S. Army in 1895. On February 27, 1890, he was brevetted lieutenant colonel in the regular army for "gallant services against the Indians under Crazy Horse on Powder River, Montana, March 17, 1876." He died in January, 1900.

[12] Richard (Uncle Dick) Closter, according to Bourke's diary, "is an old, white-haired and white-bearded man, snugly wrapped up in the Ulster blouse, made of green blanket, fur cap and heavy boots. . . . His beard is almost always smeared with tobacco juice and his kindly countenance marked by a pleasant smile."

Uncle Dick had seen service with pack trains on the Pacific Coast, in the Rocky

talion; Mr. Young's, to the Fourth Battalion; and Mr. Edward DeLaney's,[13] to the Fifth Battalion. The whole pack train was under the capable leadership of Tom Moore,[14] as chief packer. Moore, who was a native of Virginia, was a close friend of General Crook and had served as chief of pack trains under his command in previous Indian campaigns. He had lived on the Pacific Slope since the first days of the mining fever, and knew more about a mule than any other man in America. He liked to sing about the campfires at night, although there is reason to believe that his

---

Mountains, British Columbia, and Mexico, since 1848, and had had his full share of ups and downs. At the battle of the Rosebud during Crook's summer campaign, Mr. Closter distinguished himself by his sensational marksmanship. While with the other packers who were acting as sharpshooters four hundred yards ahead of the soldiers' line, he picked off several Indians on the Conical Hill, one thousand yards distant.

[13] "Young and Delaney had been with the English in India, in the wars with the Sikhs and Rohillas, and knew as much as most people do about campaigning and all its hardships and dangers." Bourke, *On the Border with Crook*, 305.

"Among the packers was an old, gray-haired forty-niner named Ed Delany who was always taken along for his stories. Ed was illiterate but he subscribed to several magazines for the illustrations. He was a notoriously poor shot but always carried a fine rifle and an ivory-handled, silver-barrelled six-shooter and wore two belts of ammunition suspended from his shoulders by leather galluses. Thirty years later when I was wearing a Sam Browne belt, I never put it on without thinking how much I looked like poor old Ed Delany.

"Ed had a fur cap and a full length overcoat made of selected beaver skins which he said he had caught on the Frazier River in British Columbia, and probably had. Ed would sit down by the fire and get out his Meersham pipe, with a silver lid and a bowl as big as an apple, and set up a fog like a stack of a Mississippi steamboat. Old Ed never had to be coaxed into a recital." Henry W. Daly, "Bear and Buffalo," *American Legion Monthly* (August, 1929), 66. Quotations from the *American Legion Magazine* and the *American Legion Monthly* are used with permission and courtesy of Joseph C. Keeley, editor of the *American Legion Magazine*.

[14] "The Chief Packer was Tom Moore and his assistant was Dave Mears. Both were old-time frontiermen. They had gone to California in 1849, making the voyage around the Horn. Tom came from Kansas, where in later years his sister, Mrs. Carrie Nation, made prohibition conspicuous, if not particularly popular, with the liberal element. Kansas had a dry law, but it made little difference in the life of the frontier towns until Carrie began calling attention to it with her hatchet. She must have broken thousands of dollars' worth of bar mirrors and glassware. Tom introduced Mrs. Daly and myself to her at Camp Carlin in 1889. I noticed that she did not attempt to carry on her reformation that close to home, for Tom had a jug of whiskey handy and said he was never without it in his house. Smoking also was one of Mrs. Nation's aversions, but you would have to get up early in the morning to see Tom without his pipe, big as a Ben Davis apple. Still, brother and sister were very fond of each other." Daly, "The Warpath," *American Legion Monthly* (April, 1927), 16.

vocal efforts were not always appreciated.[15] During his absences while buying mules in the bluegrass country of Missouri and Nebraska, the outfit was managed by "Uncle" Dave Mears.

A wagon train accompanied the column, but the wagons were slow and cumbersome and could not be used in extremely rough country.

On the road, the mules are always up with the command; there is no stoppage or delay, no double-teaming on bad hills, or bogging of wheels, so calculated to retard the progress of a command when travelling with wagons. The road has not to be repaired, or bridges thrown over gullies; if the cavalry horse can scramble over, the mule can follow with comparative ease. In an Indian country the hostiles can see the dust of a wagon train in daylight almost as far as they can detect a fire at night. The amount of dust raised by a pack train is so small as to be almost imperceptible at a moderate distance. Another not unimportant factor in favor of the success of the command in stealing a march on hostiles is the absence in the pack train of all noise, which is the usual accompaniment of a wagon train, such as the cracking of whips and rumbling and creaking of wheels.[16]

Pack mules, used for many years by General Crook, had been organized into efficient pack trains to carry supplies with the cavalry troops. The mules could keep up with the troops and could go any place a horse could go. The highly trained packers, men who made a career of "following the bell," operated the trains without the assistance of the soldiers and functioned as an independent unit. Sometimes troopers without horses were mounted on mules from the pack train. These were called the "Jackass Brigade." The true value of pack mules became apparent in the campaigns against the Indians in Arizona, California, and Oregon. At first they were owned by civilians and were "on hire" to the army, but upon General Crook's recommendation, the trains were purchased by the army and extensively used in all later Indian campaigns. However,

---

[15] Bourke, "General Crook in Indian Country," *Century Magazine* (March, 1891), 657.
[16] *Army and Navy Journal,* Vol. XIX (August 20, 1881), 58.

in some of them, only a few trained packers were used, while the troops provided most of the personnel for operation. A notable example of this was the march of General Custer up the Rosebud and over the divide into the valley of the Little Big Horn, in June, 1876. His pack train was managed by inexperienced troops taken at random from his companies, and as a result was very inefficient and straggled many miles in the rear at the time when it was desperately needed.

The use of pack mules and pack saddles has been traced back to the Arabs. The idea was carried to Spain by the Moors and used by Cortés and Pizarro in their conquests of Peru and Mexico. During the gold rush to California pack trains were imported from the Andean slopes of Chile and Peru, most of the packers being natives of those countries or of Mexico. Of Spanish origin, all of the equipment and operations of a pack train had Spanish names. In medieval Spain the retinues of the nobles included pack mules with housings similar to those of the cavalry, of rich cloth embroidered with gold or of brocade with halters of silk. The bridles, headpieces, and all the harnessings glittered with silver.

In imitation of this feudal grandeur, the California gold-rush packers from South America used riding saddles beautifully stamped or engraved by hand and trimmed with beaten Mexican dollars, cut and chased in various designs to suit their individual tastes. The bridles, bits, and Spanish spurs were chased and inlaid with silver and gold, and the spurs had a bunch of tiny spangles which were made to tinkle. The holiday costume of the packer was copied from the garb of his Spanish brother, and consisted of high-heeled top boots, a silken sash wrapped two or three times around the waist, an embroidered silk front, and a conical sombrero with a silver snake around the crown and silver braid on the underside of the brim.[17]

While operating against the Apaches in Arizona, General Crook organized his pack mules into trains so that they carried supplies along with the fast-moving columns. He made the question of mili-

[17] Henry W. Daly, packmaster, U. S. A., *Manual of Instructions in Pack Transportation.*

tary transportation the study of his life; and under his leadership, pack trains attained a high degree of efficiency. The condition of his pack mules was most jealously scrutinized by him. Crook knew every packer by name, what his peculiarities were, and how he cared for his animals. He knew every mule in his outfit. His pack trains were models after which all others in the army were later patterned.

The packers themselves were robust, hard-working, good-natured fellows, great eaters and good storytellers.[18] They afforded the comedy relief for the soldiers and did all the yelling and shouting for the command. One man to every five mules was the usual allowance in a well-regulated train. Each unit consisted of one pack master, one *cargador*—who divided the loads and saw that they balanced on each mule—one blacksmith, and ten packers, each mounted on a riding mule, together with the bell mare, ridden by the cook, and fifty or more pack mules.

A man to become thoroughly competent must have at least three years practical experience; every year's additional experience will add materially to his intrinsic value. His abilities are required to be so varied, that he must be competent to perform the duties of veterinary surgeon, farrier, harness maker, and cook—one who can roll himself up in a gunny sack with the thermometer at zero and imagine that he is warm, at least be able to sleep. His constitution must be strong enough to enable him to work hard, for a month or more at a time, with but six hours sleep, sometimes less, out of the twenty-four. He must be able to get out of bed

---

[18] "They were a good-natured, merry-hearted set of fellows, ever anxious to render service and delighted beyond expression when they happened to run across an officer desirous of jotting down the tender words of their dainty Spanish songs of love disdained and unrequited.

"First-class packers were almost invariably first-class cooks, to whose forethought and courtesy I have been indebted on many a cold, chilly night for an invigorating cup of chocolate; or nourishing plate of frijoles, dishes beyond the grasp of our boasted civilization. Americans are unequalled by any people in the world for abilities in many directions, but not when it comes to catering to the inner man. Were I at this minute called upon to choose between a cup of chocolate and a plate of beans prepared by my old friend Chileno John or Lauriano Gomez, and the same viands concocted by the most famous chefs in the land, there would be no doubt as to my decision." Bourke, "Mackenzie's Last Fight with the Cheyennes," *Winners of the West* (February 28, 1930), 8.

at any time, no matter how cold, wet, or miserable his surroundings may happen to be, and go at once to work, not merely mechanical work, but such as requires the steady application of his intelligence. The greatest difficulties which he will have to overcome present themselves when travelling over a country destitute of water. The mules on such occasions become frantic, and therefore almost unmanageable. The packer's duties thus become doubled, whilst he himself is suffering from the want of both food and water.[19]

One can imagine that long experience was necessary in learning to cope with the mules, who are notoriously the most contrary of God's creatures. In fact, the pack mule never lost an opportunity to demonstrate the natural perversity of his nature and to call down upon his head the inexhaustible fund of profanity of the packers.

They are unamiable and unattractive animals, awkward, yet "handy with their feet," and vilely discordant. The General, however, knew their value on a campaign, and had great respect for their eccentricities of manner and habit. Notwithstanding, I consider that the average mule is obstinate, and even morose, in manner, and filthy, not to say immodest, in habit. But the animal has his fine points also. He is surer, if slower, than the horse, and can live where the latter would surely starve. Ears polite would be immeasurably shocked by the sounds and observations that accompany the starting of a pack train from camp in the early morning. The hybrids are "cinched" or girthed so tight by the packers that they are almost cut in two. Naturally the beasts don't want to move under such circumstances. They therefore stand stock still. This irritates the packers, who swear in a most artistic and perfectly inexhaustible fashion. They welt the animals with their rawhides most unmercifully, and the brutes reply with their heels and the batteries of nature, in a most effective, if somewhat obscene manner. Suddenly, and generally simultaneously, they dash forward, and matters run more tranquilly during the rest of the day. Such is part of "the romance of war." The muledrivers used to have an excellent time of it, and lived far better than the soldiers. The latter were expected to do all the fighting, while the mulewhackers had the better part of the feasting.[20]

[19] *Army and Navy Journal,* Vol. XIX (August 20, 1881), 58.
[20] John F. Finerty, *Warpath and Bivouac,* 63.

The mules selected for the pack trains were from four to eight years old. If their mouths were bridle worn, they were unfit for pack-train service because when they tried to drink from a stream, the water would run out through the corners of their mouths. They had to have large bellies in order to feed upon the grass of the hills, ofttimes their only sustenance. They could not slope down to the withers because the load would then press too heavily in front. Their backs must be strong, free from blemishes or sores, and their dispositions kind and gentle. The pack animals were never hitched to the picket line. When in bivouac or taken out to graze, they were under a "pack guard." Because mules will never leave the bell mare, it alone was hobbled. The old mules of a train knew their business perfectly well and would never wander far from the sound of the bell. The inexperienced young mule, fresh from the bluegrass of Missouri or Nebraska, was the source of more profanity than he was worth. He would not mind the bell and would wander away from his comrades on herd. The packers marked him in such a manner that every packer could see at a glance that he was a new arrival, and thereupon drive him back to his proper place in the herd. They neatly roached his mane and shaved his tail so that nothing was left but a pencil or tassel of hair at the extreme end. He was then known as a "shavetail," and everybody recognized him at first sight.

One mule will not follow another mule, so that a gray mare known as the "bell mare" was added to each train. The packers, to save the inconvenience of driving and keeping the mules together, made use of the mare with a bell slung around her neck, and the mules when working at night, or in deep and crooked trails where they could not see the mare ahead, would follow perfectly contented within hearing distance of it; but woe to the unfortunate packers if, by an accident, the bell ceased to be heard by the mules.

The mules [wrote Lieutenant John G. Bourke in his diary] speedily learn the sound of their proper bell and rarely fail to heed its warning. The bell mare is ridden by the cook, an important personage in every sphere of life but notably an officer of dignity and trust in a pack train.

Mules manifest a great liking for white horses or mares and in one case that I remember in Arizona they really crushed a little white colt to death in the pack train with General Crook's expedition against hostile Apaches in 1871.

The average load of a pack mule was 250 pounds, exclusive of the packsaddle or *aparejo*, which weighed 60 pounds, and the average day's march was thirty miles but lessened to fifteen miles during mountain climbing. A pack train would average a speed of four to six miles an hour, the same as cavalry, while infantry would cover only two and one-half miles an hour.

The load was balanced on the *aparejo*, which was fitted onto the mule's back. The old style of packsaddle consisted of a couple of boards connected on top by sticks which met and crossed over the animal's back and were very hard on the mule. The loads were firmly attached to the cross sticks; and if both sides were not evenly balanced, the heavier one drew the saddle over, cutting the opposite side of the mule's back. Down steep hills, the load was forced forward on the animal's withers and caused horrible sores. During the California gold rush, when it was necessary to transport barrels of whisky, billiard tables, cooking stoves, mirrors, and provisions over the summits of the Nevada mountains for use in the mining camps, improvements were made by the freighters and a more humane *aparejo* was devised.

It consists of a long and very strong sack of leather about twenty inches wide and from fifty-four to sixty-two inches long. There is a seam which runs from the rear of this sack and terminates in a peculiarly shaped double seam at its front which, when the aparejo is ready for use, protects the withers of the mule from being pressed. This seam divides the sack into equal parts, leaving one for each side of the animal. Into these sacks from the inside are first placed willow or ash sprouts, running lengthwise and carefully placed at equal distances, thus creating a stiff and even surface on the outside; on the inside of these and toward the mule's back are placed layers of soft springy hay, varying from two and a half to four inches thick, the variations in thickness being governed in each case by the peculiarity of the conformation of the back of the mule, for which the particular aparejo is intended. A wide crupper is attached to the outside of this sack, which extends back over the hips, thus presenting a broad surface which prevents chafing. A canvas cover is placed over these sacks to protect the leather.

The aparejo is now ready for use. . . . It protects the mule's sides as well as the back; it presents four times the number of square inches for equal pressure to the animal that the saddle does; the peculiar shape of the aparejo affords an opportunity to balance the load; thus one hundred pounds on one side can be made to ride with sixty on the opposite as well as if they were of equal weight, thus preventing any unequal strain on the animal. In the field, when working every day, a bruise or sore on a mule's back can be cured in the following manner: when it first appears, which it does by becoming inflamed, the hay is removed from the interor of the sack in the place which has been the cause of the bruise, thus leaving a space which, when on the mule's back, forms a kind of cup over the injury without pressing or further irritating it. Again, no matter how badly shaped a mule's back may be, an experienced packer can manipulate the filling in the sacks so that it will fit his back as nicely and smoothly as a glove.[21]

The *corona*, which was used to wrap up the cargo, consisted of four plies of blankets, sewed together and lined with light canvas; it was wider than the *aparejo*, but not so long. The outer blanket was usually of a bright red color, gorgeously ornamented, and often wrought with odd and fantastic designs. The packers would spend odd hours of loving toil upon the *corona*, working the representations of some animal, bird, insigne, or legend with silken thread of various colors. After the cargo had been taken off, the *corona* was removed and placed double on top of it, with the figures up. On the halter of the mule, which was fixed permanently on its head, the packers, after fitting an *aparejo* to his back, cut the corresponding number in the strap which passed over the jaw. By this means, each mule always had the same adjusted *aparejo* placed on it. As the matching numbers were either raised or cut out, there was no liability of making mistakes even when working at night.

The *sobrejalma*, or overcover, which supported the *aparejo*, was made of stout canvas, faced with leather, and of the following di-

[21] *Army and Navy Journal*, Vol. XVIII (July 2, 1881), 1010.

mensions: length, seventy-six inches; width, thirty-two inches; thickness, three inches. This was made to double in the middle of its length and was secured to the animal by the *cincha,* or belt, of canvas passing around the girth.

On the march, camp was made at two or three o'clock in the afternoon in order to avoid the extreme heat. On arrival at camp, the loads were taken off and the *aparejos* removed and placed side by side in the form of an arc. When standing on the ground they resembled miniature A tents, being about thirty inches high and some twenty inches wide at the bottom. The mules were turned over to the guard, and everything belonging to the pack train was so arranged that no matter how dark the night was, there would be no confusion in case of their being ordered to move.

At night the bell mare was picketed, and the mules grazed around her all night, without ever wandering far enough from her to be beyond the reach of the sound of the bell. There were only two meals a day, the large meal being at night after camp was made. Breakfast was cooked at the same time and kept warm until the next morning so that there would be little delay in breaking camp. After supper the men congregated around the campfires, had a short session of storytelling or singing, and went early to rest.

At three o'clock in the morning the camp would be roused up, and after a hasty breakfast, the column was on its way by six o'clock. When the mules were caught, they were driven up to the convex side of the arc, their heads pointing towards the center of the circle over the *aparejos,* and were kept standing in this position while the pack master, with the halter straps on his arm, walked along on the inside of the arc and, by means of a spring on the end of each strap, snapped one in the halter of each mule as he passed. A man followed who tied the mules together. Commencing at the mare, which was held or tied in her proper place, he tied the halter strap of the first mule to that of the bell mare, the strap of the second mule to that of the first, and so on until the chain was complete, thus securing each mule without difficulty. The packers, who worked in pairs, unfastened the lower mule, leading him around in front of the others, until they arrived at his *aparejo.* After the mule had been blindfolded with the *topajo,* a leathern blind, the sweat cloth was placed upon the withers followed by two saddle blankets. Next came the *sobrejalma* doubled crossways, upon which was mounted the *aparejo.* The *corona* was placed over the *aparejo,* and then the *cincha,* which was ten inches wide, passed loosely over the *aparejo* but not attached to it. This served, when tightened, to equalize the pressure on the animal's back and sides, and at the same time, to allow a wide surface for the mule's belly. While the packers were thus engaged, the pack master was receiving the loads which were being brought in by the soldiers from the different companies, and he arranged them so as to secure a load for each mule.

The manner of packing is as follows: the load is divided into two as equal parts as possible. A loop of a rope is then thrown from one side to the other across the aparejo, the loads are then placed on the animal's back by the two men, one on each side, the loop is then passed back over the load, one of the ends passed through it and then firmly tied to the other one; this is called "slinging." The load is now simply resting on the aparejo, without being attached to it, in which position it is balanced. Next a long rope, to one end of which is attached a short leathern girth with a brass hook at the end of it is used, the girth passing under the mule's belly, and the rope thrown in a peculiar manner into a kind of loose knot over the load, which, when tightened, holds the cargo firmly in its proper place. This knot is elsewhere referred to as a diamond hitch. In this manner howitzers, Hotchkiss guns, bacon, flour, corn, ammunition, blankets, and in fact every description of camp supplies are thus packed over mountains and valleys, where the uninitiated gentleman from the East would be afraid even to lead his horse.[22]

After being loaded, each mule was turned loose; when all were loaded, the packers mounted their mules. The cook took the bell mare and started off, the most energetic mules close behind her, and so on, until the lazy fellows, or those most heavily loaded, brought up the rear about 150 yards behind the bell, but never farther, all being strung out in single file. The packers rode to the left of the train at intervals of from 20 to 30 yards, each man

[22] *Ibid.*

keeping his eyes on the mules ahead of him. When he saw a load that was not riding properly, he notified his nearest neighbor of the fact, and they both rode ahead, and jumping off, each took a side of the trail, where they waited until the arrival of the mule they wanted. Closing in on it, they led it to one side, where they loosened up the lashing, rebalanced the load, and having again tightened the lash rope, turned the animal loose. All this was done in less time than it takes to tell it. The mule, on getting away, started after the bell; by the time the packers had mounted their saddle mules and overtaken him, he would have regained his position in the train.

While the wagon train and pack train brought up the rear, the column was led by a number of scouts and guides who were familiar with the Powder River country. Captain Azor H. Nickerson, aide-de-camp to General Crook, had assembled about thirty-five of these men from the settlements below Fort Laramie and from the Indian agencies. A band of ten scouts came from Fort Robinson in Nebraska under the leadership of Louis Richaud.

Col. T. H. Stanton [wrote Mr. Strahorn in his dispatch of February 29] is Chief of perhaps as fine a corps of scouts as has ever been organized in an Indian campaign—especially if experience goes for aught. Among the twenty-five or thirty selected, are such men as Jules Ecofee, who has seen almost a quarter of a century of service as scout, guide, etc., in the Rocky Mountain country; Ben Clark,[23] from Indian Terri-

[23] As the troops were moving out from Fort Fetterman at the start of the campaign, Lieutenant Bourke wrote in his diary, "Ben Clarke has been on many scouts and campaigns against the hostile Indians of Texas, Indian Territory, Kansas and Colorado, attracting the favorable attention of such distinguished officers as Gen. Sheridan. He is not acquainted with the Big Horn country but his natural faculty for learning locality is so great that he may safely be considered our best man." However, Frank Grouard, who was familiar with the country, was soon recognized as the head scout, and Ben Clarke was mentioned no more in the accounts.

In later years, Henry W. Daly, who had joined General Crook's pack train shortly before the Rosebud campaign, remembered the famous scout, "Old Ben Clark has been dead now for twenty years, but were you to see him as I have seen him a great many times with a pair of worn jeans tucked in his boots, a greasy hat and a weeks growth of beard, you might mistake him for a second-rate cowboy who couldn't make enough to keep up appearances. Yet Ben Clark was one of the famous scouts of the west." Henry W. Daly, "Scouts—Good and Bad," *American Legion Monthly* (August, 1928), 24.

tory, for a long time one of Gen. Crook's principal scouts, and sent for by the General for this expedition; Baptiste Poirrier, a well-versed French frontiersman, and for a long time one of the scouts at Fort Laramie; Speed Stagner, post guide at Fort Fetterman, and Louis Richaud, a halfbreed Sioux, who was scout on the expedition of Generals Smith and Connor.

However, Lieutenant Bourke was not impressed with the scouts, and wrote in his diary:

They are as sweet a lot of cut-throats as ever scuttled a ship, halfbreeds, squaw men, bounty jumpers, thieves and desperadoes of different grades from the various Indian Agencies. . . . I do not mean to reflect upon Col. Stanton for the personnel of his corps d'elite most of which was recruited before his assignment to its command . . . but a respectable minority were men of high type of character, of great previous experience and likely to be of inestimable use in any sudden emergency.

Other scouts named in the various accounts were Louis Shangrau, John Shangrau, Charlie Jennesse, Charles Richard, Baptiste "Little Bat" Garnier, Tom Reed, Joe Eldridge, John Provost, Mitch Shimmeno, Jack Russell, John Farnham, and Frank Grouard. Most of these men lived on the flats a short distance down the river from Fort Laramie and were descendants of some of La Ramie's associates. They were a mixture of French and Indian blood and lived with Indian women. The band of scouts under Louis Richaud did not arrive until after the command had left Fort Fetterman, and joined the column at Sage Creek.

In his dispatch of February 29 to his newspaper, Mr. Strahorn reported that friendly Indians stopped at the post with accounts of unusual activity among the hostile camps to the north:

It is quite evident, from the movements of peaceably disposed Indians, that hostile bands have an inkling of the fact that a demonstration is to be made against them. Several days ago Plenty-of-Bears, an Arapahoe Chief, with ten or a dozen lodges of followers, came here and said he was anxious to always be at peace with the "Great Father," that he was then on his way over to Red Cloud Agency to attest his sincerity in the matter. When questioned about the Indians against whom we are to proceed he replied: "Minneconjoux heap braves. Many lodges. Makum tired countum." Black Crow, another Arapahoe Chieftain with thirty-six lodges, also came in a day or two ago, and is now encamped near by on the Platte. He, too, is very much afraid something unpleasant is about to happen, and says he is on his way to the Agency. He intimates that Indian runners have already conveyed intelligence of an anticipated move by the military from this point to the northern tribes. In addition to these facts pointing to the arousing of the Indian suspicion, we have positive information that the Minneconjoux and other tribes are already overrunning the northern frontier, and that numerous depredations have recently been committed by them. General Crook therefore discovers that instead of taking the Indians by surprise they have almost anticipated him by first opening the ball thus early in the season.

On February 29, Lieutenant Bourke noted in his diary that "weather is now changing, sky cloudy and leaden in appearance, wind chilly and damp. Indications of a snow storm approaching. Command is all encamped (with exception of the 2 infantry companies) on the bank of the North Platte River with system and order rapidly asserting themselves. We expect to get off early tomorrow morning, March 1st."

Chapter 3 THE MARCH TO POWDER RIVER

GENERAL Crook had determined to follow the old Bozeman Trail leading in a general northwesterly direction from Fort Fetterman: the Montana Road which ran through Sioux territory, passing by the sites of old Fort Reno, Fort Phil Kearny, and Fort C. F. Smith, which had been abandoned in 1868, and terminated at the mining center, Virginia City. By following this road the command would have easier grades, better water and wood, and fords across the larger streams.

On March 1 the command moved off in fine style. Officers and men were in good spirits; and horses, chomping on their bits, were eager for the journey. The snow storm of the night before had ceased, and upon the serene sky not a trace of clouds could be seen.

When the soldiers left the fort, they did not follow the road northward past the Hog Ranch. Since the river was deep in front of the fort, the troops took the road westward across La Prelle Creek and marched south of the river for two miles. At the point where the river was wide and shallow with a good rock bottom, the column crossed. Marching straight north for several miles, they struck the Bozeman Trail, which bends to the northwest at the Hog Ranch. After the line had closed up, the column extended for a little over two miles. The band of scouts were first in line, ten long companies of cavalry next, two companies of infantry following; then the ambulances, wagon train, pack train, and the herd of sixty or seventy beef cattle in the rear. The cattle were to be slaughtered along the way as occasion demanded. The first day of march was only fifteen miles, and at one o'clock camp was made on Sage Creek. Here was found an abundance of grass, but water only in a few pools and no fuel except sagebrush.

According to Lieutenant Morton's map, the official map of the course followed by the expedition, the Sage Creek camp was east of the road and north of the creek. As the campsite must have covered an area of at least one-half mile square, it was probably in the fork of Sage Creek about one mile east of the present road. Wherever possible, the soldiers would camp in a fork where one stream joined another in order to have greater access to water. The Sage Creek camp was one commonly used on the Bozeman Trail, since it was one easy day's march from Fort Fetterman for a wagon train and infantry.

The next morning, breaking camp quite early, the column was on the road at sunrise. After they had marched ten or twelve miles, fine views of the Black Hills were obtained seventy miles to the northeast. Pumpkin Buttes, four large elevations resembling in shape the vegetable of the same name, were visible forty miles to the north, and Laramie Peak could be seen to the southeast. When the column reached Brown Springs (which was named after Lieutenant John R. Brown of Company E, Eleventh Ohio Cavalry, who was killed here by Indians in July, 1864), it turned to the northeast, leaving the Bozeman Trail, and followed down the valley three or four miles to its junction with the Dry Fork of the Cheyenne River. This stream cut its narrow bed through hills and bluffs so rugged that at many points it could not be approached. Camp was made on a tongue of land at the fork where the water was deeper and clearer than that farther upstream to the west. There was a good crossing here, and the trail led northwest over the bluffs back to the main road. It is apparent that this spot was an old campsite because burned rocks, glass fragments, cans, and other debris are still scattered about. Brown Springs was usually the second campground out from Fort Fetterman, but General Crook must have thought there was not enough water there for all of the animals and decided to go on a few miles farther to the Dry Fork.

The March to Powder River

The first incident of the campaign occurred that night, and Mr. Strahorn described it in his dispatch of March 3 to his newspaper:

At about two o'clock this morning, when the entire camp was wrapped in deepest slumber, and when all but the sentinels and herders were sleeping in as fancied security as though yet at Fetterman, we went through the novel sensation of a modern Indian stampede. There were a number of unearthly yells as if from a man surprised, several rifle shots in quick succession, an Indian whoop, a cloud of dust, and a man was dangerously wounded, a herd of fifty cattle and a horse vanished, and that is what we know of a stampede. The wounded man, a herder, who is shot through the lungs, says he saw two or three Indians creeping toward him through the sage brush, and his yells and the rapidly succeeding shots were the result. The entire command was instantly aroused, and the order to "fall in" came almost upon the heels of the alarm from several captains. But immediate pursuit was not allowed, as that would have been next to a hopeless undertaking. At break of day, however, a company of cavalry, headed by two or three of our best trailing scouts, took the track and were soon going at high speed over a neighboring plateau. A very short time has elapsed, and now, as the sun has reddened the east and is just peeping out upon the scene of its widespread blush, the pursuers enter the almost deserted camp with the information that the cattle are on their way back to Fort Fetterman, where, it is to be hoped, their safe arrival will be as greatly appreciated as would have been their onward march with us. We have less now to retard us, but, alas for the rarity of Indian charity, we are out of beef and have a wounded man on our hands—all this, too, within thirty-two miles of the fort. It is thought that the Indians, observing the sudden alarm of the camp, were fearful that in trying to get away with so much booty they might lose their own scalps, and so made tracks in another direction with their stolen horse. Indian signs were numerous and fresh in almost every direction, and that they—the savages—are watching our every movement in spite of all precaution, is indisputable.

The loss of the beef herd was more serious than was realized at the time. The herder who was shot through the lung was John Wright. He was carried along with the column in an ambulance. It is extremely doubtful that the beef herd ever reached the fort thirty-two miles away with no one to drive them there. It is more probable that they were rounded up by the Indians and driven to the nearest village.

On March 3 the command marched eight miles to the Middle Fork of the Cheyenne River and seven more to the North Fork. Camp was made six miles farther on at Buffalo Wallow, a pleasant little cove on one of the forks of Wind River. In the forenoon, from the top of a prominent mesa, the men had their first view of the Big Horn Mountains, a resplendent range stretching off for over one hundred miles along the northwestern horizon.

The next day, after a march of twenty-one miles, the command made camp on the Dry Fork of Powder River. In the afternoon an Indian smoke signal was observed on the apex of a high hill far to the front. That night an Indian crept up through the grass and was discovered by a sentry, who immediately fired. Next morning it was found that three or four Indians had been taking observations on the outskirts of camp.

On March 5 the column moved fifteen miles down the valley of the Dry Fork of Powder River in the face of wind and snow from the northwest, and camped in a wooded stretch of bottom land which was on Powder River across from the ghostly relict of old Fort Reno. Many lodgepole trails had been seen, and during the march two Indian bucks mounted on fleet ponies were observed in the distance. They waited until the head of the column approached within one thousand yards, then scampered rapidly over the hills and were soon lost to sight. General Crook would not allow any pursuit, as he said it would break down at least twenty horses. Such cautiousness would also lead the Indians to believe that the soldiers were in fear of them, and it was hoped that they would become emboldened to approach more closely in larger bands and make an attack upon the troops.

That evening, General Crook sent out a small party of picked scouts, mounted on Indian ponies, down the Powder River to look for Indian villages. Pickets were posted three hundred yards in front of camp, and about eight o'clock a sentry of Major Coates's[1]

---

[1] Captain Edwin M. Coates, born in New York, was appointed a second lieutenant in the Second Cavalry, from Illinois, on August 5, 1861. He was transferred

company discovered three mounted Indians approaching him from the Fort Reno side of camp. The sentry opened fire upon them; instantly a brisk fusillade was commenced from other Indians hidden on two sides of the camp. The bright campfires were put out, but not before the Indians had obtained the range; they kept up a deliberate and accurate fire for thirty or forty minutes. The soldiers fell in line but did not answer the fire of the Indians at first—because the flash of their rifles would have provided good targets for the enemy—but later fired several volleys. The plan of the Indians had been for the three to advance into the bivouac and, by shouting, shaking of buffalo robes, and shooting, cause a stampede among the horses and mules. With many hundreds of animals wild with terror rushing through and over tents and picket lines, the soldiers would have done well to save their own lives. In the resulting confusion the bold intruders could easily escape to their comrades at the other side of camp; and together they could seize upon the herd and leave the soldiers afoot. This scheme was frustrated by the vigilance of the sentinel and by the fact that the horses and mules had been picketed instead of being allowed to run at large in camp. During the attack the soldiers obeyed orders with coolness and precision, despite the fact that many of them were imperfectly drilled recruits. Corporal Slavey of Major Coates's company of the Fourth Infantry was wounded slightly in the cheek, and there were many close calls. After remaining under arms about half an hour, the line was withdrawn, leaving the pickets posted at suitable points.

The scouts who had been sent out earlier had advanced five or six miles when a halt was made to rest. Discovering the lights of the rifles back at the camp and surmising that Indians were attacking it, they decided to return in the hope of aiding the defense of the camp by approaching the attackers from the rear. They arrived about midnight, too late to be of assistance, but General Crook

to the Twelfth Infantry and served all through the Civil War. He was brevetted captain on August 1, 1864, for gallant service in the Battle of the Wilderness and during the campaign before Richmond, Virginia. On March 23, 1869, he was transferred to the Fourth Infantry, where he served for many years on the western frontier.

expressed his satisfaction with their behavior. The rest of the night passed quietly.

The soldiers were impressed with the coolness and imperturbability of the General, who had retired to rest shortly before the firing began. After expressing his satisfaction with the way Colonel Reynolds had posted the vedettes, he explained the Indian strategy to his officers. Divining that there would be no serious action that night, he turned over and went to sleep.

Everyone in the command evinces a commendable eagerness to encounter the enemy [wrote Lieutenant Bourke in his diary] and a confidence of success which is half of the victory. If we can find the Indians there will be another "Black Kettle" affair to impress upon them the folly of waging war upon the whites. . . .

One exception must be made when speaking of the good spirits of all the Expedition—the exception I am sorry to say is our colored cook "Jeff" whose culinary efforts have earned a praise which cannot be shared by his patriotism or valor. What fear nature first placed in his breast has been greatly developed under the arduous instructions of Col. Stanton and other friends of the freed man, along with us at this time. The very name of an Indian stops the circulation of his blood, and at night his terror is almost laughable. The stories told him are frightful enough but lack the element of probability and veracity. . . .

March 6th. Everybody awoke at a very early hour. Our cook Jeff had not entirely recovered from the fright last night's events had occasioned. For that reason we were willing to accept with patience and with charitable good will any shortcomings in the culinary arrangements of the morning. To our surprise, however, our generosity had no occasion to manifest itself. In truth the breakfast today excelled any we had seated ourselves to on the whole trip. The cold bracing air sweeping down from the mountains exhilarated us wonderfully and was eagerly used as an excuse for the ravenous appetites which consumed fabulous quantities of biscuits, butter, meat, potatoes, eggs, and dried stewed apples washed down by copious draughts of excellent hot and strong coffee. We soon crossed the ice and water of Powder River. . . . The bed of the stream is mainly quicksand and has the reputation of impassability except at the ford which we used. Upon climbing the opposite bank our advance entered the ruins of old Fort Reno. Nothing now remains but a little of

Fort Riley, Kansas, Museum
COLONEL
JOSEPH J. REYNOLDS.

National Archives
MAJOR T. H. STANTON.

Library of Congress

FRANK GROUARD. *From a sketch by Charles St. George Stanley, in* Frank Leslie's Illustrated Newspaper.

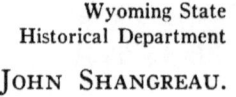

Wyoming State Historical Department

JOHN SHANGREAU.

the stockade formerly surrounding the post, part of the bake-oven, the chimney of the trader's store and one or two of those belonging to the officers' quarters. . . .

From the crests of the bluffs overlooking the Powder a magnificent view was obtained of the Big Horn Range. Piercing far above the superincumbent clouds the snow-capped eminences seemed so many sentinels guarding the country at their base. Heavy belts of black pine and junipers brought into bold contrast the glaring white of the summits. . . . All day long we pursued our way over a very good road, without rocks or breaks to impede the progress of the trains. . . . Two or three of our guides went off on each flank and by afternoon were successful in bringing down three nice fat antelope which will help to vary the bill of fare most pleasantly. . . . Indian signal smokes were to be seen all day away off on our right, and once or twice our guards noticed signals flashed across country. These signals are made by the reflection of the sun from the small round looking glasses Indians wear about their necks and are flashed according to some pre-arranged system.

The column made camp on the banks of the Crazy Woman's Fork about 4:00 P.M. after marching about twenty-five miles.

The rivers in this area had been named by the Indians. Powder River derived its name from the peculiar black, mellow soil found on its banks which had the appearance of black gunpowder. The Indians believed that this soil could be transformed into gunpowder; and although all of their attempts failed, they clung to the belief that this could be accomplished if the right process were found. Tongue River, the "Talking River," was so named because of the distinctness of the echoes which resounded from its rocky walls. Crazy Woman's Fork was so called because one of their women betrayed a monomania for being indiscriminately married —something that an Indian believed must arise from a crazed state of mind. Sequestered Hanging Woman's Fork came from the sad history that a beautiful Arapaho maiden had long ago committed suicide, at the end of a lariat over its banks, because her tribe wanted her to marry at least once against her wishes. Wooden Leg Creek received its homely cognomen simply because a Sioux brave there lost one of his legs by freezing, and showed his ingenuity in carving a frostproof limb from one of the many cottonwoods that overhung the stream.[2]

The country was becoming so rough that General Crook decided to leave the cumbersome wagon train under guard of the two infantry companies, and to strike out with the cavalry and pack train. At sundown the officers gathered in a semicircle in front of General Crook's tent to receive their final instructions. All baggage was to be inspected, and each man could have one buffalo robe or two blankets and no more. No tentage was allowed, but every man might take a piece of shelter tent, and every two officers one tent fly. These were to be carried by the pack train together with an extra one hundred rounds of ammunition per man. The men were to carry nothing on their persons but their arms, one hundred rounds of ammunition, and the clothing on their backs. Rations for fifteen days, consisting of hard bread, half-rations of bacon, coffee, and sugar, together with one-sixth rations of grain, 26,000 pounds, for the animals, were to be packed on the mule train. The wagon train and the two infantry companies under command of Major Coates were sent back to the site of Fort Reno to entrench and await the return of the column. Dr. Ridgely remained with the wagon train, charged with the care of a few cavalrymen found to be unfit to proceed and the wounded herder, John Wright, who was doing well. A .45-caliber pistol ball had passed through the edge of his lung at an angle. Dr. Ridgely received careful instructions to establish a field hospital to be in readiness on the return of the troops because it was probable there would be many requiring medical attention.

March 7 was devoted to the preparation for the active campaign, and at dark that evening the five squadrons of cavalry moved out on the first night march amid murmurs of hundreds of farewells and good wishes to carry the war into the Sioux country. The long dark column marched northward across plains, over rugged hills and through dark gulches, occasionally winding around the brinks of dangerous precipices, the men groping carefully for footholds. During the night a mule broke his back descending an icy ravine.

[2] Bourke, Diary.

The March to Powder River

At 4:00 P.M. the next morning the command was halted on the banks of the Clear Fork of the Powder River, having covered thirty miles during the night. After a few hours' sleep the troops were awakened by a bitter, pelting storm of snow driven by a cold wind which extinguished the cook fires and froze the beans, coffee, and bacon. The command moved down the valley of the Clear Fork five miles to the mouth of Piney Creek and camped the rest of the day in a pleasant cove. The storm continued all night and the next day. The snow was five or six inches deep but in many places was piled high by the piercing winds.

As we were without tents [wrote Lieutenant Bourke in his diary], we had nothing to do but grin and bear it. Some officers stretched blankets to the branches of trees. Others found a questionable shelter under the bluffs. One or two constructed nondescript habitations of twigs and grass, while General Crook and Colonel Stanton seized upon the abandoned den of a family of beavers which a sudden change in the bed of the stream had deprived of their home. To obtain water, holes of suitable dimensions were cut in the ice here found to be 18 inches thick. . . . Everyone welcomed the advent of night which enabled us to seek such rest as we could find and clad as last night in the garments of the day, officers and men, wrapped up in blankets from the pack train found rest but not much repose. Our men shared with their animals their own scanty allowance of blankets as the bad weather and poor rations have made our animals look gaunt and travel worn. Mustaches and beards were coated with pendant icicles several inches long.

The troops were astir before daylight on March 9 and soon were ascending the valley of Piney Creek. After a few miles they crossed over a high, badly broken divide and proceeded some fifteen miles farther, the snow and piercing blasts opposing every forward step, to the head of Prairie Dog Creek, where camp was made in a secluded ravine with the mercury showing six degrees below zero. Twenty scouts were sent ahead at nightfall to prospect the way and to guard against alarming any Indian encampments which the soldiers expected to find at any moment.

The next day the command marched twenty-two miles northward

down Prairie Dog Creek in the face of a severe storm to a point near the Tongue River, where camp was made. During lulls in the storm the little prairie dogs could be seen running around in the snow to and from their holes, marking the snow in every direction with their tracks. The ground was extremely slippery and icy, and men and horses were constantly slipping and falling in crossing the abrupt *arroyos* cutting across the trail every few hundred yards. Corporal Moore, of Lieutenant W. W. Robinson's Company D, Third Cavalry, was severely injured when his horse lost its footing and fell upon him. He was carried on a trail stretcher constructed for him and dragged behind a mule.

The animals had no trouble on level ground; but whenever a little gulch or piece of ground covered with ice was crossed, every company commander and every trainmaster watched with anxiety. The mules did better in this respect than the horses. Many a hearty laugh resulted from seeing the mules cautiously approach the edge of a ravine and then, after having considered the situation, fold their hind legs under them, stiffen their forelegs, and slide to the bottom like a boy coasting down hill.

That evening the scouts returned and reported that the Indians had fled down the Tongue River. They had found a recently deserted Indian village of sixty tipis with many freshly picked buffalo skeletons. A young puppy strangled to death and suspended from a tree by a piece of rope indicated that they had left in great haste, since choked pup, cooked whole in a pot of boiling water, was a rare delicacy among the Sioux.

On Saturday, March 11, the sun shone out bright and clear, but the mercury in the thermometer had shrunk low into the bulb. The command marched down to Tongue River and followed the stream northward into Montana Territory, crossing it five or six times. The guides explored as far west as the Rosebud River, but no Indian signs were seen in that direction. That night the mercury congealed in the bulb, but fortunately no one was frozen, and the casualties from cold up to that date amounted to a frosted ear and finger, both cases very slight. Cooking breakfast during this cold weather was a problem Bourke described in his diary:

The March to Powder River

Our cook must first chop with an axe the bacon which overnight has frozen solid as marble; then if he has made any "soft bread," i.e. flour bread baked in a frying pan, he has to place that in front of a strong fire for a few minutes to thaw it so it can be eaten. Fork and spoon are heated in ashes to keep them from freezing the skin of the lip and tongue. Breakfast is apt to be no meal at all unless the eater displays great adroitness and agility. First the cook spreads down a long piece of canvas for a table cloth arranging upon it tin cups, plates, knives and forks in proportion to the number in the mess. A huge mess pan of boiled or baked beans, flanked by salt and pepper bottles and several platters of hard tack, or if the cook has had time to make it, soft bread baked in a frying pan, is placed upon the canvas, followed by hot coffee, crisply fried bacon and generally stewed dried apples. To the inspiring cry "Grub pile," "Yars yer hash," "Sup-pah," etc., the wolfy appetites of the packers press forward to the festive board. Old hands who know what cold weather is, now seize their plates and give them a twirl or two in front of the fire and in like manner knives, forks and spoons are heated and the work of carnage commences. This is not the proper place to specify the quantities of solid food consumed at each meal by a hard working packer; the amount would almost certainly do a small family for a day. The afternoon meal is ready without appreciable delay; hunger gives place to satiety and for a brief interval we gather around the fire to narrate occurrences of the march or exchange the song or story. Well has the Spaniard observed: "a full belly makes contented heart."

There was no noon meal on the march and seldom one in camp in the field. The men ate morning and night, cooking only in the evening. When supper was out of the way, breakfast was prepared and kept over until morning.

The march of the twelfth brought the command twenty miles down the Tongue River, which was crossed eighteen times during the day. Its valley gradually narrowed down to a little gorge bordered by bluffs of red and yellow sandstone between 150 and 200 feet high, well fringed with scrub pine and juniper trees. The cold weather continued.

During the night [wrote Mr. Strahorn in his March 13 dispatch] two men belonging to one of the pack trains grew as uncomfortable as the balance of the shivery command and singularly enough each blamed the other for his discomfort, never dreaming that mercury was congealing and that spirit thermometers would have registered 40 or 50 degrees below zero beneath his blanket. After fighting around an hour or two, and wasting a vast amount of scientific profanity, the two freezing packers after years of warmest friendship, agreed to part. Their scanty supply of blankets was divided, each took up his portion and moved some twenty paces in an opposite direction, the frozen ground and snow creaking underfoot like a rusty hinge, and the air thick with frost. Again lying down in plain view of each other the divorced packers every moment growing colder, commenced thinking of how beautiful it is for brethren to dwell in unity together—or something to that effect—when it is so unmercifully cold. Then each would wonder how long the other would "grin and bear it," whether it would be better after all to commence making overtures looking to a speedy consolidating of personal effects—especially blankets. Soon there was a rolling and cramping, and unmistakable grunting, and finally at 2 o'clock A.M., both sat bolt upright; for fear of freezing a good intention by undue procrastination they then rose to their feet as one man, icy blankets were lifted from the icy ground, and the twain came to "right shoulder shift" with military precision; without a word they strode rapidly toward each other and when they met as they had parted Hans threw down his blankets, Pat and Hans lay down in one time and two motions and Pat pulled his offering in the shape of blankets up very carefully up over both. Then for the first time since the pangs of parting the intensity of feeling broke out in words for each. Pat said:

"Hans?"

"Wot?"

"It's damned cold, ain't it?"

And then Hans said:

"Pat?"

"Pwhat?"

"Ve has peen damt fools, ain't we?"

They are about as good judges of cold weather now as any other men on the expedition. Hans, evidently a sacrilegious wretch, upon leaving Fort Fetterman marked on his knapsack the words, "Big Horn or Hell," but after breathing the Montana atmosphere for a few days, defaced the inscription and wrote underneath, "Hell Froze Over!"

The March to Powder River

On March 13 the weather moderated, although remaining cloudy and threatening. Bourke reported on this date that the rations were one-half gone. During the cold weather his bottle of ink froze and burst, and he had to finish his diary in pencil. The command moved twelve and three-eighths miles farther down the Tongue River, passing by hundreds of acres covered with large cottonwood trees which had been felled by Indian women so that the ponies could browse upon the tender young shoots and branches. Upon the barkless whitened trunks appeared many curious drawings of men and animals executed by the Indians. Several old buffalo had been shot and were served up on every mess canvas, and while the meat was tough, fibrous, and lean, according to Lieutenant Bourke, it was an excellent substitute for no meat at all. Guides were sent out in advance to scout northward down to the Yellowstone River under orders to rejoin the command in two days, farther down the Tongue River. Near the camp of the thirteenth, on the summit of a small knoll, was found red paint material which the Indians used in rendering their persons savagely beautiful. An excavation some twenty feet square in the mound of dark red clay indicated that the Indians had for years obtained their supply of ochre here. Eighteen miles farther down the valley was a similar deposit of white clay from which white and other colors of paint were made by the rude processes of the natives.

During the march Lieutenant Bourke was looked after by his warm friend Richard Closter, leader of one of the pack trains. In later years, while in a reminiscent mood, Bourke remembered the devotion shown him by the old man:

"Uncle Dick" Kloster, one of the pack train veterans now passed away, presents himself to my recollection clad from head to heel in fur and blanket lined canvas, a muskrat cap on his head, while from eyes to breast extends a snow white beard matted like a board with frozen tobacco juice; that was during the severe privations we underwent in Montana during the early months of 1876, marching on half rations with the mercury in the thermometer frozen solid. Every afternoon, the moment the column made camp, out came my notebook to record the events of the day—in ink until the intense cold broke the bottle and afterwards in pencil as well as numbed fingers would permit. After first looking to his mules, Dick would hurry to my side, doing everything in his power to add to my comfort; sometimes he would pile up *aparejos* (a form of pack saddle) to keep the fierce north wind from carrying me bodily away, or build a fire at my feet to prevent my toes from freezing—always something.[3]

Observing that Bourke was continually making notes for his book, Closter, who had never seen his name in print, requested that his name be put in the book. Upon learning of the death of the old man, Bourke recalled the incident:

When I told the dear old soul that not only his name but full references to his valuable kindness as well, would appear on a prominent page, the smile that overspread his face almost cracked the frost on his beard. "Look, Uncle Dick, here's your name—see for yourself!" This recognition roused his generous good nature to a paroxysm of enthusiasm; he multiplied his efforts and ventured now and then to offer bits of information, some of consequence and others not, but all most gratefully received.

I once overheard him confiding to an open-mouthed packer that "Me'n the Capt'n air getting up a book 'bout the Injuns an' mos' everything," and my last parting word from the old man was, "Cap, don't forgit that thar book outfit."

No, Uncle Dick, I have not forgotten; and I do hope that from the packer's paradise to which I am sure you have gone, and where your honest soul would be grieved if you did not find abundance of grass and water for your mules, no flies to bother them, the very best rations for your men—beans and bacon, "yeast powder" bread, dried apples, coffee, chocolate and an occasional "snootful" of something to drive away malaria—you may be able to read these lines.[4]

After the march ten miles down Tongue River, camp was made on the fourteenth on the left bank opposite the mouth of Pumpkin Creek, also named Red Clay Creek. In an abandoned Indian village

[3] Bourke, "Mackenzie's Last Fight with the Cheyennes," *Winners of the West* (February 28, 1930), 8.
[4] *Ibid.*

nearby wood piled up by the dozens of cords was found. A human arm belonging to an Indian and still in a fair state of preservation was picked up in the village. It had been amputated at the elbow, and two fingers were missing, apparently the result of a shotgun blast. The weather was cloudy with a keen wind blowing from the north. Bourke reported that the pack trains now had very little to carry, and the mules pressed closely upon the heels of the cavalry companies. As an example of the great variation in temperature in this region, the thermometer showed ten degrees below zero at seven in the morning, and fifty-two degrees above zero at three in the afternoon. Because this was the place where the scouts were to return to the command, the soldiers remained in camp all day on the fifteenth, glad of the chance to rest after the grueling march.

At 4:00 P.M. on the fifteenth, the guides returned and reported that they had made a complete examination of the Tongue River valley as far north as the Yellowstone River but had found neither Indians nor villages. The tribe of Crazy Horse must undoubtedly be located farther east in the Powder River country since all of the more recent trails led that way, all of the buffalo seen and the fresh game trails pointed in an opposite direction, and no Indians had been found to the west or north. General Crook determined to remain in camp until morning and then march eastward to the headwaters of Otter Creek, on the divide between the valleys of the Tongue and Powder rivers. Otter Creek, a little mountain-locked stream which flowed northwest into the Tongue River, was so named not because of an abundance of sporting otter but because some ambitious Indians, putting in a hard winter's work, had managed to catch three of the animals down near its mouth.

The command had breakfast at five the next morning under a clear, bright sky and broke camp at eight, moving easterly up the valley of Pumpkin Creek. After a march of twenty miles over pine-covered ridges and valleys, the soldiers came down into the valley of Otter Creek where camp was made. As the soldiers were descending a steep mountain overlooking the valley, two horsemen were seen trotting their ponies leisurely down along the creek;

and by the aid of glasses the welcome intelligence soon passed along the line that they were Indians.

Frank Grouard,[5] naturally assuming leadership of the thirty-four scouts accompanying the column because of his extensive knowledge of this country, was the son of a Creole father and an Oglala woman and had spent many years roving this area in the camps of Sitting Bull and Crazy Horse. After some misunderstanding with the Sioux, he returned to civilization and got a job as a scout with General Crook. Grouard was one of the controversial figures of the period. His real name was Walter Brazeau, but the Indians called him "The Grabber." Physically he was impressive, being six feet in height and weighing over two hundred pounds. His complexion was very dark; and in order to explain that he was not of Indian blood, he gave out the story that he was born in the Sandwich Islands. In later years his biography was written by Joe De Barthe and published under the title *Life and Adventures of Frank Grouard*. In this book Frank tells about the discovery of the two horsemen:

Just as I came on to hills leading to Otter Creek or just before, I got off my horse and crept up to the hills to look up and down the creek with my glass. Up the creek about five miles from where I was, I saw two Indians trailing a buffalo or some animal track. They were tracking down the creek towards where I was. I watched them very close, all their movements, and was sure just as quick as I watched them awhile that they were out hunting and that they had come from their village. It was quite a ride to the command, and I didn't suppose it would come to where I was until between one and two o'clock. I thought the Indians would

---

[5] During the 1876 campaigns Grouard proved to be an invaluable scout and adviser to General Crook. When the Indians found that the soldiers had used him as a scout in order to seek them out in their native haunts, they were furious. He had lived so long among them that he had acquired all of their habits and traits, as well as knowledge of their favorite campsites. However, there were other scouts and soldiers who believed that he was still friendly to the hostile Indians and purposely misdirected the troops or gave warning of their approach. After hostilities ceased, Grouard was employed as scout and interpreter by the army for life at $150 per month, upon recommendation of Crook and in recognition of his services. In later years he quit the government service at Fort McKinney and went to Pine Ridge Agency to live.

have plenty of time to get out of sight of the command before it reached there. Well, I must have been watching them for about three hours. I did not dare to move or show myself, but I was looking at the Indians through my glass at this time, watching every move. When they had got almost opposite me, they stopped their horses all of a sudden and looked towards me. I was not over a mile and a half from them and could almost see their features through the glass. All of a sudden they commenced whipping their horses. There were some pines right ahead of them, and they ran in behind them and got off their horses, crept up on to the brow of the hill, and looked towards me. I could just see the top of their heads. I thought to myself, "What if they should see me?"

Well, I soon found out what it was that attracted their attention. Pretty soon here comes all those scouts, running their horses across the hills. They were scattered for two miles along the hill in plain view of the Indians, who stopped and pretty soon started for the timber, but instead of going back the way they came, they went in a northeasterly direction, towards Powder River, and I knew they were going on to the main trail to Powder River. In fact, when I saw that the scouts had scared the Indians, I waited until they had got up to me. Then I took four of them and started after the Indians to keep them out of sight of the command. The Indians didn't wait for us but just kept going. But they were out of the way of the command. They didn't see it. I was satisfied that they couldn't recognize whether we were Indians or whites. Probably they would think we were a war party of Crows and go for camp as fast as they could. We went across Otter Creek for convenience. The command had got there, and I told the General about it. It made me mad because the scouts had got away from the command. I told him that if he had kept the scouts away, the Indians would not have known of our coming, and it would have been no trouble getting into their camp.

The General said he gave them orders but they escaped the command. He said he didn't think the command was so close to me as it was. I explained that they were getting close to the Indians and I could not tell how near we were and that was the reason I had asked him to keep the scouts with the command.

General Crook was afraid that the village would be apprised of the approach of the soldiers by the two Indians and would decamp. Orders were issued for a forced night march, and the scouts were sent out for a few miles to prospect the route toward the Powder

River. General Crook designated three squadrons consisting of about three hundred men to make the attack. The second and fourth squadrons under command of Captain William Hawley[6] and Captain T. B. Dewees,[7] respectively, were to remain in charge of the pack trains and camp equipage, under General Crook, while the first squadron, consisting of Companies M and E, Third Cavalry, under Captain Anson Mills; the third squadron, consisting of Companies I and K, Second Cavalry, under Captain H. E. Noyes; and the fifth squadron, consisting of Companies F of the Third Cavalry and E of the Second Cavalry, under Captain Alex Moore, were to make the advance under command of Colonel Reynolds. The troops composing the attacking force were to carry nothing but their arms, an extra supply of ammunition, and rations for the next day so that there would be no dead weight to retard their movements. Medical supplies were again divided, and Dr. Stevens was to remain with General Crook, while Dr. Munn would accompany the attacking force. General Crook offered Colonel Reynolds his choice of remaining with the smaller force or of commanding the attacking force, and of course Reynolds decided to go forward. Lieutenant Bourke says that Crook wanted to give Reynolds an opportunity to distinguish himself and to dispel the adverse publicity he had received as commander of the Department of Texas. This may have been true, since the hostile Indians were believed to number not more than five to eight hundred warriors in all and to be scattered into little bands which the troops could easily subdue. It was believed that a swift march that night could overtake

[6] Captain William Hawley was born in Washington, D. C., and served as a private in Company H, Third Battalion of D. C. Infantry from April 15 to July 15, 1861. He was commissioned a second lieutenant in the Third Cavalry on August 5, 1861, a first lieutenant on the same date, and a captain on February 15, 1864. After the war he served on the border and was commissioned a major in the Third Cavalry on March 20, 1879. He was retired June 14, 1879.

[7] Captain Thomas B. Dewees, a Pennsylvanian, entered service as a private but was commissioned a second lieutenant in the Second Cavalry in October, 1861. He was brevetted captain on June 9, 1863, for gallant services in the battle of Beverly Ford, Virginia. After the Civil War he was stationed at many western border posts and engaged in many Indian skirmishes. He died July 5, 1886. Captain Dewees, the bluff and hearty type, was a good storyteller. His infectious laugh and amiable manner made him popular with the men around the campfires.

the Indians, thought to be under the leadership of Crazy Horse, somewhere on the Powder River, thirty miles distant. It was understood that the two forces would rendezvous at the mouth of Lodgepole Creek, also known as Clear Fork, on Powder River, and that the first arrival would await the other there.

In a general way the purpose of the attack was to capture the Indian village, kill or capture as many Indians as possible, run off their pony herd, and do them as much damage as possible. General Crook later claimed that he gave specific orders to Colonel Reynolds to capture the pony herd and carry off the meat and provisions so they could be used by the troops. Colonel Reynolds denied that specific orders were given him and maintained that the main objective was to do the Indians as much damage as possible and that the specific means by which this was accomplished depended upon the circumstances and were of necessity left to his discretion.

General Crook was criticized for dividing his command and sending only six companies of cavalry after the Indians. When asked his reason for this action during the court-martial proceedings against Colonel Reynolds, he replied: "It was so very cold and the ground was frozen and it was very difficult for the animals to go up an incline of ten degrees. It was so smooth after a few had gone over it, making it impossible to take the pack train, so the command was divided."

The scouts returned and reported that the trail of the two Indians left the valley about two miles farther up and followed the north branch of Otter Creek. After the horses had been fed and the men had partaken of a hearty repast, the three squadrons set out at 5:20 P.M., following the trail of the two Indians in the snow, up the north branch of Otter Creek to its head and then across the divide into the valley of the Powder River.

In his dispatch of March 18 to his newspaper, Robert A. Strahorn gave a graphic account of the night march.

Without doubt, the most remarkable event of General Crook's present campaign was the night march commenced early on the evening of the 16th inst. As a matter of history it well deserves a place by the side of any similar incident known to frontier service; and if the three hundred gallant and uncomplaining spirits who participated in its thrilling scenes had nothing more whereof to tell in future bivouacs around more peaceful fires, this would be enough. A hard day's march had just been accomplished, men and beasts had earned the hearty fare, and the bed of frozen ground that usually were their lot; but the circumstance narrated in my last changed the aspects of affairs. A leader like General Crook was in search of just such circumstances, and if there were any complaints heard in connection with the swiftness of his movements, they came from those whose lot it was to remain behind. Therefore about two hours after reaching Otter Creek, with darkness already shadowing the gulches, the three squadrons pushed silently forward. A cutting breeze with its usual perversity in these parts, drove the falling snow directly in our faces. The storm, without even a moonlit sky above, served to deepen the gloom so rapidly that we were little more than out of sight of the campfires left behind until the blackest of nights was upon us. Riding at the head of the scouts in company with Col. Stanton and Lt. J. B. Bourke, the latter Aide-de-Camp to General Crook, I had, during the night, an excellent opportunity of witnessing the truly remarkable achievement of Frank Gruard, our principal guide and trailer. His knowledge of the country had been noteworthy ever since the opening of the campaign, but the duty he was now called upon to perform was of just the nature that would have bewildered almost any one in broad daylight. He had orders to follow the "back trail" of the two Indians we had seen early in the evening, lead where it would. This he did through the entire night in the face of a storm that was constantly rendering the pony tracks of the two savages less distinct while it was also hourly increasing the tedium of travel. Over rugged bluffs and narrow valleys, through gloomy defiles and down breakneck declivities, plunged the indomitable Frank; now down on his hands and knees in the deep snow, scrutinizing the faint footprints, then, losing the trail for an instant, darting to and fro until it was found, and again following it up with the keenness of a hound and a fearlessness that would have imbued almost anyone with fresh vim and courage. Nor should we forget his valuable assistants, Baptiste Garnier, Jack Russell, Baptiste Pourrier, Louis Gingros, and others of our keen-eyed scouts who were practically indispensable. With such unfailing celerity was the trailing accomplished that during almost every hour of the long night order would come from the rear to halt in order that the command might be kept "closed up."

The March to Powder River

Towards morning the clouds commenced breaking and soon the sky was almost clear but with the change came the most intense cold we had ever experienced, and were it not that the almost exhausted men were compelled to walk and lead their horses much of the way, on account of the roughness of the country, many cases of freezing must have been recorded. The worst was yet to come. At four in the morning we halted upon what seemed the apex of the entire region. We had at last been ascending quite rapidly nearly all night and now by the aid of the dim starlight, and through the thick frosty atmosphere, we could look down, down, as far as the strained vision would reach, into a wilderness of mountains, forest and vale. How to get down, and at the same time be morally certain of striking the Indians at once, was the question—for we knew that somewhere through that mass of rocky upheavals must flow the Powder. Again the ever ready scouts were to show us their true worth, and, with Frank in the lead, off they bounded, to find or make a way. Near the summit upon which we had thus briefly halted was a deep narrow ravine. In order to have his men as well sheltered as possible while waiting, General Reynolds ordered the command to take position therein and dismount. Here a scene was presented which we cannot forget. The cold grew in intensity, and exert ourselves as we would to keep up a circulation, it seemed almost unbearable. The fatiguing marches of the day and night, the great strain upon the nerves caused by the loss of sleep and the continuous cold, the hunger, too, making itself felt, and our not being permitted to enkindle a single fire, however small, on account of the danger of alarming the foe—all of these influences combined told severely upon the strongest physiques. Stalking my way up and down the gulch in which the shivering men and horses were crowded like bees in a hive, I had no trouble in discovering how they were bearing up under such difficulties. There were very few complaints, but every few moments some poor fellow would drop into the snow, "just for a minute, you know" and when at once shaken up by his more determined comrades, would make all sorts of excuses to be allowed to enter that sleep, which if undisturbed, would have known no waking. Officers were everywhere on the alert to keep their men upon their feet, and, thanks to this general watchfulness, no cases of amputations are yet known to be necessary on account of freezing, although nearly all of us are now nursing frost bitten feet, faces, or ears. At daylight the returning scouts reported the discovery of a trail leading down to the river, and the stream was yet some three or four miles distant. An advance was at once ordered—an order that was obeyed with more than usual willingness.

During the night march the horses suffered greatly, not only from the cold, but also from straining themselves in climbing up and sliding down the glassy slopes in the line of march. Small crevices, not more than three or four feet deep, stopped the march for several minutes until an examination would reveal where a passage was feasible without incurring the risk of breaking the animals' backs. Grouard soon discovered that the Indians belonged to a small mounted hunting party of thirty or forty, and their trail was found. As the light became stronger, the command advanced along the trail more rapidly until a dense column of smoke was seen arising before them in the distance. This was soon found to come from "coal measures" on fire.

One of the scouts who went ahead to locate the village was John Shangrau, who was one of the party which came from Fort Robinson and joined General Crook at Sage Creek. In later years he described the incident when interviewed by Judge E. S. Ricker at Allan, South Dakota, on November 5, 1906. Judge Ricker,[8] a justice of the peace at Chadron, Nebraska, wrote down in pencil tablets the stories told him by Indians and French-Indian scouts around Pine Ridge Agency concerning the events of the early days. Judge Ricker planned to incorporate these accounts in a book about the Indian wars, but he died May 17, 1926, before the book was written, and the tablets are now in the custody of the Nebraska State Historical Society. History owes Judge Ricker a debt of gratitude for his painstaking labor in preserving material which would otherwise have been lost. In addition to writing down the

[8] Eli S. Ricker was born in Maine on September 29, 1843. He was a Union soldier in the 102nd Illinois Infantry, serving over three years during the Civil War. He was eventually admitted to the bar in Iowa in 1884, and in 1885 located in Chadron, Nebraska. He served three terms as county judge in Chadron and for a time was in the newspaper business. About 1900 he began to devote his time to the collection of information on Indian-white relationships, interviewing Indians and others who had figured in the Indian wars. His activity in this field brought him to the attention of the Indian Bureau, and he was appointed clerk in the archives of that bureau. He held this position for about ten years, resigning in 1920 and returning to his home in Grand Junction, Colorado.

words laboriously in longhand, he had to travel on horseback, or in a horse and buggy, many miles from Chadron in order to get to the homes of his informants on Pine Ridge Reservation. It must have been quite a task in those days to locate the individuals and arrange for the services of an interpreter. It is to be regretted that Judge Ricker was unable to make use of his splendid material. The John Shangrau account is as follows:

It got so they could hardly see the tracks, then one of the scouts walked until he was tired, then another would change off and so on; about daylight they got on the ridge of Powder R. the soldiers were 3 or 4 miles behind the scouts; here the latter made a fire to warm themselves, as it was a pretty cold night. While making a fire Louie Shangrau and Frank Gruard were sent on so they could see Powder River bottom, promising to stay there until they returned. Both came back saying there was a camp, for they heard the horse bells; but they couldn't see the camp for the darkness. Frank Gruard was sent back to Crook to hurry and come up as they had discovered the camp. Meantime they sent Louie Richaud and Louie Shangrau back to the river to see if they could not see the camp. Before the troops arrived these 2 scouts had returned and it was daylight. They reported a big camp. They said they counted 51 lodges. Then the troops arrived. Louie Richaud told Reynolds about the no. of lodges and where the camp was. All moved towards the camp trying to reach it before sunrise.[9]

Frank Grouard continued with his version of the discovery of the village:

I came to the Powder River divide some six miles from Powder river, about 3 o'clock in the morning, and went on to locate the village, leaving the command six miles to the rear to await my return. One of the men with me was Buckskin Jack, a notorious scout (who is now travelling with Buffalo Bill), then a young man. He might be called the "Midget of the Plains." The other man's name was Phoenix. He was hanged afterwards down on the Yellowstone for horse stealing.

[9] Ricker, "Narrative of John Shangrau," *Interviews,* Tablet 27, 58–81. All quotations and material from the Ricker *Interviews* are used with the permission and courtesy of the Nebraska State Historical Society.

Just at daylight we came up a hill above Powder River. There was an immense fog, so thick I could not see anything. It had raised out of the river, but I could hear the bells of the Indian ponies. Of course that satisfied me that there was a village there. I sent Buckskin Jack back after the command, telling him to bring them up as soon as possible, while I went down and located the village. I could not tell where it was, on account of the fog. I was up about one thousand feet, and it was straight down to the village. I got about half way down the hill when the fog raised, so that I could look in under it and see the village down below me, about a mile off. I could see the tops of the lodges, and the horses, and could hear the Indians talk. An Indian was haranguing the camp, and it was from this one that I learned that a part of the Indians had gone back on the trail to find out who we were, for they had seen us on Otter Creek; but instead of going the upper trail, they had gone the lower one, so we had missed them. I found this out through the crier. I could hear it as plain as could be. I could not tell how large a village it was from where I stood. They had camped in a low bed of a river, or where a river had been perhaps a hundred years ago, right under a big bank. The Indians had camped in the circle of this old river bed. There was timber scattered all through the bottom, and they were camped amongst this timber. I supposed there were some one hundred lodges, and from seven hundred to one thousand Indians. I came back up on the hill. Just as I reached there, Col. Reynolds and his company came up close to me. Said I: "Colonel, here are the Indians. Now, that I have found them, all you have to do is fight them."[10]

The trail the troops had followed lay approximately along the site of the present road leading over the divide from Otter Creek. The ravine where they had stopped was six miles from Powder River. When the scouts brought back word that a large Indian village was near, it was about 6:30 or 7:00, a little before sunrise, and the command had stopped for a rest, with the head of the column upon a plateau a mile and three-quarters west of the river and north of the road. A thrill of excitement ran through the command; they could hardly realize that at last they had come upon the Indians in their chosen retreat. Some men eagerly questioned

---

[10] De Barth, *Life and Adventures of Frank Grouard*, 95.

Grouard about the apparent strength of the enemy, while others examined their weapons and the fastenings of their saddle girths.

The soldiers were halted in a long column of twos with Captain Moore's battalion in the front, Lieutenant Rawolle's company leading; Captain Mills's battalion second, with his company leading and Lieutenant Johnson's company following; and Captain Noyes's battalion in the rear, with his company leading and Captain Egan's men following. At the decision to attack the village immediately, Lieutenant Charles Morton, the adjutant, and Colonel Stanton were sent back with orders to the battalion commanders to assemble their troops on the plateau by companies, in columns of twos abreast of the leading company. Accordingly, Captain Moore's Company F of the Third Cavalry was brought up to the south of the leading company, while Captain Mills' Company M of the Third Cavalry came abreast to the north of it. Next in order toward the north came the columns of Company E of the Third Cavalry under Lieutenant Johnson, Company I of the Second Cavalry under Captain Henry E. Noyes, and Company K of the Second Cavalry under Captain James Egan. By 7:00 A.M. all six companies were in parallel columns of twos facing east. At the foot of the mountain on which they were assembled lay the Indian village for which they had searched so long.[11]

---

[11] The highly detailed account of the battle and retreat to old Fort Reno which follows is taken from microfilm copies of Records of the War Department, Office of Judge Advocate General, *Court Martial of Captain Henry E. Noyes*, RG 153, GCM PP 5473; *Court Martial of Colonel Joseph J. Reynolds*, RG 153, GCM QQ 26; and *Court Martial of Captain Alexander Moore*, RG 153, GCM QQ 27. As the campaign was believed to have been a failure, charges were filed and tried by general court-martial involving Captain Noyes, Colonel Reynolds and Captain Moore. The testimony of the witnesses was taken down in longhand by a court reporter and, despite the obvious conflicts in the evidence and the sharp exchanges between counsel and witnesses, it furnishes a complete and accurate account of the action. Where there is a conflict in the accounts, it is so indicated, while matters not in dispute are stated as factual. Dialogue is taken directly from the microfilm, and where portions of the testimony are quoted, they are copied without correction from the original as taken down by the court reporter. Where sources other than the trials are used, they are indicated.

Chapter 4 THE ATTACK ON THE VILLAGE

WHILE the troops were being brought up, Colonel Reynolds and Captain Moore formulated plans for the attack. The village and terrain were only partially visible because the morning mists had not yet risen. A smoky haze hung over the village, and there were two or three inches of snow on the ground. Reynolds questioned Frank Grouard about the best mode of approaching the village and immediately made dispositions for the attack. Since the nature of the ground over which the troops had to approach the village was unknown and could not be ascertained from the top of the mountain, directions in general terms were given.

The scouts reported that the village was on the creek bottom behind the mountain they were on and recommended that the forces be divided so that one could go down the north side of the mountain and the other down the south ravine, both striking the village simultaneously from opposite sides. Colonel Reynolds, in the belief that the village lay at the east base of the mountain, adopted the plan of the scouts. However, the village was actually a mile farther off than Reynolds was told by the scouts, and a half-mile to the north behind another mountain. This misunderstanding of the terrain was the cause of the miscarriage of the plan to attack both ends of the village at once.

The clearest explanation of the situation was given by Lieutenant Charles Morton in his testimony in the trial of Captain Moore:

The Attack on the Village

Capt. Egan was to go around on the right [south] of the village which was supposed to be on the creek bottom—it was not visible at the point where he [Reynolds] gave the instructions—that Capt. Moore with his dismounted battalion was to go around to the left [north] of the village and receive the Indians as they fled from the village. *Question.* Can't you state more definitely—did you understand where Capt. Moore was to take up a position. *Answer.* It was simply a relative position—it was not a designated point. At that time Col. Reynolds did not know where the village was—its exact locality—I heard the guide tell Col. Reynolds it was behind a large hill that we had seen him on before his return. Afterwards we found it was not behind that hill. It was a relative position. *Question.* If he charged in a position perpendicular to the village, Capt. Moore was to be opposite them. *Answer.* Yes, sir, it was a relative position he was to take. *Question.* Did the accused [Moore] with his command take that position as ordered. *Answer.* As I understand his order, he did not in my opinion.

Questions by the Court—Could the accused have known exactly the point opposite where Capt. Egan charged. *Answer.* I don't think he could have.

Questions by the Judge-Advocate—Wherein did he fail if he did not. *Answer.* The village was not located as I presumed Col. Reynolds understood it to be. It was not behind the hill the guide told him it was, and upon which information Col. Reynolds had acted, but was at least a mile farther, and behind some other hills. It was lower down [north of] the river, I can't say immediately behind it, though we had to cross that hill.

The mountain on which the soldiers were assembled sloped down abruptly and terminated in a steep bluff at the riverbank. The north side of the mountain descended abruptly to the valley of a small dry creek, now known as Thompson Creek, which ran southeasterly, reaching the river four hundred yards south of the village. The valley was several hundred yards wide north of the mountain, but at the mouth it was half a mile wide. On both sides of the mountain rocky gorges descended sharply to the valleys below.

As both ravines actually came out south of the village, all the troops struck the village from the southwest, the column going down the south ravine making a long, useless detour in that direction. The column going down Thompson Creek soon discovered the true location, while the other did not see the village until it arrived on the divide south of it, after making the detour. All were surprised to meet in the valley of Thompson Creek where they had thought the village was. With the ravines sloping down toward the southeast, it would have been difficult to determine definitely from that angle of vision whether the village was in the valley of Thompson Creek at the foot of the mountain, or north of it—assuming that it was visible.

The village was located within a bend of the river in a large grove of cottonwood trees on the west side of the river. It was described as "elliptical" and "in the form of a horseshoe," two hundred yards wide by six hundred yards long, lying parallel with the river. East of the river, which was frozen over twenty inches thick, lay a flat area one mile wide. West of the village was another steep mountain separated from the mountain occupied by Reynolds by the valley of Thompson Creek, which came down from the northwest. The mountain west of the village extended for at least one mile north of it, while on the south side of this mountain were five spurs jutting southward into the Thompson Creek valley.

Colonel Reynolds decided that Captain Egan's white horse troop would make the charge through the village because they still had their pistols. At Otter Creek it had been decided that the attack would be made with carbines, so all the other companies had left their pistols with the pack train. Captain Noyes's company was to accompany Egan down the south ravine and, when it came out at the south edge of the village, was to cut out the pony herd which was grazing along the river, while Egan was to drive the Indians out of the village onto the mountainside where the dismounted companies on the north side would be waiting to capture them as they ran out.

Captain Moore's battalion was to go down into the valley of Thompson Creek, get as close to the village as it could without being discovered, dismount, and await the charge of Captain Egan. When the charge was made, it was to rush in and capture the Indians as they retreated up into the ravines on the side of the mountain opposite the north edge of the village. Captain Mills's battalion

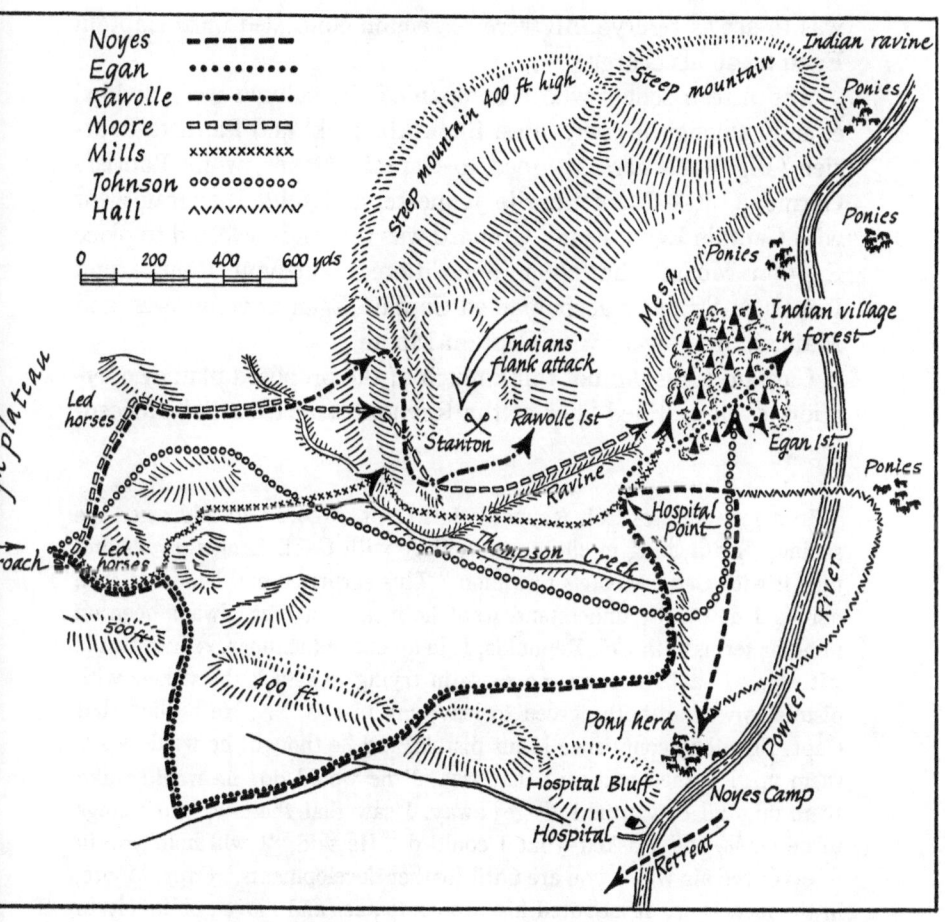

THE POWDER RIVER BATTLEFIELD

was to act as reserve. All were to remain concealed until Captain Egan made his charge.

The fifteen scouts who accompanied the column were divided equally among the companies. Buckskin Jack[1] and Baptiste Pourrier (Big Bat) were assigned to Captain Noyes, while Baptiste Garnier (Little Bat), Charlie Jennesse, and John Shangrau went with Captain Egan. Frank Grouard was the guide selected to place Captain Moore's battalion in position. Lieutenant Bourke and Robert A. Strahorn accompanied Captain Egan as volunteers, and Major Stanton went with Captain Moore.

Captain Mills did not think much of the proposed plan of operation, as he testified later at the Reynolds court-martial proceedings:

> In a few minutes Col. Reynolds left Capt. Moore and addressed me saying: "I am going to charge the village with Capt. Egan's pistols and take it with Capt. Moore's battalion." This surprised me. I did not then nor do I now quite understand what he meant: having always been on familiar terms with Col. Reynolds, I, in an excited manner, remonstrated with him. I said there was no sense in trying to attack the village with pistols as we had both agreed to leave my pistols. . . . He replied that Capt. Egan had confidence in his pistols, and he thought he would wake them up. I turned and said that was all he would do: he would wake them up, and they would all get away. I saw that there was no change to be made, and I asked what I could do. He said, "I will hold you in reserve: remain where you are until further developments." Capt. Moore, in the meantime, dismounted his two companies and moved obliquely to

---

[1] Jack Russell was named "Buckskin Jack" by Magliorie A. Mousseau of White River, South Dakota, because he wore buckskin clothes. Russell, born in Missouri on November 8, 1847, ran away from home at the age of fifteen. He worked around Denver and Cheyenne until 1864, when he went to work for John Richaud, Sr., at the ranch on the north fork of the Laramie. John Richaud, Jr., took such a liking to Russell that he adopted him as his brother after the Indian fashion. In 1865, Russell helped tend bridge near the present site of Casper, Wyoming, for John Richaud, Sr., but when the river fell, he went to Deer Creek and went to work for Jules Ecoffee and Adolph Cuney. In the summer of 1875, General Crook sent word to Russell to report to Big Bat and Little Bat at Red Cloud Agency. They showed him a paper stating that Crook wanted the three to go north as scouts for the troops and to bring others with them. When they got to Fort Laramie, they found the troops camped there. Russell also served as a scout in the Rosebud and Slim Buttes campaigns in 1876.

The Attack on the Village

the left. Capt. Noyes came up with his battalion, Capt. Egan following him, moved on in the direction of the village. Lt. Morton, having returned from communicating with Capt. Noyes, rode up to me and said, "the Colonel is going to make a fix of it." At Lt. Morton's request I went to see Col. Reynolds but could not change the disposition.

Captain Mills and Lieutenant Morton[2] believed that more troops should be dismounted and that another company should go in with Captain Egan to clear the Indians out of the brush which surrounded the village. Colonel Reynolds did finally dismount Captain Mills's company and agreed to send Lieutenant Johnson's company if needed. It was well established that the best way to fight Indians was for cavalry to dismount, as an accurate fire could not be directed from horseback. This was particularly true in rough country where it was impossible for cavalry to charge.

While waiting on the mountain, the soldiers were boastful and overconfident. Captain Moore expressed great anxiety to get an opportunity to crawl in close to the enemy and give them what he called a "blizzard" and to get a "bucketful of blood." The troops were drawn up in the center of a flat area about a mile in diameter, but five hundred yards in their front rose a small bluff which was on the eastern edge of the mountain. Curving around the foot of this bluff was a deep ravine, one end of which ran northeasterly down the mountain on one side, while the other end ran southeasterly down the other side of the mountain to the valley below. As the companies filed off, the clouds and mists began slowly to separate. Every moment of darkness was precious, as so much depended upon the suddenness and unsuspectedness of the attack. It was long after sunrise when the final preparations were completed for the attack.

[2] Lieutenant Charles Morton was born in Ohio, but served with the Missouri Infantry and Engineers during the Civil War. He was appointed to the Military Academy in 1865 and upon graduation in 1869 was commissioned a second lieutenant in the Third Cavalry. On September 25, 1876, he was appointed first lieutenant and on February 27, 1890, was brevetted for gallant services in action against hostile Indians in Tonto County, Arizona, on June 5, 1871. Morton had a long and successful career in the army and eventually became a general officer. He died in Washington, D. C., on December 20, 1914, at the age of sixty-nine.

Captain Moore's battalion, with Frank Grouard as guide, went down a side ravine on the north slope of the mountain into the valley of Thompson Creek. The gorge was so steep and rocky that the men had to pick their way down on foot, leading their horses. They climbed a hill south of the creek and dismounted, leaving their horses with every eighth man, who acted as horse-holder. It took about an hour to make the descent, during which time Moore questioned Grouard about the village. Grouard told him that "the whole kaboodle was there—Sitting Bull, Crazy Horse, and all."[3] After the men dismounted, Grouard left them and rode down toward the village where he was later seen among the pony herd. The hill where the troops dismounted was out of sight of the village and about a mile from it. The men were here only a short time when Colonel Reynolds rode up and told Captain Moore that he was so far back that he might as well be in Texas. By this time it was broad daylight. All must have realized that the village was not where it had been supposed to be, and that it would be impossible to attack the village from the north. Moore, leaving his horses with the horse-holders, advanced his battalion down Thompson Creek over some small foothills and climbed a wooded spur about six hundred yards northeast of and across the creek from his first position. Colonel Reynolds then rode back to Lieutenant Johnson's company, which was just appearing in the valley to the west, and accompanied it towards the village. Captain Moore's company was the first to climb the ridge and took position in line on the south end of the crest, while Lieutenant Rawolle's men followed and lined the crest next to Moore's company on the north. After securing permission from Captain Moore, Lieutenant Rawolle sent Sergeant Lewis Gilbert, Private Kingsley, and another private, the three best shots in his company, to a point on the next spur about 150 yards to the east as sharpshooters to pick off the Indians. The men lay down on the snow on the slope of the ridge to keep out of sight of a few Indians who were visible in the pony herd. From this position the men could look over the intervening spurs and plainly see the village a thousand yards away.

[3] Testimony of Captain Moore in the Reynolds court-martial trial.

The Attack on the Village

When Captain Moore decided to remain on this ridge, Major Stanton said to him, "We might as well be in Cheyenne as here. The Indians will all escape."[4] Moore refused to move forward, saying that if he did so his men would be discovered by Indians in the pony herd. Stanton then went to Lieutenant Rawolle[5] and said, "Rawolle, that place [meaning the point occupied by Sergeant Gilbert's party] is in the rear of the village, why don't you go there?"[6] Lieutenant Rawolle told him that Captain Moore was his commanding officer and that he received his orders from him. Stanton replied, "I am going in the direction the troops should go if I have to go alone."[7] He went over to Sergeant Gilbert, sitting in a clump of bushes with his men, and told them to be quiet because he had seen an Indian; they waited a few minutes. After being joined by Lieutenant Sibley,[8] the group advanced to another point one-half mile east and a little north of Captain Moore's position, about three hundred yards from the village and on the side of the mountain overlooking it. It took about ten minutes to go from Moore's ridge to this place. Here the group remained behind a little point concealed by bushes until Captain Egan made his charge.

Just before Stanton left the ridge, Lieutenant Rawolle and Captain Moore saw dismounted troops approaching from the south and starting to come up the same ridge. They remarked that the

---

[4] Testimony of Major Stanton in the court-martial trial of Colonel Reynolds.

[5] Lieutenant William C. Rawolle was appointed to the army from New York and served all through the Civil War with a brilliant record in the Second New York Artillery. At the end of that conflict he had attained the rank of brevet lieutenant colonel. Since he was a native-born Prussian, the military life appealed to him, and he was commissioned a lieutenant in the regular establishment. He was called from his station at Fort Sanders to command Company E of the Second Cavalry on the Big Horn Expedition. After a long career in the army, he died in June, 1895.

[6] Testimony of Major Stanton in the court-martial trial of Colonel Reynolds.

[7] *Ibid.*

[8] Lieutenant Frederick Sibley was born in Texas and graduated from the Military Academy in the class of 1874. He was brevetted for gallantry in action on the Little Big Horn River in July, 1876. This affair, which was commonly known as the "Sibley Scout," was a reconnaissance through Indian country by a small band sent out by General Crook. After abandoning their horses, they miraculously made their way on foot back to the camp on Goose Creek without losing a man. Sibley in later years attained the rank of a general officer and died on February 17, 1918, at the age of sixty-five.

ridge had as many men as could be concealed there, so Captain Moore went down to have an interview with Captain Mills to stop him at the foot of the hill.

Meanwhile, after Moore's battalion had filed down the mountain, Colonel Reynolds advanced Noyes's battalion eastward to the ravine leading down the south side of the mountain. While superintending the crossing of this deep gorge, Reynolds sent for Captain Mills and his company and ordered them to dismount, leave one man to hold ten horses, and follow and support Captain Moore. Captain Mills left his horses with the horse-holders as directed, on the edge of the gorge; and, as it would be hard work to climb down the rocks, he ordered the men to take off their overcoats and put them in a pile. The forty-eight overcoats left on the mountain were never recovered, and it has never been explained why they were not brought down with the horses later on.[9] The company then descended into the gorge, down the opposite side from that followed by Noyes's column, into the valley of Thompson Creek, where they saw Moore's battalion climbing the side of the ridge where it took position.

[9] In September, 1958, I covered this area to try to find some trace of the missing overcoats. After driving about a mile up the valley of Thompson Creek, I climbed the mountain along the edge of the ravine which Mills had descended. Upon reaching the top, I found myself in the ravine which circled around the north, west, and south sides of the little hill which was at the eastern end of the mountain. Toward the west was the plateau on which the command had been drawn up in parallel columns of companies. At the edge of the plateau and overlooking the ravine was the shelf where Mills had left his led horses. Noyes's battalion had gone down the south ravine, while Mills went down the ravine to the north. In tracing his course by his map, I found that there was a little bench leading around the hill toward the east which one would naturally follow in going toward the village. However, this bench led to a ridge leading northeast down the side of the mountain, which was in plain sight of the village. In order to remain concealed, Mills cut back northwest to the ravine which he descended. From his account it is evident that the overcoats were piled at the edge of the ravine before the men climbed down into it, and from his map this point is several hundred yards down from the top of the mountain and about one hundred yards down from the bench. When the holders brought the led horses down, they undoubtedly took the easiest and shortest route around the bench and down the ridge, which Mills did not dare take. The men, being in a hurry and each having a number of horses to lead, had little inclination to detour several hundred yards to gather up overcoats. They did well to get down at all. One horse did get away from them, but Mills sent a trooper to bring it in. Although I found no trace of the overcoats, this is a reasonable explanation for the failure of the horse-holders to bring them down.

The Attack on the Village

When I got near the foot of that mountain [Captain Mills testified], Captain Moore came halfway down and motioned me not to come forward; supposing there was danger of being discovered, I directed the men to halt and lie down. I went myself up the mountain to see what was the difficulty. I went about half way up the mountain and Captain Moore said to me, "there is no use of your command coming up here, you can't get into the village this way, there is an impassable ravine between me and the village." I replied that I was ordered to support him and asked him what I was going to do. He said he had taken a position that overlooked the village, within 150 yards of it, and he intended to remain there until Captain Egan began to charge and then fire into it. I told him I had no orders to give him, but it was evidently our business to get into the village, and there ought to be some way to get in. He said it was impossible to cross the ravine, and there was no good in coming up there. I rather forced myself up there, though he did not want me to come. After I got to the crest I had a full view of the village, and it appeared to me to be a full mile distant. It was a large village. I said it was utter folly to stay there; if we could not get in that way we must get in some other way. If he fired from there his bullets would not reach the village and would only warn them of our presence. He said he had some sharpshooters in advance and they would pick off the Indians. I did not see them, and told him that was not the question. We were to get in and do something. After while he said, "if you will take your company to the right I will follow." I thought from his demeanor that he would fire from the mountain, and I told him by all means not to fire, and made him promise that he would not fire from that position but would follow me. I moved my company around and got as far as I could so as not to have it entirely in view of the village and ordered the men to lie down and await the approach of Captain Egan. All the rest of the troops were out of sight except Captain Moore's battalion of two companies. We lay in the snow until I saw Captain Egan appear around the spur of a small mountain across the creek which I had followed down, with Captain Noyes directly behind him. Almost at the same time Lt. Johnson with E company and Colonel Reynolds and Lt. Drew appeared to the left, coming around the spur of another mountain.

Colonel Reynolds had told Captain Mills on the mountain to report if he wanted Lieutenant Johnson's company, and whether mounted or dismounted. Captain Mills wrote out the note to Reynolds at the dictation of Captain Moore and gave it to Lieutenant Paul,[10] who was standing by, to be delivered. Captain Mills later saw the note delivered by Private Robb[11] to Colonel Reynolds down in the valley. The note, written before Captain Mills saw how far away the village was, apparently stated that they did not need Lieutenant Johnson's company because the three companies were within 150 yards of the village. During the conversation with Captain Moore, Mills's company was 100 or 150 yards off. Mills motioned to them to come on and they arrived before the talk ended.

Back on the mountain, Colonel Reynolds returned to Lieutenant Johnson after the companies of Noyes and Egan were across the deep gorge and told him that he would make the best use of him he could. Colonel Reynolds then started this company down a side ravine leading to the valley of Thompson Creek, the same one taken by Moore's battalion, while he rode on ahead to the hill where Moore's men had dismounted. After telling Moore that he might as well be in Texas, he rode back to the foot of the mountain where Johnson's company was just appearing to the west and accompanied it towards the village, riding on the south side of Thompson Creek.[12] When Reynolds and his escort were close to the village, but hidden from it by spurs from the mountain, Captains Egan

[10] Lieutenant Augustus C. Paul, born in New York, was appointed captain of the Twenty-third Kentucky Volunteer Infantry on May 16, 1861. He was brevetted major of volunteers on March 13, 1865, for gallant services during the Battle of the Wilderness, and lieutenant colonel of volunteers for services at Spottsylvania. He was commissioned second lieutenant in the Third Cavalry in 1869, and served in that regiment until his resignation from the army on May 24, 1881.

[11] As there was no "Private Robb" mentioned in the muster rolls of the expedition, it is believed that this was Private George Raab of Captain Mills's company, who had enlisted in New York City on January 9, 1874.

[12] The routes the various companies followed down the mountain are taken from sketches made by the soldiers. While none of them are completely accurate, those portions of each which had been in view of the artist are correct. Captain Mills's map, which was used at the Reynolds court-martial, is fairly accurate in showing the area in which he operated, but the area south of Thompson Creek and the indicated route of the attacking column are erroneous. The map used at the Noyes court-martial is correct in showing the area south of Thompson Creek and the route taken by the attacking column, but is not accurate as to the rest of the field. Lieutenant Bourke made a sketch in his diary showing the march of the attacking column and the dismounted line of Egan's troops when support failed to arrive. The lines of march and the features of the terrain have been confirmed by reference to aerial photographs of the area and by many weeks spent on the field.

The Attack on the Village

and Noyes were mounting their companies on the south side of Thompson Creek, but closer to the village. Captain Egan saw Johnson's company five hundred yards to his left and sent Frank Grouard to tell it to halt so as to keep out of sight of the village during the charge.

By the time the attacking column appeared over the bluffs to the south, it was about nine o'clock and the sun was high in the heavens. The men on the slopes had been waiting in position for half an hour. In the pony herd a few Indians, both men and women, were leading the animals to water and taking charge of them. Over the crest of the steep ridge, the young Indian men could be seen in the valley below, moving about in the village among the tipis, while their horses and mules grazed quietly on the banks of the river nearby. The soldiers had not yet been discovered, and they waited expectantly for Captain Egan to make his charge.

After crossing the deep gorge on the mountain, the attacking column, composed of the companies of Captain James Egan and Captain Henry E. Noyes, struggled southward in file over a rugged series of brakes, ravines, and gulches. The horses were compelled to take terrific plunges down icy canyons and to pick their way through fallen timber and over dangerous rock-strewn chasms. One horse slipped on the rocks and broke its neck. In thirty minutes the column had floundered to the bottom of the south fork of the dry ravine south of the divide. It then turned northeast, the men leading their horses, and followed the ravine past the mouth of the north fork up onto the divide. It was now 8:30 A.M.

Here, scarcely hid by a low bluff [wrote Mr. Strahorn in his dispatch of March 18], we could look over and see the village spread out in full view, yet nearly a mile distant. Its position was such as a more civilized Chieftain might have selected, and our crafty Crazy Horse rose considerably in our estimation as with one long, eager look we took in those points which particularly interested us now—its adaptability for speedy abandonment rather than its strength. Looking down the valley, between us and the camp lay a long wide stretch of bench land, a natural pasturage; meeting this, and with an elevation from 10 to 12 feet lower was a narrow belt of bottomland, with the river washing it on the right.

At the limit of the view, where the river swept quite closely around the base of a high and very rugged mountain, and on our side of the stream, lay the object of so much toil and search. The 100 and odd tepees were nestled quite cosily in a grove of large cottonwoods and on the lower and river side were sheltered by a dense growth of willows. Scattered here and there quietly feeding along both banks of the stream, were bands of hundreds of ponies.

Not the slightest mistrust or alarm was apparent in this forest home and it was undoubtedly as clear a case of surprise as there is on record. Arms were hastily inspected, belts filled with cartridges, and overcoats and other impediments to hasty movements strapped to the saddles.

The column remained behind the bluff about half an hour, because an Indian getting out the ponies was in sight. During the wait one of the scouts, Baptiste Pourrier,[13] was sent eastward along the ridge to examine the terrain. After he had reported that the Indians could not escape in any way on that side after the advance was made, Captain Noyes moved the battalion up into position.

The command then advanced northward over the divide, around the west side of the spur of a small mountain, and down a ravine several hundred yards west of the present road in columns of twos, with the two companies abreast and five yards apart. Some men

[13] Baptiste Pourrier was one of the famous scouts and interpreters of the period. He was called "Big Bat" to distinguish him from another famous scout and hunter, Baptiste Garnier, who was known as "Little Bat." Pourrier was born of French parents in St. Charles, Missouri, on July 16, 1843. His father died when he was two years old, and he lived with his mother, two brothers, and one sister until he left home at the age of fourteen. Obtaining employment with John Richaud, Sr., whose home was also in St. Charles at the time, he made the long journey by wagon train to the present site of Casper, Wyoming, where he arrived in October, 1858. Near here Richaud operated a toll bridge and engaged in various enterprises. Big Bat worked for many years in this vicinity hauling wood, trading with the Indians, and taking care of horses for freighting outfits. He became closely allied with the Richaud family and married a daughter of John Richaud, Sr., in 1859. In 1858, Bat moved to Fort Fetterman, where he was employed to run the mule train by John Richaud, Jr., and Hi Kelley, who had the wood and hay contract. In the fall of 1869, the Richaud family, including Big Bat and his wife, moved to Richaud Creek, a tributary of the "Chug." In the spring of 1870 he was employed at Fort Laramie as scout and interpreter at $100 a month. He served there until 1876, when General Crook employed him as a scout for the campaigns of that year at $150 a month. After the Indian wars, Big Bat lived on the Pine Ridge Reservation, where he died. See Ricker, "Life of Big Bat as Told by Himself," *Interviews,* Tablet 15, 75 ff.

Bureau of American Ethnology

LITTLE WOLF.

Bureau of American Ethnology

WHITE BULL.

The Attack on the Village

were mounted, while others were leading their horses. Captain Egan's company was on the right, Captain Noyes's on the left. When they reached the valley floor, the column turned eastward along the base of the divide until it arrived south of the village. Here the command again turned northward and upon reaching Thompson Creek halted and mounted its horses. The steep ravine, ten or twelve feet deep and forty or fifty feet wide, had to be crossed in single file. At this point Frank Grouard joined the command after having appeared from among the pony herd. Lieutenant Johnson's company was coming down Thompson Creek about five hundred yards to the left, so Grouard was sent to tell Johnson to halt his men while the charge was being made. The double column of twos advanced northward along the edge of the mesa. The men were not in sight of the village because the edge of the mesa to their front and right shut off the view. When a short distance from the village, Captain Egan formed his men in a company front, while Captain Noyes's company remained in column of twos. While forming the line for the charge Captain Moore's battalion and Captain Mills's company were seen lining a ridge to the left.

Captain Egan's line advanced at a walk until it reached the abrupt decline at the edge of the mesa, north of a sharp angle, to become known later as "Hospital Point." The men descended the steep bench, reformed the line, and charged along the south and east edge of the village. When the charge commenced, two hundred yards from the village, Captain Egan looked at his watch: the time was 9:05 A.M. Captain Noyes's company wheeled to the right and went down to the bottom land in columns of twos a little south of the Hospital Point, and formed a line so as to charge south and cut out the pony herd. Lieutenant Bourke, who was with Captain Egan, told about the charge in his diary:

The command "left front into line," was given, and the little company of 47 men formed a beautiful line in less time than it takes to narrate the movement. Egan ordered us to keep at a walk until we had entered the village or been discovered by the enemy. Then to charge at a slow trot (our animals being too tired and cold to do more) and upon approaching closely to fire our pistols and storm the village, or failing in that, to wheel around and charge back. Moving in this order, we were soon in among the herds of the ponies, which trotted off to the right and left at our approach.

An Indian boy herding his ponies, was standing within 10 feet of me. I covered him with my revolver. I could have killed him; Egan said, "Let him alone, John." The youngster betrayed great stoicism maintaining silence until we passed and then shouting the war whoop to clear the village.

The village soon appeared on our left, not so much in our front as we had thought it would be.... The lodges were sheltered in little coves and nooks among the rocks and finally protected in front by a little clump of cottonwood and a dense undergrowth of wild plum.

Running out of their lodges by dozens, the Indians who at first were greatly frightened now threw themselves behind the brush and opened upon us a lively fire which was returned with apparently good effect from our pistols as the Indians abandoned the first line of trees and took refuge further to the rear. During the 3 or 4 minutes this little affair lasted, our command behaved very gallantly. Our casualties up to this time in Egan's company alone were: 3 men wounded; one in the lower part of lung, one in elbow, and one in collarbone. Some time after this a very brave soldier, Private Schneider, was killed. 6 horses were killed and 2 wounded; not including Captain Egan's horse which was also wounded in the neck. My bridle rein was cut in two by a bullet and a number of men were shot through the clothing.

The Indians, seeing the paucity of our numbers, regained confidence and rushed forward to cut us off but we dismounted and formed a line on foot so rapidly in the undergrowth whence we opened up on them such an unpleasant fire from our carbines that the Sioux were only too glad to retire and leave us in possession of that end of the village.

As Captain Egan entered the village, Hospital Steward Will Bryan was riding beside him. As they dashed in among the lodges, an Indian came from one of the tipis, aiming to kill the Captain. Bryan, seeing that Egan was in danger, ran in front of him so that his horse received the bullet in its head, killing it instantly. Bryan ran after the Indian. He was a foot racer, but he didn't catch him, though he ran the Indian in among the lodges.[14]

[14] De Barthe, *Life and Adventures of Frank Grouard*, 97.

The Attack on the Village

Robert A. Strahorn, who was also with Egan, described the charge in his dispatch of March 18:

Revolvers were drawn, the pace was slightly accelerated, and when within less than 200 yards of the nearest tepee, the first terror-stricken savage was seen to run and loudly whoop the alarm. "Charge, my boys!" came like an electric flash from the dauntless leader, and, giving their magnificent gray steeds rein and spur and yelling like so many demons, the gallant 47 men bounded into the village with the speed and force of a hurricane. With the savages swarming out of their tepees and scattering almost under our feet, we fired right and left at their retreating forms. Our horses meanwhile worked into such a frenzy by the din of whoops and yells and discharging arms that they fairly flew over the ground. . . . The beautiful gray horses were a splendid mark for the Indians.

In charging into one of the tepees a man received a bullet through his cap. It just grazed his head, and as himself and a comrade or two rushed in to wreak their vengeance on the redskin who had fired, what was their astonishment at seeing 3 or 4 squaws, armed with revolvers, in the act of slipping through the opposite side of the wigwam by the way of a hole they had just carved with butcher knives.

These Indians may be cowardly, but they have a queer way of showing it. While in the extreme front we noticed a small band of ponies on our right that had been overlooked by the men detailed to gather them in. The main body of Indians was then on our left, and we were amazed to see a gaudily-dressed warrior, well mounted, emerge from behind a clump of bushes, tauntingly brandish his weapons, and start with breakneck speed toward the ponies, with the evident intention of making off with them. To accomplish this he was compelled to ride within a hundred yards of 15 or 20 of us and just before reaching the goal, faithful horse and reckless rider fell riddled with bullets. . . .

Private Gouget,[15] a Frenchman, of Captain Egan's company, while charging over rough ground on foot, fell, unnoticed, into a deep narrow pit. He was just tall enough to level his gun over the edge, and although the position was swept by the enemy's fire from three directions, and

---

[15] Private Theodore Gouget of Company K, Second Cavalry, had enlisted in Omaha, Nebraska, on March 18, 1875. One wonders what strange twist of fate could have caused a Frenchman to enlist in the U. S. cavalry in Omaha.

there was no one to keep him company, he thought that a good place from which to fire some 60 rounds.

Strahorn failed to mention that in the charge his horse became frightened and ran away, breaking its neck after falling over a precipice. During cavalry charges it was not at all uncommon for horses to become so excited and frenzied from the firing that they stampeded with their riders. Strahorn was fortunate that his horse did not carry him into the ranks of the enemy.

The charge carried to the north end of the village near the river, and because no other soldiers appeared for some time, the Indians rallied and were pressing the soldiers when the latter dismounted. The soldiers turned their horses over to every fourth man and formed a line facing west and a little south in the shelter of the plum copse along the border of the ice-locked channel of the river. Their position was critical, and they scanned the bluffs in vain for the sight of the promised support. Captain Egan gave the top-level account of his predicament in his testimony at the Reynolds court-martial proceedings:

My intention was to go through the village and form on the other side of it, but when I went through I found the timber was cut down, what I would call slashed timber. It was so thick that some of the men and horses fell through and could not go any farther. All that took up time, and the Indians were getting stirred up, and I found I could do nothing that way, and dismounted my men, and formed a line on front perpendicular to the line I went in on, and attacked the Indians in front, and moved up into the village, firing by volleys, and went up in the village. There was no support coming yet, and the Indians were going out into the bluffs. I could see that everything was getting out of the village except a few stragglers that were in the outside lodges, perhaps 800 yards away. The first intimation I had of any support was a few straggling shots away on my left, in the bluffs. Just after that a line of footmen came in which turned out to be Capt. Mills with the troops under him. He was the first man who came to my support. It was from 20 to 25 minutes until that support came. When I advanced on the village the women and children ran out on the opposite side to the bluffs; the warriors I had to drive out on foot. If I had been left alone I could

The Attack on the Village

not have held the village. If it had not been for those few straggling shots from the bluffs, half of my company would have been lost. I don't know who fired them. On the firing of those shots the Indians commenced to fall back and I followed them in what you might call double time and by the time Capt. Mills came in the village I was above the village facing the bluffs. Except a few on my left there were no Indians in the village then. When I got through the village and beyond it Capt. Mills joined me. His right joined my left. That was up in front of the village. When I got there Capt. Mills was coming in over the same ground I covered going into the village. . . . The first six or eight straggling shots were the first things that attracted the attention of the Indians, and I saw that was my opportunity: that some one was coming to assist me and I pressed the Indians. I did not know where they came from or who fired them.

The shots from the bluffs which disconcerted the Indians were fired by Major Stanton's little party from its vantage point fifty or sixty feet above the village and three to four hundred yards west of the south edge of it.[16] Major Stanton testified later that his party fired twenty-five to fifty shots at the Indians as they were running out of the village. When they commenced firing, they got out of the ravine in which they had been hiding and onto the open ground. The Indians escaped into several large ravines located five or six hundred yards north of his position. After Captain Egan had driven the Indians out of the village, Major Stanton and some of his party ran down the slope and entered the village as Captain Mills's men came into line.

When Captain Egan made his charge, Captain Mills's company descended the side slope of the ridge, behind which it had been concealed, into the valley of Thompson Creek and went at the double-quick eastward towards the village. It took the route which skirted the south ends of the spurs which jutted out into the valley. The

[16] This could not have been the volley fired by Moore's men, because all of the accounts agree that Moore's volley was fired just as Egan's men entered the village, twenty minutes or a half hour before. Lieutenant Rawolle did not claim that his men did the firing, and Mills's and Johnson's companies were not on the bluffs at this time. If this is true, Stanton's party did not fire when Egan entered the village as claimed, but waited until Mills was coming up in support.

company arrived in the vicinity of Hospital Point, descended to the bottom land, and went northward into the village, taking position west of Egan's line, several hundred yards north of Hospital Point. Captain Egan was undoubtedly right in saying that Mills's company joined him in twenty to twenty-five minutes, since it takes that long to walk the distance at a fast pace in dry weather.

Captain Moore claimed that while on the ridge, he detailed Sergeants Warfield[17] and Emmet[18] and six privates to advance and act in connection with the detail from Lieutenant Rawolle's company and to get as near as possible to the village. These men claimed to have got within 150 yards of the village at the time of the charge and to have entered three minutes later. This claim was not supported by any other testimony and was apparently ignored by the court. When Egan entered the village, Moore's company fired a volley from its position on the crest of the same ridge that Mills's company was behind.[19] The bullets fell short among some of the advancing troops in Thompson Creek valley. Lieutenant Morton, who was with Lieutenant Johnson's[20] company, said in his testi-

[17] Sergeant John C. A. Warfield of Company F, Third Cavalry, had re-enlisted at Fort McPherson, Nebraska, on February 21, 1873. Enlistments were for the term of five years, and because the army encouraged re-enlistments by paying $2.00 per month extra after five years' continuous service, the sergeant was drawing this amount in addition to his regular pay.

[18] Sergeant Robert Emmet of Company F, Third Cavalry, had enlisted in Philadelphia, Pennsylvania, on July 11, 1872.

[19] After the battle there was considerable controversy concerning the distance to the village from the ridge from which Captain Moore fired his volley. I located this ridge by finding on the south end of the crest thirteen .45-70 copper cartridge cases of the type used by the army at that time. On the aerial photograph the ridge is one thousand yards from the edge of the village, straight across country. Because of the steep gulch in front of it, the troops had to go several hundred yards to the south in order to avoid it. I walked at a swift pace over dry ground over the route Moore's men took, and it was fifteen minutes before I reached the road at the site of the west end of Moore's line. It must have taken the soldiers twenty-five or thirty minutes to cover the same distance on snow and ice and to take position in the ravine on the east side of the road. East of Moore's Ridge are three lower spurs jutting out from the mountain; in crossing the last one, Lieutenant Rawolle came down into the little ravine where he took position.

[20] Lieutenant John Burgess Johnson, from Massachusetts, was appointed a second lieutenant in the Sixth U. S. Infantry on September 8, 1863, and first lieutenant on February 15, 1865. After being mustered out he was commissioned a second lieutenant in the Seventh Infantry on April 23, 1866, and a first lieutenant in October, 1867. He was assigned to the Third Cavalry on December 31, 1870, becoming regi-

The Attack on the Village

mony, "When attacking the village I saw some men to left and front stooping and dodging as if bullets were falling among them. I moved out to the left and waved my hand and called out to cease firing." It was one thousand yards to the village, and the cavalry carbines were not accurate for more than six hundred yards. Colonel Reynolds asked Lieutenant Morton who fired the volley and was told that it was Captain Moore's company. Reynolds, having in mind the note he had just received stating that these men were only 150 yards from the village, exclaimed, "Oh no. It can't be."[21] After firing the volley, Moore's men could not advance directly toward the village because there was the steep ravine between his position and the next spur, at the bottom of which was a snow-filled gully which was impassable. It was necessary for Moore to follow down the south slope of the ridge, in the path of Mills's company, in order to go around the ravine. He followed down the valley of Thompson Creek, skirting the south ends of the spurs in the path of Mills's company, and took position in a ravine on the mesa facing north, with some of his men on the bottom land joining the left of Mills's line.[22]

At the time Captain Egan mounted his company, Lieutenant Rawolle, who was on the crest north of Captain Moore's company,

---

mental adjutant until his appointment as captain on April 4, 1878. He died April 5, 1896.

[21] Testimony of Lieutenant Morton in court-martial trial of Alex Moore.

[22] In covering this area I found a metal buckle from cavalry harness and, in a group on the mesa next to the bottom land, seventeen .45–70 military cartridge cases north of and along the edge of the ravine. The latter has eroded at this point, and I found several more such cartridges at the bottom of it. About one hundred yards north of the ravine twenty-six such cases were found close together. The men had apparently advanced out of the ravine and fired a volley at the retreating Indians at the beginning of the fight. Along the edge of the mesa for fifty yards north of the ravine were found twelve .45–70 cases. As this line faced west, the firing could have been at the advancing hostiles later in the action. Nothing was found north of this area which would indicate that the soldiers had advanced any farther. However, south of the ravine, and along the edge of the mesa for seventy-five yards, were found twenty-four .45–70 military cartridge cases and one .50-caliber bullet. The latter had probably been fired by an Indian; and since it was deformed in a peculiar manner, it might have caused one of the soldier casualties. This line, which faced west, extended to within seventy-five yards of Hospital Point and undoubtedly marks the position of Moore's men just before they dropped down on the bottom land when outflanked by the Indians.

started his troop forward down into the ravine. It was so steep that the men had to slide down, and when they got to the bottom, they found the deep gulch filled with snow which they could not get over. Turning to the south to go around the head of the gulch, they heard the volley of shots fired over their heads by Moore's company. Rawolle led them over the spurs, north of Mills's men; and as this took longer than marching on the flat, he arrived in sight of the village over the last spur just as Moore was putting his men in position in the ravine on the mesa. Rawolle placed his company behind a ridge on the mountainside facing north and joining Moore's line at the west edge of the mesa. The extreme left of the position was on a little point at the west end of the ridge which commanded the area to the north.[23] When Rawolle occupied the ridge, Sergeant Gilbert came down from the point which had been occupied by Major Stanton's little party, but was sent back with some men with instructions to stay there.

When the attack was made, Lieutenant Johnson's company took a wide sweep to the south, and Captain Noyes at the same time advanced his men in a company front towards the south, to enclose the pony herd. The shouting and shots attending the charge stampeded most of the Indian ponies, and Johnson's company drove to the rear about three hundred of them. Lieutenant Hall[24] took his platoon across the river and rounded up a herd of ponies over there and drove it southwesterly back across the river to the flat north of the divide and next to the river. The bluff next to the

[23] Behind the east end of this ridge, in a line about one hundred yards long and at a distance below the crest from which a man could just barely look over the top, twenty .45–70 military cartridge cases and one .40-caliber Sharps cartridge were found. Among them was a .44-caliber lead bullet, flattened out, which had obviously been fired by an Indian. One wonders if this could have been the bullet which caused the abrasion on Lieutenant Rawolle's leg. The ridge extends westward up the side of the mountain for about two hundred yards, terminating in the small peak where Major Stanton's party lay concealed. Here were found four empty military cartridge cases and one flattened-out lead bullet from a soldier's carbine. The latter apparently had been fired at Indians later occupying the ridge. The point was occupied by Sergeant Gilbert's party until they were driven off.

[24] Lieutenant Christopher T. Hall was born in Kentucky and graduated from the Military Academy in the class of 1868. Assigned to the Second Cavalry, he was promoted to first lieutenant in 1869. He resigned from the army in 1880 and died January 31, 1887.

The Attack on the Village

river here was later known as "Hospital Rock" or "Hospital Bluff." Here they were joined by the other ponies driven back by Captain Noyes's other platoon, aided by the scouts. A mounted guard was put over the herd to prevent its escape to the north and west. After sending out small squads to gather up straggling ponies, Captain Noyes, with the remainder of his company, rode up on the divide at the point where the present road crosses and watched the battle from that vantage point half a mile away.

There was so much confusion while the ponies were being rounded up that some Indians got one herd of two hundred and drove them through the soldiers' line. Captain Mills ordered his men to open and let them through. He then re-established his line because he expected an attack as soon as the warriors had led their families to places of safety among the rocks and ravines on the mountainside.

By 9:30 A.M. the Indians had been driven out of the village, and there was a complete soldier line extending from the river on the east to the point on the mountainside on the west. It ran along the south edge of the village about two hundred yards north of Hospital Point.[25] Here there was a jog in the line where it bent southward along the foot of the mesa for about a hundred yards to the ravine in which Captain Moore's men were stationed. At the west end of Moore's line was another jog since Rawolle's bluff was fifty yards north of the ravine. In the early part of the fight there was a gap in the line east of Mills while Egan was still facing west, but the companies soon formed a continuous line.

---

[25] Nothing can be found on the bottom land since it has been covered over for years by silt washing down from the steep mountain on the west. In 1923 the lowland was flooded by the river and was completely buried with mud and debris. Local residents assured me that this area has been covered by at least two feet of dirt since the battle. Large second- and third-growth cottonwoods are now growing in the bottom, but there are a few large dead trees which were there during the battle. Bullet holes can still be seen in some of them. In the early days someone started a sawmill with the intention of converting the cottonwoods into commercial lumber. Before much timber was sawed, the lead bullets lodged in the trees had ruined many sets of saws, and the project was abandoned.

Chapter 5 BURNING THE TIPIS

AS Johnson's company charged in to help round up the pony herd, Colonel Reynolds hurried into the village to survey the ground and inspect the tipis more closely. Captain Egan was engaged with the Indians at the east end toward the river; and since Captain Mills was in his immediate front, the Colonel rode over to him. The two men differed concerning the substance of their conversation and Captain Mills gave his version during his testimony at the Reynolds court-martial proceedings:

I soon saw Col. Reynolds coming up from the upper [south] side of the village, where we started. Wishing to know what was to be done, I ran to meet him. We met about the center of the village. He was very much pleased, riding his horse, and said what have you got? I said a very large village and the meat and everything. The Indians then commenced firing, and I advised Col. Reynolds to get off his horse, as he was conspicuous and they might pick him off. *Q.* Did you at that time make any suggestions to Col. Reynolds. *A.* Yes, sir, after exchanging a few words he said I want you to burn everything and get out as quick as possible to a safer camp. I said it is a very large village, rich in everything we want, and my idea is we ought to camp here and wait until Gen. Crook comes, and select all that is valuable to us, carry it away on a pack train, and destroy the balance. He said do you think we can hold the village. I said certainly. He said you may do that, make a detail and select all that is valuable and destroy the rest. Col. Reynolds then returned and I went along back and told Lt. Paul we were going to camp

Burning the Tipis

there and to make preparations to resist an attack as they would probably return as soon as they got their women and children to a place of safety, and to make a detail go out and gather up the meat and the robes; the rest was to be burned.

Colonel Reynolds claimed later that he never assented to the suggestion of Mills that they camp in the village, and that when his orders were given later to burn the village, they were not changes of orders, but the only orders issued by him on the subject. During this interview the whole line was engaged with the Indians, though not very heavily. At the conclusion of it Mills asked for Lieutenant Johnson's company to be sent to him. Colonel Reynolds agreed to issue the order when the company was no longer needed to round up the pony herd and rode over 150 yards to the west, where Captain Moore was in line with his battalion. It was now about ten o'clock, and after exchanging a few words, Colonel Reynolds rode on. After consulting with Lieutenant Rawolle, Captain Moore went to Colonel Reynolds and asked permission to send some men for the horses on the mountain. The request was granted on condition that enough men be kept to hold the line. The second interview with Captain Moore lasted only about two minutes, and Colonel Reynolds rode off and completed his survey of the field.

There were several courses of action open to him, but he had to make his decision immediately. He could camp in the village, send for General Crook, and retain some of the food and robes, as Captain Mills suggested; or he could destroy everything and return to the mouth of Lodgepole Creek in time to meet General Crook that night, as ordered. The third plan, which it was later claimed that he should have followed, was to separate the meat and robes, pack them on the Indian ponies, and take his command and all captured ponies to Lodgepole Creek that night, after destroying the village.

He reasoned that the purpose of the expedition was to attack and damage the Indians as much as possible and convince them that they could no longer live unmolested off the reservations. Colonel Reynolds had almost 300 men in his command, but one company of 50 men was not on the firing line because it had to guard the pony herd. Since the troops were fighting dismounted, every eighth man had to act as horse-holder. These, together with orderlies, took another 40 men from the line. The 90 men out of action left a fighting force of 210. No fighting was expected of the scouts and guides. The number of Indians was estimated at two warriors to a lodge, or about the same size force as the troops. Reynolds did not have enough men to surround and capture all the warriors. The battle line was half a mile long, and taking out details of men to destroy the property would further deplete the fighting force. Already the Indians were forming along the river for a charge to recapture their ponies. Colonel Reynolds decided to do as much damage as he could and get out of there as quickly as possible. He defended his decision in his statement of defense:

> After I had made an inspection of the position of the troops I surveyed with my eye the skin and canvas lodges and the surroundings including the pony herd, being driven off. I presumed as a matter of course that there must be considerable property in a village of this size, but as it was wholly impracticable for me to transport it I determined to destroy everything that we could lay our hands on and then resume the march up the river to meet the other portion of the command at the mouth of Lodgepole according to agreement. To carry out this programme and hold our skirmish line, keeping the Indians from reoccupying the village, was accordingly ordered.
>
> Johnson was sent to Mills who had previously asked for him. Egan returned from his charge and was ordered in again dismounted to the support of Mills who had called for help after Johnson had joined him. Orders were sent to make details from the companies to destroy lodges and property by burning and cutting. Some of the witnesses for the prosecution long after the transaction and having had time to compare notes and arrange a story, speak of large amounts of property.
>
> I made up my mind what to do without waiting to take an inventory of saddles, meat, or halters, and having decided to destroy everything, the more we should find the better. My point was to damage the enemy and the more I damaged him the better I would feel on that point. . . . Every man was in the fight except the horse-holders and the herd guard. I had no reserve; the destruction of the village was completed under constant fire from the Indians, varying in intensity from time to time.

Burning the Tipis

Captain Noyes had cut out part of the pony herd which was driven to the bluff to the rear, but Colonel Reynolds saw as many more ponies grazing beyond the village. Foreseeing that Captain Noyes's company would eventually be needed to hold the line, Reynolds sent orders to move the captured ponies into the river bottom, south of the promontory and tending up the river, where they could be protected by a minimum number of men.

As soon as the decision was made, orders were sent by Lieutenant Morton to all the companies to send details of men to burn the tipis and all the property in the village.

Lieutenant Johnson, while coming up into the village, received the order to dismount his company, using one holder for each eight horses, and report to Captain Mills. Upon his arrival about ten o'clock, a small herd of twenty-five Indian ponies came charging through the line from the north, and part of his company took charge of these and drove them south to the rest of the captured herd. The ponies had been frightened by the attack and ran north to the Indian positions, where they were turned back by the noise and confusion. A portion of Lieutenant Johnson's company was deployed and distributed along the line occupied by Mills's company, where they fired an average of sixty rounds per man during the engagement. The detail sent from the company destroyed tipis on the east side of the village under the direction of Colonel Reynolds.

Shortly after Mills established his line, Egan's company was withdrawn to reorganize because it had lost one-fourth of its strength. The first sergeant and eight or ten men were left to hold the position. The wounded of the company were carried back behind Hospital Point, where Dr. Munn had established a field hospital at the foot of the mesa two hundred yards south of Mills's line. Captain Egan was here looking after his wounded when he received an order from Colonel Reynolds to send twenty-five men to the support of Mills, who had again asked for reinforcements. That was nearly all the men Captain Egan had available, considering that there were three men wounded, nine horses killed or wounded, and horse-holders in the rear. After Egan had been withdrawn, the Indians crawled toward his position and fired at Mills's company from the tall grass on the right flank. About the time Private Peter Dowdy was killed on the left, Captain Mills sent Sergeant Kaminski[1] with two men to destroy some lodges on the river bank. The Sergeant was wounded above the knee joint by a pistol shot from the willows nearby.

When Lieutenant Rawolle put his company in the ravine on the extreme left, the Indians commenced firing from the rocks and ravines on the slopes of the mountainside about six to eight hundred yards distant. A number of Indian ponies clambering up the mountain were killed by his men when it became apparent that they could not be recaptured. Sergeants Land and Howard[2] and Private Pat Douglas,[3] under orders from Lieutenant Rawolle, cut out fifteen or twenty ponies under a severe fire and drove them back into the herd in the rear.

Lieutenant Rawolle stated later that the details from the companies started burning the village about half an hour after he got in line, while Sergeant Land of his company claimed that it was an hour before the burning commenced. The destruction was probably started between ten and ten-thirty.

On Captain Moore's line, half of his men were on the mesa, while the other half were below it joining with Mills's company. According to Moore, Captain Mills came to him just after they went into the village, before the fight really commenced at all, and wanted reinforcements, although there were only straggling shots at the time. Mills was told to go see Colonel Reynolds, who was close by. Later, when Captain Mills came a second time for reinforcements, Moore told him the same thing. Colonel Reynolds riding up shortly after, Moore told him that Mills had been asking for reinforcements; Reynolds said to pay no attention to these requests. Captain Egan's company was not long in the village when

---

[1] Sergeant Charles Kaminski of Company M, Third Cavalry, had enlisted in Cleveland, Ohio, on August 9, 1871.

[2] Sergeant George S. Howard of Company E, Second Cavalry, had enlisted in Springfield, Massachusetts, on October 14, 1872.

[3] Private George E. "Pat" Douglas of Company E, Third Cavalry had enlisted in Omaha, Nebraska, on February 8, 1875.

Burning the Tipis

Egan came over to Moore's line and stayed for some time. When he first came over, he slapped Moore on the back and shook his hand and said, "Old fellow, if you had not got in as soon as you did those fellows would have eaten me up."[4] While Egan was there, Moore took a carbine and fired at some Indians who had ventured down on the mesa.

Private Peter Dowdy[5] of Lieutenant Johnson's company was shot in the head about ten-thirty and died instantly. This occurred twenty to twenty-five yards in rear of Moore's line, in the village, somewhat to the left of where the fighting was at the time. About noon, Sergeant Jeremiah Foley of the same company carried the body to the rear, assisted by Privates Brannon,[6] Schubert,[7] Acton,[8] Burton,[9] Slater,[10] and Cunningham.[11] They met Colonel Reynolds riding along the line, who told them to put the man behind the bluff (that on which Noyes was guarding the pony herd), cover him with some buffalo robes, and report back to their commander. It is not clear what Private Dowdy was doing so far from his company, although during the engagement the men were commingled, especially while burning the village.

Shortly after Private Dowdy was killed, Captain Moore sent Sergeant Land and a detail between ten-thirty and eleven o'clock

---

[4] Testimony of Captain Alex Moore in the court-martial trial of Colonel Reynolds.

[5] Private Peter Dowdy of Company E, Third Cavalry, had enlisted in Baltimore, Maryland, on February 11, 1875.

[6] Private Michael Brannon of Company E, Third Cavalry, had enlisted in Boston, Massachusetts, on February 5, 1875.

[7] Private William Schubert, Company E, Third Cavalry, had re-enlisted for the second time at Fort Sanders on November 3, 1873. As a private he was entitled to the regular pay of $13.00 per month, paid bimonthly, together with $3.00 extra for having had over ten years' continuous service.

[8] As no "Private Acton" is mentioned in the muster rolls, it is believed that the soldier referred to was Private Daniel Ackley of Company E, Third Cavalry, who had enlisted in Boston, Massachusetts, on February 19, 1875.

[9] Private Henry Burton of Company E, Third Cavalry, had enlisted in Boston, Massachusetts, on December 31, 1874.

[10] Private Benjamin F. Slater of Company E, Third Cavalry, had enlisted in Louisville, Kentucky, on December 10, 1875. After the campaign was over, he and two of his comrades deserted on April 17, 1876, at Fort D. A. Russell.

[11] Private Charles Cunningham, of Company E, Third Cavalry, had enlisted in Cincinnati, Ohio, on November 3, 1875. He deserted with Private Slater on April 17, after they had returned to Fort D. A. Russell.

for the horses which were still up on the mountain. While starting out to the rear at the foot of the mesa, they were accosted by Captain Mills, who was having difficulty in keeping his men in line. Captain Mills ordered them back in the line because the Indians were gathering in his front and right to recapture their ponies and drive the soldiers from the village. Sergeant Land told him that they had been detailed by Captain Moore to go after the horses. Captain Mills reported later that there were ten to fifteen men in the detail and that he let some of them go after the horses but forced the rest of them into his line.

The Indians who had been accumulating in Mills's front finally made their charge to get a herd of ponies near Mills's right, toward the river. It was claimed that the herd was not captured, but the Indians apparently captured some cavalry horses, since some of them were later taken from the Indians by General Crook's detachment.

It was generally agreed that during the fight the soldiers fired too rapidly. Colonel Reynolds sent Lieutenant Morton twice to caution the officers to compel their men to fire carefully and not waste ammunition. Captain Noyes, who watched the battle from afar, observed that the soldiers fired fifty to one hundred shots to the Indians' one. Dr. Munn,[12] who was very busy building travois for the wounded at Hospital Point, noticed that the firing was very rapid. While Captain Moore was nearby, around eleven o'clock, Dr. Munn told him that his men were wasting ammunition, but Moore replied that he would tend to that part of the business if Dr. Munn would tend to his. About this time Dr. Munn observed Captain Moore with a pistol in his hand talking excitedly to Colonel Reynolds. The conversation lasted fifteen or twenty minutes, but Dr. Munn was too busy to hear it.

It was about this time that it became apparent that Captain Moore would be unable to maintain his position on the bluff and mesa. Colonel Reynolds ordered that the hospital be moved to a

[12] Dr. Curtis E. Munn was born in Vermont and was appointed assistant surgeon in the Massachusetts Volunteers, with whom he served all through the Civil War. He was commissioned assistant surgeon in the regular army on November 16, 1868, and served on the western frontier for many years.

Burning the Tipis

point behind the bluff where Captain Noyes was herding the pony herd, later referred to as "Hospital Rock" or "Hospital Bluff." There were only the two hospital sites, but the men may have stopped between the two points. While Hospital Point is shown on all the maps and is easy to find, the site of the hospital south of the bluff is unknown.[13]

While the battle line was engaged in holding off the Indians, the details from the companies were engaged in the destruction of the Indian property and tipis. The latter were large conical tents made of canvas obtained at the agencies and elk and buffalo skins procured by the chase. These were supported by a number of ash and fir poles, meeting in a point at the top and radiating out at the bottom until the floor had a diameter of eighteen to twenty-five feet, while apertures at the apex allowed egress to the smoke ascending from the fire at the center of the floor. The entrance was through a small trap door of skin at the side. Major Stanton counted a total of 105 tipis in the village, including those sheltering dogs, ponies, and brood mares. Lieutenant Morton and Frank Grouard reported eighty-four lodges in the village. John Shangrau told Judge Ricker that there were fifty-one lodges and that the Indians were Oglalas. He possibly meant there were fifty-one lodges of Oglalas. There were forty new canvas tipis at the south end of the village. The discrepancy in the number of lodges reported is probably accounted for by the inclusion or omission of the small shelters used by the unmarried warriors, called "wickiups."

Everything was wet and hard to burn, but the tipis were so full

[13] I have made a close search for the exact spot on which this hospital was located but have not found any material evidence which would indicate where it was. There were two dead men left there close enough to the passing troops so that they could be identified by them. The dead were undoubtedly stripped and dismembered after the troops moved out. The area around the bottom of the bluff has been covered over several feet deep by earth washing down from the steep sides of the bluff. Fence posts close to the south foot of the bluff stand only two feet above the ground. There is an old abandoned county road which comes around the foot of the bluff on the south and east side, which probably covers the place where the hospital was. It comes along a little bench not far from the trail the soldiers must have followed in retreat, and there is a little nook just around on the south side which is large enough for two dead men and four or five wounded. It is the first likely spot out of sight of the village.

of powder, caps, and fixed ammunition that after a fire was started they all exploded. When the kegs of powder exploded, the lodgepoles, thick as a man's wrist and at least eighteen feet long, would go sailing up into the air, and upon descending would smash all obstacles in their way. Fortunately no one was injured by the falling debris. First of all, the tipi poles were torn down and pieces of dry cottonwood found outside each tipi were piled on. The saddles, robes, and everything else were added to make it burn. The green meat was nicely cooked by the fire, but that which was dried and packed in little sacks and all that was partly dried was rendered unfit for use. Major Stanton and Lieutenant Morton agreed that there was enough buffalo and deer meat and other provisions to feed the whole command from three to five days. Lieutenant Morton estimated that he saw two to three thousand buffalo robes there. Captain Egan stated that he saw "any quantity" of riding and pack saddles and headgear destroyed, together with at least fifty travois. After the burning there was much green meat on the ground only partly burned. Major Stanton reported that he did not see any firearms except one or two old muskets, but stated in his testimony that "there were all kinds of provisions. There was even coffee, flour, tobacco, meat, and some chickens. I saw a soldier carrying off a chicken or two."

Robert A. Strahorn's dispatch of March 18 described the luxuries found in the village and several incidents which occurred during the burning:

> With all the scenes of native splendor, and luxury our fancy had pictured, this Powder River reality yet excelled, yet astonishes. In the more than one hundred large tepees totally destroyed were beds of furs and robes, that, to a soldier, looked simply fit for savage Gods; war bonnets and squaw dresses regal in the construction and decoration, requiring months for making, and worth from five to ten ponies each; cooking utensils that an ordinary housewife would not need to be ashamed of; tons of dried and fresh meats, and occasionally dried fruits; every tepee an arsenal within itself with its kegs and canisters of powder; its large supply of bar lead, caps, and fixed ammunition; and then piles of such miscellaneous articles as axes, knives, saddles—over 125 of these—buck-

Burning the Tipis

skin clothing of every description, moccasins, beautifully ornamented saddle bags, sewing outfits, and really everything any frontiersman would need to insure his comfort. With the exception of a few robes and other trinkets removed by the troops, these vast stores, in many instances the accumulation of a life time, were piled upon the dismantled tepees, and the whole reduced to ashes. In the case of the generous pieces of nicely dried meat the action was particularly unfortunate, as the troops needed such provender badly, and General Crook had especially impressed upon the minds of the officers the importance of saving it. . . .

We failed to see the white girl who was known to be with this tribe. She was captured when only 2 or 3 years old from Mormon emigrants, it is believed, and is now 20 years of age. Frank Gruard, who, while a prisoner here, saw her daily, says she is quite handsome, has a very pleasant disposition, and is esteemed and guarded as the richest treasure by her dusky companions. He never knew them to insult or mistreat her, and she is not obliged to perform any of the common labor of the squaws, most of her time being spent in doing fancy bead-work, embroidery, etc. Yet, not knowing a word of English, and having no knowledge of a more convenient sphere, she often, by her listless and unsatisfied manner betrays a desire to leave the tribe, or at least to make some change for the better.

Among the domestic animals about the village, we noticed several broods of chickens and a number of fine dogs. The conduct of several of the latter seemed particularly strange. Lying by the side of their master's tepees when we arrived, they would not change their position one iota, as its domicile was torn down and with its effects set on fire. The great faithful fellow would still remain motionless as a statue, heedless of coaxing, gazing wistfully without a growl at the bands of the destroyers.

It took longer than expected to complete the destruction of the village. Reynolds had trouble keeping the men from pilfering. They would delay the firing of the lodges to bring out robes and meat, but Reynolds required them to throw these things away, permitting them to retain a piece of meat which could be conveniently carried. Reynolds, with one orderly, was the only soldier supervising the burning of the village, the other officers being on the skirmish line. The Indians became bolder and, creeping among the logs, trees, sage brush, rocks, and willows which were found from one end of the line to the other, would pick off the men from concealed positions. Most of the village was burned by eleven o'clock, but the work of destruction continued until the tipis and property were reduced to ashes. One tipi was left untouched so as to provide shelter for an old Indian woman who had been shot in the thigh and left behind. She told Frank Grouard that Sitting Bull's village was situated about sixty miles down the river, while it was Crazy Horse's village which was being destroyed. Grouard claimed that he knew this was the village of Crazy Horse by the horses, and that he knew every horse there.[14] The other guides reported that the Indians in the village were Oglala Sioux, Minneconjou Sioux, and Northern Cheyennes. One or two lodges of Sitting Bull's band were there and about the same number of Indians from Red Cloud Agency who had come in that morning to trade.

Up until eleven o'clock Colonel Reynolds had been fully occupied with destroying the village and maintaining the skirmish line. Now that his primary object had been accomplished, the problem was to withdraw his men as soon as possible. This could not be done until the led horses of the three companies could be brought down from the mountain. The horses of Captain Mills's company were on the little shelf at the top of the mountain a mile and three-quarters away, while those of Captain Moore were still on the hill near the foot of the mountain. No men had been left to protect the horses except for the horse-holders, who had eight horses each in their charge. Bringing these horses down the mountainside, with the possibility of the Indians attacking and stampeding them, was a delicate operation. Colonel Reynolds stated that the withdrawal was delayed two hours because of the great difficulty in getting the horses down from the mountain.

During this period the skirmish line had to hold the Indians back. Lieutenant Rawolle had sent several messengers back for his horses, and one of them, Sergeant Land,[15] said it took an hour or more to

[14] De Barthe, *Life and Adventures of Frank Grouard*, 98.

[15] First Sergeant William Land of Company E, Second Cavalry, had re-enlisted at Fort Laramie on November 6, 1873, and because he had over five years' continuous service he drew the extra $2.00 per month. The first sergeant was the headman of

get the horses of his company down. Lieutenant Bainbridge Reynolds said no men of Captain Moore's company left the skirmish line except three or four who had been sent for the horses.

The Indians became bolder during the last several hours of the engagement, and the soldiers had a hard time holding their positions. At first the Indians had fired wildly and without much effect, but later their aim improved. Colonel Reynolds said they were reinforced from time to time by returning hunting parties. The evening before, according to Frank Grouard, forty warriors had been sent out to find the soldiers but missed them by going up the lower trail. It seems more probable that it was the return of this party which turned the tide of battle.

During the early part of the action, Lieutenant Rawolle had ten to twenty men spaced at different places on the bluff and six to eight men up on the point. While the village was being destroyed, Rawolle held the bluff although the men came down from the point. The bluff, which was about three hundred yards long, rising to the peak at the west end, was particularly vulnerable to a flank attack because it was commanded on the west and north by other peaks and ridges higher up on the mountainside. About noon, some of the warriors worked southward along the side of the mountain, protected by the unevenness of the ground, and obtained an enfilading fire on the men on the bluff. Some of the men fled and joined Moore's company in the ravine on the mesa, but when a soldier was wounded on the bluff, the rest of them retired. The Indians occupied this ridge and poured in a fire on the men on the mesa so that they went down on the bottom land and formed a line facing west. The river had formerly run around at the foot of the mesa, cutting out a low place next to the bank. This was a secure place, although exposed to long-range fire from the rocks on the mountainside. Since Moore's battalion was now out of sight of the Indians on the bluff, the latter concentrated their fire obliquely from

his company, taking orders only from his commissioned officers. As he had direct control and contact with the men, he was of necessity a rugged individual. It is said that in the cavalry the first sergeant had to lick all the men in his company before they would obey his orders.

the rear upon Mills's battalion in line. Captain Egan's company, which had been sent back into the line to reinforce Captain Mills on the right, was flanked from the river and fell back so that its line was parallel with the river and facing it. The Indians at this point had crawled up in the long grass and the thickets bordering the river and compelled the line to swing back and face them. At this time the soldier line was in the form of an inverted U with Captain Mills's battalion farthest advanced. Later, Captain Egan's men were again withdrawn, and because there was no protection on that flank, Mills bore the brunt of the enfilading fire from east and west. He repeatedly sent back for reinforcements, which Colonel Reynolds did not have to send. Some of Mills's men were absent from the line, engaged in plundering the lodges. In one instance he found several of his men carrying buffalo robes to the rear and had to threaten them with his shotgun before they would return to their places in the line.

Finally, in exasperation, Captain Mills went back 150 to 200 yards to the clump of trees near Hospital Point, where Captain Moore had position, to try to get him to advance back on the mesa where he had been before. Captain Moore refused and stayed with his men in the line under the mesa. One of the most controversial matters in the campaign was the conduct of Captain Moore at this point, and it was the subject of a court-martial proceeding against him which came to trial the following January. Although there was much bitter feeling which split the officers into two camps and gave rise to many biased and conflicting statements, there is no substantial difference in the various eyewitness accounts.

Captain Mills, in his official report, gave the most complete account of the action after the destruction of the village:

Gen. Reynolds then returned near the lower end of the village when I reported to him that Egan and Moore were not treating me right that Egan had entirely left my right and that Moore was falling back on my left, that it would take some time to destroy everything that they ought to be made to hold their ground and that I had no command over them. He replied that we would talk about that some other time that Egan had

Burning the Tipis

done so well in the charge that he did not like to call on him for any more work, but that he would send Noyes as soon as he could. . . .

I called out . . . to Captain Moore that if he would keep the men in the bluffs he could get the Indians sure . . . and fearing that he might not hear me I sent Pvt Shore[16] Co E, 3rd Cavalry, who returned with a message from Major Moore that he understood it and would attend to it. Seeing they did not go back and the bullets coming close and low and low down from both flanks, I sent Lt. Johnson to tell Gen Reynolds that Moore had fallen back that both our flanks were exposed and that unless I was supported I would have to fall back, at this time I think there was a gap [from the west end of Mills's line to the north end of Moore's line] of 150 yards entirely unoccupied. Lt. Johnson returned with a message to the effect that Noyes would soon be up to support me, about that time I asked Lts Morton and Bourke to carry for me the same message, but received no answer.

About this time one of Egan's men was mortally wounded. I ordered some men to carry him to the rear and sent a man for Dr Munn, and seeing Gen Reynolds coming up I went to meet him. He saw them carrying him and asked how badly he was hurt. I told him that I thought he was mortally wounded. He told me to ascertain if he were dead. I called to the Sergeant who said he was almost dead when the General ordered him left where he was. . . . About that time I met Egan who said Mills if you want more men on your right I will send them. I replied that I certainly did and a short time before we retired eight or ten men came up and joined.

The man who was carried back mortally wounded was Private George Schneider[17] of Egan's company, who had been shot through the neck. He was left at Hospital Point, where he soon died. Private George H. Maitland of Egan's company testified at the Reynolds court-martial that a sergeant of his company had told him that he and a detail of men had buried Private Schneider. Maitland did

[16] Private Alexander Shore of Company E, Third Cavalry, had enlisted in Indianapolis, Indiana, on July 29, 1870.

[17] Private George Schneider of Company K, Second Cavalry, had re-enlisted at Omaha Barracks, Nebraska, on September 14, 1872, and was drawing the $3.00 per month extra for having had over ten years of continuous service. One wonders why Schneider remained a private after such long service. Most of the men who had had over five years of service were noncommissioned officers.

not see him buried, and there is little reason to believe that he was buried. Major Stanton said that as he left the field he saw two dead men, one of Egan's company, lying back of a little point where there was a hospital. Schneider was the only man killed in Egan's company, and as he was not buried by the time of the retreat, he was probably not buried at all. Captain Egan testified that he left one dead man just above the hospital—two bodies were left there together. Captain Mills said that he told the men who were carrying Schneider to "drop him and get back to their places" after Reynolds gave the order to leave him where he was. One might surmise that Schneider's body was carried back to Hospital Bluff when the hospital was moved there. Captain Mills's testimony continued:

By that time, the place was becoming very hot, and seeing that I could not remain there, fearing I would be surrounded by Indians coming in on the right and left, I saw Lt. Bourke and sent a message by him to Col Reynolds that I could not stay there if I was not supported on the right and left. After that I saw Lt. Morton and told him that Col Reynolds must make these men keep their places.... While these men were carrying that wounded man to the rear, the Indians all the time firing on them, I saw Col Reynolds coming and ran down to meet him, and told him I could not stay there without support. I then returned towards my own command. Seeing that Col Reynolds would not compel Capt Moore to hold his position, I went to see him myself. I found him at the upper corner of the village, about 600 yards in rear of my position, with all his officers and a great part of his battalion firing at the mountain at long range. I should say that previous to this time while I was near the left of my line a corporal by the name of Lang was wounded in the foot, and I saw them carrying him to the rear, and at that time the men on the mesa and the broken washes broke and ran towards the hospital. Before the wounding of that man, about half a dozen Indians came down towards those men occupying the mesa, and were dancing and making themselves quite conspicuous, and I directed some of my men to fire at them. About that time, the corporal being wounded, the whole line fled up the bed of the river towards Captain Moore. I ran to the extreme left of my line and called out to them for God's sake not to abandon that position, that if they remained there they could kill the Indians as

Burning the Tipis

they came down. Some of them halted and listened to me, but went on apparently under orders. *Q.* Did you have any conversation with Capt Moore the time you saw him. *A.* Yes sir. I went close up to him and in an excited manner said to him, "Major Moore, how is it all your officers and men are here. There is no use for them here. There is a fight going on in front, and I am hotly pressed. I have no right to give you orders, but I ask you as a brother officer to come and sustain my left." He looked me squarely in the face and made no reply whatever. I turned on my heel and seeing one of my own sergeants among his men drove him back to the command. I then went back and told Lt. Johnson we were not going to receive any help, and we must make dispositions to get out of there. I went along the line and called to the men that we were going to retire from the village, that we would all go at the same time, firing a volley first, and move off slowly and to see that all were taken away. *Q.* In response to the appeal to Capt Moore for assistance did he assist you. *A.* No sir, not in the least; they were firing but they could not see the Indians on the mesa, because they were so close under the bluff. They could see Indians farther to the right, about 1000 yards off and were firing at them, but the Indians on the mesa were about 150 yards off my left flank, but not visible to those men. *Q.* State what effect the withdrawal of those troops from that position on the bluff had upon your position. *A.* It rendered it perfectly untenable if I was to continue the destruction of the property.

Captain Mills was in error when he stated that he went six hundred yards to the rear to find Captain Moore. Throughout the court-martial proceedings and in his map, Mills insisted that his line was along the north edge of the village. All other witnesses maintained that it was along the south edge of the village, a contention that is borne out by the fact that military cartridge cases have been found on a prolongation of the south edge of the village, but none have been found near the north edge of the village. In Mills's map the south end of Moore's line was near Hospital Point. In his testimony Mills assumes that he, being at the north end of the village which was 600 yards long, went back 600 yards to Hospital Point, where he found Moore. Actually he went south 150 to 200 yards.

The conversation between Captain Moore and Captain Mills occurred about noon. Lieutenant Rawolle stated that about eleven o'clock, while he was down seeing Captain Moore about arrangements for bringing the led horses down, he overheard this interview, and that Captain Moore told Mills to go see Colonel Reynolds, who was not over seventy-five yards distant. Lieutenant Rawolle and Captain Mills both stated that they entered the village at eight-thirty, which was just an hour earlier than shown by Captain Egan's watch. On the basis of Egan's watch, the interview took place an hour later, or at twelve. Captain Mills stated that Colonel Reynolds first promised to send Noyes's company in support at nine-thirty, which by Egan's time would be actually at ten-thirty. When Lieutenant Bourke carried Mills's message to Colonel Reynolds asking for reinforcements, the latter replied that he would support Captain Mills directly and that he would move out some of the men that were with the herd as soon as he could. Bourke then noticed that Captain Noyes's men were unsaddled and did not appear to be in readiness for action.

The battle line was described by Lieutenant Morton in his testimony:

In the latter part of the action the men were spread out fan-shaped—I could not say the line was continuous. The Indians got around and occupied a position near where Moore's battalion formerly held position. I believe we killed an Indian there. I was in the village when that shot killed the Indian. I think I was with Capt. Moore at the time the shot was fired and saw the Indian drop. Mills and Moore protected each other. I don't know that one position was any safer than the other—the whole village was in range. There was a little gap between Mills' and Moore's line. The position of Moore protected Mills from that oblique fire. The Indians making the oblique fire on Mills were actually a little to the right and in front of Moore's line. No effort was made to drive the Indians from the bluff except by concentration of fire. The Indians got off on the left and rear—almost in the direction we entered the village from. Our position was in a semi-circle.

Lieutenant Paul said that when the company retreated from the bluff they went toward the rear in the direction of Hospital Rock, two or three hours before Noyes came up to relieve the line. Lieutenant Paul's company was in the village from nine-thirty to two-thirty. Lieutenant Sibley said Moore's battalion fell back only once, at a distance of two to three hundred yards, about one o'clock—just before the village was evacuated. Private Michael I. McCannon[18] was reported killed by a gunshot wound near the east end of Captain Mills's line by Captain Moore, his company commander. His body was never recovered. Colonel Reynolds testified that he did not see Captain Moore near Hospital Rock during the battle, but that Captain Mills was very much excited all through the day and kept sending for reinforcements although he was in no more danger than any other company, having suffered no serious losses during the day.

Lieutenant Johnson was sent twice to Reynolds for support. The second time he told Colonel Reynolds that Moore had fallen back and that Mills's battalion was being fired at from three sides and unless reinforced would have to fall back. Reynolds replied, "That can't be so. Here comes Noyes now to reinforce you," and added that Mills was to withdraw his battalion to its horses.[19] Johnson reported back to Captain Mills, but when Noyes's men did not appear immediately, Mills gave the order to retire after waiting another ten to fifteen minutes. The company had gone but a few yards when Captain Noyes appeared with thirty-five of his men dismounted to hold the skirmish line while the other five companies withdrew. He had been delayed because his company had unsaddled and was making coffee when the order came to hurry to the front. Captain Mills then put his men back on the line, while Colonel Reynolds placed Noyes's men in position a short distance south of the village. When Noyes's men had formed, Captain Mills withdrew but halted his company about five hundred yards in rear of Noyes. Mills returned to Captain Noyes and told him where to look for danger. The Indians were in the grass on the right and

---

[18] Private Michael I. McCannon of Company F, Third Cavalry, was a raw recruit who had enlisted December 1, 1875, at Boston, Massachusetts.

[19] Testimony of Lieutenant Johnson at the court-martial trial of Colonel Reynolds.

The Reynolds Campaign on Powder River

left, and if the men went forward they would be killed. Colonel Reynolds then directed the men to get their horses as quickly as possible so the command could move to Lodgepole Creek. At this time Captain Mills requested permission to go after his overcoats which were still on the top of the mountain, but Reynolds said the hills were full of Indians and refused permission.

When questioned as to the location of Captain Moore's line when he arrived at the village, Captain Noyes testified as follows:

> When the withdrawal commenced Capt Moore was right about where the ruins of the tepees were at the south side of the village—actually in the village—right exactly where Capt Egan had charged through the tepees. He was right on the line—the general direction of the line was southwest and northeast, facing the bluffs the Indians were in. I saw Moore among the ruins of some of the tepees. He was not on the bluff to the left of the village as his line ran out to the sage brush mesa, his right extending towards the river, and on his left were other troops. A few men on the left of Capt Moore were on a picket on that little bluff. His line ran out at nearly right angles, it was an angle of 60 degrees to it.
> Q. At that time was Capt Moore's company and Captain Moore himself 150 to 300 yards to the rear of the line occupied by Capt Mills' troops.
> A. No sir, I considered the troops were in a continuous line, as much so as considering the fact that the men sought individual shelter. They were all facing the same general direction—there was a bulge in the line. . . .
> When I got to the village things were rather quiet. Occasionally there would be a shot from the Indians which was answered from our line. . . . I was there from ten minutes to a half hour—I did not lose any men. . . . The line was not straight as the men took shelter behind stumps, trees and other things. . . . Moore's line faced north and a little to the west—the line was not semi-circular, but something in that shape. As the Indians were in different directions both Mills and Moore were equally near the Indians. Mills was facing one lot of Indians and Captain Moore another, and perhaps Egan another—I was not on the right of the line.

From this description, the "picket on that little bluff" must have referred to men at Hospital Rock. It could not have been the bluff previously occupied by Rawolle's company because that had long

Burning the Tipis

since been occupied by the Indians. It seems clear that when Moore's battalion was outflanked by the Indians, it withdrew to the shelter of the mesa where a new line was formed extending from the vicinity of Mills's left in the south end of the village southward toward Hospital Rock. At the end of the fight there were eight to ten of Captain Egan's men extending in a line southward from the east end of Mills's line, facing the river and in rear of Moore's line.

Chapter 6 THE PONY HERD

AFTER the Indian herd had been stampeded up the river bottom by Captain Noyes during the initial charge, it was driven into the hills and left under the guard of the scouts, the soldiers being sent out in small squads to gather up the straggling ponies. When all had been collected, they were herded half a mile west of the river on the bluff. At this time Captain Noyes received his order from Colonel Reynolds to take the herd to the south side of the promontory where the bluff, later known as Hospital Rock or Bluff, came down to the river. In following this order Captain Noyes apparently brought the herd back over its trail on the north side of the bluff; but when about to cross the river, he received another order to hold it in the bottom just south of the point and guard it there. Instead of driving the herd across the river and then back westward around the point, he left it north of the point in the angle formed by the steep bluff and the river, with mounted guards protecting it on the open side on the north.

It was now about eleven o'clock. Most of the tipis had been burned, and there was only desultory long-range skirmishing. Captain Noyes, misinterpreting the message from Colonel Reynolds, inferred that the latter intended to camp at or near the village. Believing that the battle was about over, he left eleven men with the scouts to guard the pony herd, detailing eight more to assist them. He took the rest of his company, which contained a total of

The Pony Herd

fifty-one men, seventy-five yards across the river, where he thought it safe to encamp, and ordered it to unsaddle. The river at this point was frozen solid enough to permit the passage of mounted troopers, but they had to pick their crossing places. The horses were hobbled and lariated, and the men made coffee and rested. It had been Captain Noyes's practice to permit his men and horses to eat and rest whenever possible. The horses had been under the saddle for twenty-six hours and had had no forage since the camp at Otter Creek. The men had ridden fifty-five miles without rest since early the morning of the day before and had not eaten since the previous evening.

The soldiers had not captured all of the Indian ponies. Colonel Reynolds stated in his official report that while yet on the mountain before the charge, he saw other pony herds grazing beyond the village and that the animals captured did not include more than half of the number seen. Captain Mills testified later that from his own observation there were altogether fifteen hundred to two thousand animals, both above and below the village, of which six to seven hundred were captured by the troops. When he first arrived on the battle line, the Indians drove one herd of two hundred ponies through his position. On his map, Captain Mills indicated three Indian herds north of the village, two on the west side of the river, and one on the east side. Most estimates of the number of ponies captured varied from six to eight hundred.

In the court-martial of Colonel Reynolds the government contended that instead of burning everything, he should have loaded up the captured meat and supplies on the Indian ponies and brought them along to feed the command, which was very short of food. General Crook, Major Stanton, and Lieutenant Bourke testified that it would have been entirely practicable to have done this, but did not attempt to explain how it could have been done during the engagement. The packers and the pack mules had been left behind with General Crook, and Captain Noyes. Lieutenant Rawolle, and Lieutenant Drew, who were in direct charge of the pony herd, were quick to point out the difficulties involved in such an attempt.

Captain Noyes, after stating that the herd consisted of six to seven hundred ponies, testified as follows:

Q. What did they [the Indian horses] consist of. *A.* There might be one fourth or one sixth was ponies, the balance were colts and yearlings. *Q.* Did you see any mules. *A.* I saw one gray mule. *Q.* Suppose there had been a large amount of meat, provisions, and pack saddles, would it have been practicable under all the circumstances, to have loaded these on the animals. *A.* Not if we were to get to the mouth of Clear Fork that night. We would have had to catch the ponies, saddle them, and load the meat on them. *Q.* Were there men enough to perform that duty and at the same time protect themselves from the Indians. *A.* Not within a reasonable time. It would take a long time. *Q.* Were the ponies wild. *A.* Like all Indian ponies when white men come around them, they don't smell what they are used to, and it would be difficult to get them up. *Q.* Would it be difficult to catch them and saddle them. *A.* Yes sir. I know that I had two of them lariated for myself and they bolted into the middle of the herd as soon as the rope went over their heads.

Lieutenant Rawolle stated that because there were no packers with the command, it would not have been practicable to load the meat on the ponies, even if there were no Indians about. Since the meat and supplies were half a mile away, the ponies would have to be brought to the village increasing the danger of their recapture. He estimated that one-fourth of the herd were colts, or yearlings and the rest were ordinary Indian ponies, with a few American horses.

Lieutenant George A. Drew,[1] the quartermaster of the expedition, agreed with Captain Noyes and Lieutenant Rawolle. He testified that it would have been a very difficult matter to load the ponies, since they were very wild and running in all directions. The scouts had been trying to catch ponies out of the herd for their

[1] Lieutenant George A. Drew, born in Michigan, was appointed second lieutenant in the Sixth Michigan Cavalry with which he served during the Civil War. He was brevetted lieutenant colonel of volunteers on March 13, 1865, for distinguished services in the Shenandoah valley, and colonel of volunteers on April 9, 1865, for gallant service in the campaign against Richmond, Virginia. He was assigned to the Third Cavalry on January 1, 1871.

Captain Anson Mills.
From Anson Mills,
My Story (*1918*).

Library,
Colorado Historical Society

Captain
Henry E. Noyes.

Photograph by the author

Looking north from Rawolle's ridge in the foreground to the site of the village in the trees on the right.

Photograph by the author

Campsite near the mouth of Lodgepole Creek on the night of the battle.

The Pony Herd

own use, but had been unable to do so. The provisions might have been loaded and taken away, but he estimated that it would have taken a day to do it.

Sergeant Land stated that he saw five or six mules in the herd. Mr. Strahorn testified that many of the horses, ponies, and mules were of the best class and were identified as belonging to various stockmen on the Colorado and Wyoming frontier. It was suggested by the government that the dried meat was carried off after the battle of Slim Buttes on September 9, 1876. Captain Noyes pointed out, however, that in that case the meat was packed by regular citizen packers accompanying the soldiers who, being skilled in packing, did it rapidly, and the pack mules of the expedition were used. In that engagement fifteen to sixteen hundred soldiers captured a village of thirty-five tipis, so it was not a case in point. Since most of the captured herd on Powder River were colts and yearlings, and the balance consisted of mules, American horses, and ponies, it is probable that the war ponies, which were most valuable to the Indians, were among the herds north of the village which were not captured.

About noon, Colonel Reynolds sent Corporal Meagher[2] back to Captain Noyes with the order to leave the pony herd and bring his company to the village, but the order did not state whether the company was to come mounted or dismounted. Captain Noyes sent word that his company was unsaddled and was making coffee but that it would be up in a few minutes. Shortly after, a messenger came from Dr. Munn to Captain Noyes with word that Colonel Reynolds had ordered Noyes's company to the village and that Dr. Munn was bringing his wounded men to the bluff. When Reynolds received Noyes's reply, he was exasperated and sent Corporal Meagher back with the peremptory order to come at once, dismounted. Noyes received this order ten to fifteen minutes after the first one and for the first time realized that he was needed on the skirmish line. Colonel Reynolds later filed charges against Captain Noyes, claiming that the unsaddling rendered the com-

---

[2] Corporal Thomas Meagher of Company I, Second Cavalry, had re-enlisted at Fort Sanders on February 8, 1875.

pany incapable of defending the pony herd against an attack and of responding to any emergency call which might be made upon it. "The unsaddling was, under the circumstances, blameworthy, but as no evil came of it, and his [Noyes's] general conduct was so entirely satisfactory and praiseworthy, no notice was taken at that time of the unsaddling."[3] Captain Noyes contended that it would take only three to five minutes to saddle up his horses and that in this case it made no difference because he was ordered to the village dismounted. Upon receiving the last order, he immediately started for the village, leaving his horses lariated and hobbled.

While the troops were hard pressed to hold the Indians back and after orders had been sent to Captain Noyes to hurry his troops to the field dismounted, the horses coming down from the mountain were in imminent danger of being captured and stampeded by the Indians, who had made their way around the left of the soldier line on the mountain west of the village. As the led horses were approaching on the flat, some Indians appeared on the plain attempting to cut them off. To prevent this, Colonel Reynolds went in person to the horse-holders of Egan's and Johnson's companies and ordered them to tie their held horses to trees, seize their carbines and run up on the plain and fire at the Indians. This was done under the immediate direction of Lieutenant Morton, and the Indians were driven back. The horses of the three companies were brought in safely just as Captain Noyes arrived on the ground with his troops. The horses of Captain Moore's battalion were the last to come down, with those of Lieutenant Rawolle's company in the rear. One can imagine what a precarious job it was for each of the horse-holders to lead seven frightened animals through the confusion and tumult of the attack. From Mills's map it appears that they were brought down the valley of Thompson Creek to the bottom land under the mesa. Some of them were driven to Hospital Rock and some close behind the line, where they awaited the arrival of their riders.

Captain Noyes arrived on the skirmish line about one o'clock,

[3] Testimony of Colonel Reynolds at the court-martial trial of Captain H. E. Noyes.

The Pony Herd

one hour after the first summons. Nine of his men had been left to help guard the pony herd, while six of his company were straggling but reported on the line within a short time. With Captain Mills constantly calling for reinforcements, one can understand Colonel Reynolds' chagrin upon learning that Noyes's company was unsaddled and eating its lunch.

Just before Noyes's company came up, Captain Egan was getting his led horses from where he had left them in the morning. Colonel Reynolds told him to be ready to move out of the village as soon as he could. While mounting his men, Captain Egan saw Noyes's company coming up on foot and forming a line in front of where he was. "I heard Captain Noyes call to Colonel Reynolds as he was moving back and say to him I only want an opportunity to saddle up my horses. I rode out to meet Colonel Reynolds and asked him if Capt. Noyes was unsaddled. He said he supposed so, or said yes. I said the Indians would play the very mischief or something that way, and asked permission to remain where I was with my company and come out with Capt. Noyes, and see that the company was saddled up. Col. Reynolds said certainly, he was glad of the suggestion and told me to remain, and he rode off to where the other companies were forming and mounting. . . . I left the village in front of Capt. Noyes' company and moved across the river out of the village and formed a line alongside of where Capt. Noyes' company was unsaddled, and remained there until the last of the men were saddled up."[4] A cavalry company which had to saddle and mount its horses in the face of the enemy was in a vulnerable position, and unless protected by other troopers, could have been stampeded and captured. Egan stated that his company and that of Noyes left the village at two and were the last to leave it.

Meanwhile, Lieutenant Rawolle had received orders from Captain Moore to take out half of his company, mount them after the horses came down, and have the other half ready to mount as soon as Moore gave the order to do so. Rawolle's horses, the last to arrive, were back there but a few minutes when the first half of the company, under Sergeant Land, mounted and followed the

[4] Testimony of Captain Egan at the court-martial trial of Colonel Reynolds.

trail through a little piece of timber and down to Hospital Rock. Here they halted, dismounted, formed a skirmish line, and waited for orders. Since Lieutenant Rawolle stated that his was the last mounted company to leave the village, the company of Captain Moore must have moved out before it. When the other half of Rawolle's company had passed, the skirmish line was relieved by Captain Egan, who in turn formed a line to protect Noyes's company while it was mounting. Land's detachment then crossed the river and deployed as a skirmish line, waited until all others had passed, and then, being the last in line, followed as rear guard. As the soldiers left the village, forty to fifty Indians entered it from the bluffs.

After the troops had passed through Captain Noyes's skirmish line in the village, it gradually fell back about three hundred yards, where it remained until all others were mounted. Dr. Munn, who had built travois to carry his five wounded men on, placed them in readiness to move with the column. There were two dead men on the side of Hospital Rock, Privates Peter Dowdy and George Schneider, but Colonel Reynolds told Dr. Munn that the retreating column could not carry them off. Dr. Munn thought that they were left on account of the excitement prevailing there.

Captain Mills's battalion withdrew from the line when Noyes's company came up and retreated to their horses, which were in the river bottom on the north side of Hospital Rock. When the men were mounted and were about to cross the river, Blacksmith Glavinski[5] came up to Captain Mills and reported that Private Lorenzo E. Ayers[6] of Mills's company had been left wounded on the field near the east end of the line. Mills turned to Colonel Reynolds, who was close by on his horse, reported to him, and asked what could be done. Colonel Reynolds was very much annoyed and said it was too late to do anything about it and directed Mills to proceed. At that moment, Corporal Dennis Giles of Captain Moore's company was passing by on his way to the village where he had been sent by

[5] Blacksmith Albert Glavinski of Company M, Third Cavalry, had enlisted in Pittsburgh, Pennsylvania, on December 1, 1873.

[6] Private Lorenzo E. Ayers of Company M, Third Cavalry, had been in service about a year, having enlisted in Boston, Massachusetts, on February 27, 1875.

The Pony Herd

Captain Moore to find if any of the men of his company were still on the skirmish line. Captain Mills told him to give his compliments to Captain Noyes and request him to bring off the wounded man. Captain Mills then started for Lodgepole Creek at one-thirty at the head of the column, accompanied by Colonel Reynolds, Lieutenant Bourke, Lieutenant Morton, Lieutenant Drew, and Frank Grouard, with Lieutenant Johnson's company next in line. It was cold and snowing. In order to go around Hospital Rock in the bend of the river, they first crossed to the east side, then recrossed south of the Rock and marched southward on the west side of the river.

Corporal Giles and Blacksmith Glavinski went back together and found Captain Noyes on the line, which at that time had retreated about three hundred yards from the village. Captain Noyes refused to try to rescue the wounded man and sent back word to Mills that he was unable to take the man off and that it was up to Mills to take his own wounded off the field. The Indians had re-entered the village and were congregating in front of Noyes's line, which was spread very thin. It was at least three hundred yards away from the wounded man, who was probably dead by this time anyway. In the controversy which arose later as to the responsibility for leaving Ayers on the field, Captain Noyes claimed that at the time he received the message, Captain Mills was only seventy-five to eighty yards in the rear moving away toward his horses, and that he supposed that Captain Mills had come back and removed the man. Lieutenant Morton, however, stated that it was while the head of the column was standing on the ice of the river that Glavinski came up to Captain Mills and reported that the wounded man had been left on the field. If this was true, Captain Mills was too far away to go back to the rescue.

When Captain Mills was two miles on the march, Private Jeremiah J. Murphy,[7] of his company, came riding up to him and reported that Private Ayers had been scalped. Private Ayers, Murphy, Maitland, and Blacksmith Glavinski, who had been posted

[7] Private Jeremiah J. Murphy had enlisted in Boston, Massachusetts, on February 13, 1875.

The Reynolds Campaign on Powder River

in a little valley and did not see the retreat, knew nothing about it until Ayers was wounded and called for help. When they looked around, there was no one to help. Glavinski, not seeing anything of the company, ran as fast as he could about five hundred yards to where he found Captain Mills. Private Maitland said later that the Indians were about a quarter of a mile from the men, firing as they came. The soldiers returned the fire as well as they could until the Indians were within seventy-five yards of them. They had to save themselves; and when they retreated, the Indians followed until they came up to Ayers and then commenced dancing about him. Private Murphy described the incident later in his testimony:

We were all there and the command was ordered to retreat and we did not hear the order given. We called for help but there were three or four of us: all the rest had gone. Q. How was he wounded. A. He [Ayers] was shot through the leg and through the hand. He fell when shot through the leg and could not walk. Q. Who remained with the wounded man: who was with him last. A. I was with him last. Q. Under what circumstances did you leave him. A. I could not get him away, and the Indians were coming so close that I had to get away. Q. How near were the Indians when you left him. A. About a dozen of them were about 75 yards off. Q. What did he say to you. A. He called for help but no help was coming, and he said I might as well get out of there, as there was no use in two of us getting killed. Q. Then you left. A. Yes sir. Q. What did you see there after you left. A. I ran into some bushes, and they quit firing at me and I saw them circling around the wounded man—ten or fifteen of them. . . . Q. How long after you saw the Indians around that man until you reported to Capt Mills. A. About half an hour.

For their heroism on this occasion Private Murphy and Blacksmith Glavinski were awarded the Congressional Medal of Honor.

Finally Private J. J. Murphy was the only man . . . left not disabled. When the wounded man called to him in a heart rending voice: "Oh Murphy; for Mercy's sake, do not leave me in their hands," Murphy fearlessly turned back, lifted the groaning man to his shoulders and

The Pony Herd

tried to make his way through the advancing savages, who poured a rain of bullets at him. The wounded man was again hit, and Murphy's carbine stock smashed by a rifle-ball. He managed to draw his pistol, and fired until the last cartridge was spent; then being without ammunition, and seeing absolutely no chance of saving his comrade, he was compelled to abandon him, and succeeded, to the surprise of the officers, who watched his movements, in reaching his comrades. His uniform was pierced by several bullets, but the brave man escaped unscathed. For his heroism, so gallantly displayed, he was awarded the Medal of Honor.

Among those men who covered the retreat and fought the attacking Indians with the utmost intrepidity, showing a seeming reckless courage, was Blacksmith A. Glavinsky of Co. "M," Third Cavalry, who had to be recalled several times by his officers from self-selected exposed positions. He also earned the Medal of Honor.[8]

There were four soldiers killed and six wounded in the engagement, and Colonel Reynolds included in his official report the list of casualties:

Killed.	Private Peter Dowdy, Company E, 3rd Cavalry.
	Private Michael McCannon, Company F, 3rd Cavalry.
	Private L. E. Ayers, Company M, 3rd Cavalry.
	Private George Schneider, Company K, 2nd Cavalry.
Wounded.	1st Lieut. W. C. Rawolle, 2nd Cavalry [contusion on left leg from rifle ball].

[8] Beyer and Keydal, *Deeds of Valor*, II, 205–207. In paying tribute to Private Murphy and Blacksmith Glavinski, a reconstruction of the incident involving the death of Private Ayers is attempted. It is claimed that a squad of men from M Company was sent ahead of the line to an advanced post and there was cut off by the Indians. Four men were killed, while the rest managed to escape. A sketch accompanying the text shows the four dead men lying together, with Private Murphy listening to the plea of the wounded man. The advancing Indians are only about twenty yards off. The picture is accurate so far as the terrain is concerned and shows the spot where the present monument is located. So far as is known, there was no one killed on this spot as it is west of the north edge of the village and up on the mesa, far in advance of the soldier line, and after a careful search, no relics of the battle have been found here. Private Ayers was the only man killed from Company M, the others being killed elsewhere and earlier in the fight. Ayers was not killed up on the mesa but down in the village. At the time Private Murphy left the scene, the advancing Indians were about seventy-five yards distant. In the sketch there is no snow on the ground, and the men are not even wearing their blouses.

Sergeant Chas Kaminski, Company M, 3rd Cavalry.
Corporal John Lang, Company E, 2nd Cavalry.
Private John Droege,[9] Company K, 2nd Cavalry.
Private Edward Eagan,[10] Company K, 2nd Cavalry.
Private Patrick Goings,[11] Company K, 2nd Cavalry.

Two of the killed Dowdy and Schneider were brought off the field and left on the Hospital ground, there being no available means of burying them or transporting them. The other two, McCannon and Ayers, were not brought from the picket line, nor seen by their Company Commanders at all when or after they were killed. The wounded who could not ride were brought away on travois partly improvised on the ground by the Surgeon and his assistants and partly taken from the village. In this manner they were safely but with great difficulty transported to the ambulance at Reno 101 miles.

Nearly all of the casualties were incurred near the east end of Captain Mills's line, where it was flanked by Indians firing from the willows and tall grass on the riverbank. Private Peter Dowdy was killed near the west edge of the village, and Corporal Lang was wounded on Rawolle's bluff. Lieutenant Rawolle sustained a superficial injury on his left leg while on the bluff at the west end of the line. In the muster rolls of March 31 all of the wounded were listed as "sick in hospital" or "sick" with the exceptions of Farrier Patrick Goings and Lieutenant Rawolle. The former had received a rifle ball in his left shoulder. Since the wound caused him but little inconvenience, he had returned to duty on March 18. None of the wounded died of their injuries. Private Eagan had received a penetrating wound in the abdomen, the .45 pistol ball coming out of the ribs. Private Droege was shot in the left elbow joint, the large-caliber rifle ball causing an abrasive fracture. Surgery was performed and the arm dressed on the battlefield. Corporal

---

[9] Corporal John Droege of Company K, Second Cavalry, had enlisted in New York City on June 21, 1875. He became company saddler on April 1, 1876.

[10] Private Edward Eagan of Company K, Second Cavalry, was one of the raw recruits who enlisted on February 5, 1876, at Fort Laramie.

[11] Farrier Patrick Goings of Company K, Second Cavalry, had re-enlisted at Fort Laramie on January 22, 1874, and was drawing re-enlistment pay.

The Pony Herd

John Lang,[12] whose ankle bone was shattered near the end of the fight, wrote from Sioux City, Iowa, in the February, 1925, issue of *Winners of the West*: "I with the other wounded received such aid as was available, and made as comfortable as a campfire, blood-soaked blankets, and hot coffee would afford. Thus ended March 17, 1876. I entered the hospital at Fort Russell, Wyoming, on April 8th, being 21 days on the road after the fight. I was discharged eleven months later, able to walk with the help of crutches."

After the battle there was a rumor through the camp that two men had been buried in the ice. Blacksmith Albert Glavinski testified that he had heard that two men were buried under the ice but that he had not seen them buried. O. C. C. Pollock,[13] "a high private in the rear rank of Company M, 3rd Cavalry," wrote from Connorsburg, Pennsylvania, in the November, 1926, issue of *Winners of the West*: "In that fight we lost two men, who were given a soldier's burial, a hole was cut in the ice, which was two feet thick and they were given a cold bath." It is difficult to credit the rumor since there is no direct evidence to support it.

Lieutenant Bourke reported in his diary that after the village had been taken, he found to his great surprise that his right great toe and the adjoining one were so frozen that he could not walk.

It was then found that a great many of our people had been severely hurt by the severe cold. In order to make the charge as effective as possible, we had disrobed and thrown to one side, upon entering the village, all the heavy or cumbrous wraps with which we could dispense. The disagreeable consequence was that many had feet and fingers, ears and noses frozen, among them being Lieutenant Hall and myself. Hall had had much previous experience in the polar climate of these northwestern mountains, and showed me how to treat myself to prevent permanent disability. We found an air-hole in the ice, into which we thrust feet and hands, after which we rubbed them with an old piece of gunny-

[12] Corporal John Lang of Company E, Second Cavalry, had enlisted at Omaha Barracks, Nebraska, on January 20, 1875.
[13] O. C. C. Pollock is not listed in the muster rolls of any of the companies in the battle, but may have been there under an assumed name.

sack, the roughest thing we could find, to restore circulation. Steward Bryan, who seemed to be full of resources and forethought, had carried along with him a bottle of tincture of iodine for just such emergencies; this he applied liberally to our feet and to all the other frozen limbs, and thus averted several cases of amputation.

When the command reached camp that night, Dr. Munn was a busy man. In addition to the wounded, he had to treat sixty-six cases of frost-bitten fingers, noses, legs and ears. Two men were unable to ride because of inflammatory rheumatism. Dr. Munn was assisted by Hospital Steward Bryan, who had had his horse shot from under him during Egan's charge.

Chapter **7**   **IN THE INDIAN CAMP**

LITTLE is known about the Indian side of the action, and most of the accounts are conflicting. The Indians did not regard it as important, and Grinnell dismisses it with a few lines to the effect that a village of Sioux and Cheyennes were attacked but that no Indians were killed.[1] It was considered at the time as an unsuccessful attempt to exterminate the Cheyenne tribe and the prelude to the battles to come. The soldiers and their scouts thought they had struck the village of the famous Oglala war chief, Crazy Horse,[2] but the evidence is overwhelming that it was a Cheyenne village with some lodges of visiting Sioux. It is unlikely that Crazy Horse was present, as his village seems to have been three days distant toward the northeast, although there is evidence to the contrary.

Ever since the treaty of 1868, most of the Sioux and Cheyennes had been friendly with the Great White Father and were content

[1] G. B. Grinnell, *The Fighting Cheyennes*, 334.
[2] Crazy Horse was a prominent headman and warrior-chief of the Oglala Sioux. Born in Rapid Creek Valley, South Dakota, in about 1840, he was a strange youth and man, becoming one of the four hair shirt or scalp shirt men in his tribe. In many forays and battles he was chosen leader without opposition. He fought his enemies at a point and time of his own choosing and always with success. His brother, Red Feather, and his head soldier, He Dog, claimed that they had seen nine horses shot from under him in battle, and that whenever Crazy Horse came on the field everybody became brave. He was in command of the Indians on the bloody fields of Rosebud, Little Big Horn, and Wolf Mountain. After surrendering to the government in the spring of 1877, he was treacherously killed by a soldier's bayonet at Fort Robinson, Nebraska. See Sandoz, *Crazy Horse,* and Ricker, "Narrative of Chips or Encouraging Bear," *Interviews,* Tablet 18.

to remain on the reservations where they were fed and clothed at government expense. Some preferred staying in during the winter months until the grass was green, subsisting upon the food furnished, and then joining the roving bands. Those who followed the old free way of life were permitted by the treaty to go from their reservations into the hunting regions westward as far as the Big Horn River and to gather meat and skins there at all times "as long as peace conditions continue therein." These were the bands which were hostile to the government and wished to avoid all contact with the whites. They had been off the reservations for years and included the disaffected elements of all tribes who had flocked to the standard of Sitting Bull, resenting the invasion by the white man. They had seen the white tide push them farther and farther back into the wilderness. Their hatred had been eloquently expressed by Gall, the great orator and war chief of the Hunkpapa tribe of the Sioux, before the Fort Rice peace commission of 1867. Baring his chest to show the bayonet scars which had been inflicted by a soldier at Fort Berthold, he addressed the assembled throng in terms of burning reproach:

> This is our land and our home. We have no exact boundaries, but the graves of the Sioux Nation mark our possessions. Wherever they are found the land is ours. We were born naked, and have been taught to hunt and live on the game. You tell us that we must learn to farm, live in one house, and take on your ways. Suppose the people living beyond the great sea would come and tell you that you must stop farming and kill your cattle, and take your houses and lands, what would you do? Would you not fight them?[3]

In the fall of 1875 this band of from forty to fifty-five lodges of Cheyennes left Red Cloud Agency to hunt the buffalo which would provide them with food, clothing and fuel for the winter ahead. They had forty new canvas tipis furnished by the agency, and an ample supply of guns, ammunition, powder, and lead. Old Bear

[3] *South Dakota Historical Collections,* I, 151. Gall *(Pizi)* was born on Moreau River about 1840. He surrendered to the Government in 1880 and died December 4, 1894. He was buried at Wakpala.

and Little Wolf⁴ were the old-man chiefs of the band, while Two Moon⁵ was a young subchief. Ice, also known as White Bull, and Maple Tree⁶ were the medicine men. The band travelled northwest to the hunting grounds and from time to time was joined by lodges of Sioux. The Oglalas had been the closest friends of the Cheyennes, while the Minneconjoux were next in their friendly estimation. The Oglala intimacy had begun in the days of Fort Phil Kearny and Fort C. F. Smith. These military posts were located in what was Oglala and Cheyenne hunting country, so the two tribes worked together in driving out the invaders, the Oglalas making war against Fort Phil Kearny and the Cheyennes against Fort C. F. Smith. There were many intermarriages between Cheyennes and Oglalas

---

⁴ The four old-man chiefs of the Northern Cheyenne tribe at this time were Old Bear, Dirty Moccasins, Little Wolf, and Dull Knife. Dirty Moccasins and Dull Knife were still at the agency on March 17, 1876. Little Wolf and Dull Knife had been soldier-chiefs and were noted men in the tribe. Little Wolf was head of the Elk Warrior Society and was an organizer and always led his men in battle. Dull Knife was a noted warrior but did not plan his battles and did not lead his men. Little Wolf was arrogant and impatient of those not following his orders; however, his manner became milder after he was chosen one of the principal chiefs. Although he was fifty-five years of age in 1876, he was probably in command of the Indians on March 17, as stated by Short Bull. In 1879 he got drunk on white man's whisky and shot Famished Elk in the back, killing him. Because of this he lost his standing in the tribe and was no longer chief. He died in 1904 at the age of eighty-three and was buried on a hill overlooking the Rosebud valley. See George B. Grinnell, *The Cheyenne Indians* (New Haven, Yale University Press, 1923).

⁵ Two Moon was born about 1847, so was twenty-nine years of age at the time of the battle. He was one of the nine little chiefs of the Fox Warrior Society. Several years later when the Cheyennes surrendered at Fort Keogh, Two Moon was made head chief of his tribe by General Miles. According to John Stands-In-Timber, the historian of the Northern Cheyenne tribe, Indians never pronounce the plural, so the name was "Two Moon" and not "Two Moons."

⁶ In the letter of George Bent to George E. Hyde dated March 13, 1914, Maple Leaf was described as a ventriloquist who made the Cheyennes believe he could communicate with the spirits. Although blind, he would talk with the spirits to find out how the warriors would fare on the warpath. He could throw his voice to the top of the lodges, and when the poles were tied together it gave a very realistic effect. Since many things happened just as he predicted, he exercised a large influence over his tribe.

"Maple Tree, the Cheyenne, born late 1700's, died about 1885, and was called Box Elder (both trees having sweet sap), or just Tree. Later he was also known as Brave Wolf (not the later Brave Wolf, born 1833, died 1908), and Blind Bull in the very last of his years, when blind. He was a great medicine man." Letter dated November 22, 1958, from Mari Sandoz to the author.

and much visiting back and forth, which cemented their alliance more firmly.[7]

In the early part of the winter the band was encamped on Otter Creek, and then moved westward over to Tongue River. On January 28, 1876, the new agent at Red Cloud Agency, James S. Hastings, reported that the Cheyenne camp was located in the Powder River region at least one hundred miles northwest of Bear Buttes. The couriers who had been sent to the camp had not been heard from but were expected daily. Nothing had been heard from Sitting Bull's camp, which had separated from the hostile encampment on Powder River. Crazy Horse and Black Twin, Oglala Chiefs, were en route southward to Red Cloud Agency, but their progress was retarded by deep snow. When heard from, this band was at Bear Buttes, about one hundred miles distant.[8] The report was in error in stating that the Oglala chiefs were coming in to the agency since instead of moving the short distance south to Red Cloud Agency, they went northward to the Powder River country. The Indians did not choose to come to the agencies and were not impressed by the government's threats to send soldiers after them.[9]

At the earliest signs of the breaking-up of winter, the warrior Last Bull and his family joined the camp of the Cheyennes with the news that the soldiers were coming to fight all Cheyennes and Sioux who were off the reservations. The Indians at first did not believe this report because they were where they had a right to be under the treaty; but when it was later confirmed by three Cheyenne chiefs, Spotted Wolf, Medicine Wolf, and Twin, the band decided to stay where it was—on the Powder River forty to fifty miles south of the mouth of the Little Powder. Hunting parties were on the lookout for white soldiers, and the old people kept themselves in readiness for immediate flight.[10] When returning hunters brought word that soldiers had been seen coming in the

---

[7] Thomas B. Marquis, "Forcing of Tribe from Black Hills Country Provoked Trouble," *Billings Gazette,* July 17, 1932.

[8] Report of James S. Hastings, United States Indian Agent, to Hon. J. Q. Smith, Commissioner of Indian Affairs, *House Exec. Doc. 184,* 44 Cong., 2 Sess., 25.

[9] George E. Hyde, *Red Cloud's Folk,* 254 ff.

[10] Thomas B. Marquis, *A Warrior Who Fought Custer,* 161.

In the Indian Camp

general direction of the camp, it was decided to move northward down the river to join the camp of the Oglalas under Crazy Horse.[11] Camp was finally made in a sheltered spot on the west side of Powder River where there were plenty of cottonwood trees to furnish subsistence for the ponies and wood for the campfires. In later years some of the band claimed that they were slowly coming in to the agency in accordance with the ultimatum,[12] but as they were actually headed north at the time of the attack, it is difficult to accept this statement.

Early in March, a courier named "Crawler" arrived in the camp of Crazy Horse with the message from the agency: "It is Spring; we are waiting for you." He Dog, the brother chieftain of Crazy Horse, decided to comply. He borrowed one of the buffalo ponies of Crazy Horse, a spotted one which was very fast, because he would badly need lodge skins before arriving at the Agency.[13] He Dog, accompanied by Crawler, came to the Cheyenne camp with his eight lodges and was there when the attack occurred.[14] It is generally believed that Frank Grouard, upon seeing the Oglala lodges and the spotted pony of Crazy Horse, assumed that this was the village of the chief. Grouard was also in error in stating that Sitting Bull and "the whole Kaboodle" were there. He contradicted himself when he later told that Crazy Horse refused to divide food and clothing with the Cheyennes when they fled to him. It is impossible to credit any story of Grouard's relating to Crazy Horse because Grouard's life was never safe so long as the chief lived. In the early days, Grouard had killed several mail carriers in Montana and had reached the Oglala camp just a jump ahead of the troopers, who were ready to shoot him down if he resisted arrest. Crazy Horse had taken him into the tribe and protected him until there had been trouble with some of the tribesmen when Grouard fled to civilization.

Two lodges of Sioux arrived from Red Cloud Agency two days before the attack with goods and supplies to trade with the village.[15]

[11] *Ibid.*, 163.
[12] Letter of Mari Sandoz to the author, dated October 7, 1958.
[13] *Ibid.*
[14] Mari Sandoz, *Crazy Horse*, 304.

The number of lodges thus identified in the village was 65. The soldiers counted 105 lodges which probably included the wickiups of the unmarried warriors. Of the 40 lodges (or wickiups), some were undoubtedly ceremonial lodges and those used for brood mares, foals, and dogs, while others were lodges of friendly Oglalas and Minneconjoux who were visiting the Cheyennes. Although the main camp of Crazy Horse was located toward the northeast on a creek which ran westward to Powder River, some of his band may have been visiting friends and relatives in the Cheyenne camp. John Stands-In-Timber, the Cheyenne historian, told the author that it was a Cheyenne village but that many Sioux were there. The soldiers in believing they had struck the village of Crazy Horse of necessity depended upon the opinions of Grouard and the scouts. None of them claimed to have actually seen the chief there, and neither Crazy Horse nor any of his band ever admitted being there (except, of course, He Dog with a few of his lodges). The old squaw who told the soldiers that it was the village of Crazy Horse may have been in the group with He Dog or with other visiting Oglalas, or may have been, in fact, a member of his band.

That it was a Cheyenne village is attested to by Kate Big Head, a sister of White Bull (Ice), who said that it consisted of forty family lodges.[16] Iron Hawk, one of the seven-star soldiers having highest authority among the Sioux, told Dr. Ricker, "He was living on Powder River with some Cheyennes and a few Oglalas. He was living on the game which they hunted, this particular time of which he speaks was in the spring when there were many hunting in the early morning. About when the sun was rising he heard there were soldiers surrounding them and they began to shoot. The fighting lasted all day long until the sun was down. The Indians left their tepees and their horses and fled on foot north to the Blue Earth, a stream at the point of it and escaped."[17] The Cheyenne warrior Woodenleg, who was also present, said there were forty

[15] Bourke, *On the Border with Crook*, 277.
[16] Thomas B. Marquis, *She Watched Custer's Last Battle*, 2.
[17] Ricker, *Interviews*, Tablet 25, 127.
[18] Marquis, *A Warrior Who Fought Custer*, 161, 169.

In the Indian Camp

lodges of Cheyennes and three or four lodges of Oglalas.[18] The report of the agent at Cheyenne River Agency dated April 19, 1876, stated that the brother of Bull Eagle, a Minneconjou, had left the hostile camps on April 9 and brought the information that it was not the Crazy Horse village that Reynolds struck, but fifty-five lodges of Cheyennes and ten lodges of Oglalas and that Crazy Horse at the time of the fight was with the main camp on Powder River.[19] The report of Lieutenant W. P. Clark of September 14, 1877, contained information which he obtained after the surrender of the Cheyennes at Fort Robinson, Nebraska. He said the village was composed of sixty Cheyenne lodges under Old Bear and fourteen Sioux lodges under He Dog.[20] The discrepancy in the number of lodges is not unusual; it all depends upon whether the wickiups of the young warriors are included.

The only direct evidence that Crazy Horse was present is contained in several letters of George Bent, an educated French-Southern Cheyenne Indian, to George E. Hyde. In the letter of April 2, 1914, Bent wrote: "The soldiers attacked Maple Tree's village and some Sioux under Crazy Horse. Northern Cheyennes done [*sic*] all the fighting with troops. Crazy Horse, Tall Sioux says ran up bluff with one of his sons on his back he was among the women and children upon bluffs behind rocks. Tall Sioux tells me Tall Sioux is Northern Cheyenne and not Sioux."[21]

In the Bent letter of March 13, 1914, Bent refers to the fight of Colonel Reynolds with eighty lodges of Northern Cheyennes under Maple Tree. In the letter of April 18, 1914, Bent says that Powder Face and others said that Crazy Horse acted cowardly in this fight on Powder River. Powder Face (apparently a Cheyenne warrior) shot an officer; Yellow Eagle, Bull Coming Behind, and Pow-

---

[19] Report of Lieutenant Ruhlen to Acting Adjutant General, Department of Dakota, AGO Records in Mil. Div. of Mo., Doc. Files, Box 169, Special, Sitting Bull Band.

[20] Report of Lieutenant W. P. Clark, Dept. Platte, Doc. Files, Letters Rec'd., 1877, Doc. No. 4601DP77.

[21] Quoted with permission of the Western History Department, Denver, Colorado, Public Library, which has custody of the letter.

der Face counted coup on this officer. One Cheyenne by the name of Whirlwind was killed in the fight.[22]

According to the Cheyennes the man carrying the children, one after another, into the rocks during the fight was Little Wolf.[23] It is probable that the Crazy Horse referred to in the Bent letters was not the famous Oglala war chief, who had no children, but another Sioux of that name. George Bent, in his letter of November 6, 1914, told Mr. Hyde that the Northern Cheyenne warriors who had fought beside Crazy Horse all thought more of him than of any other Sioux. Bent could not have been referring to the same man whom he had described as a coward in his letters of the previous April. The name "Crazy Horse" was common among the Sioux, and in 1889 there were four Sioux on the Pine Ridge and Rosebud agencies important enough to sign the treaty that year with that name, although the war chief was long dead. There was also a prominent Hunkpapa by that name.[24] It is difficult to believe that it was the famous Oglala war chief who was branded as a coward in the Bent letters.

In 1931 the Cheyennes told Mari Sandoz that Two Moon was really the head of the band that Reynolds struck and that Little Wolf was just visiting, as his band was not there. He Dog told her that Two Moon was away but may have come in during the night.[25] However, in the Short Bull-Hinman interview, Short Bull, brother of He Dog, said that the chiefs of the Cheyennes were Little Wolf and Ice.[26] Since Little Wolf had been a warrior chief before becoming an old-man chief, it is probable that he led the fighting.

The day before the attack, some Cheyennes hunting antelope at the head of Otter Creek west of the camp saw the soldiers and urged their horses back to warn the camp. Some of the horses became exhausted, so their riders had to come in on foot. It was

[22] The Bent letters of March 13, 1914, and April 18, 1914, are used by permission of the Yale University Library, New Haven, Connecticut.
[23] Letter of Mari Sandoz to the author, dated October 7, 1958.
[24] *Ibid.*
[25] *Ibid.*
[26] Short Bull–Hinman Interview, Sunday, July 13, 1930, with John Colhoff as interpreter, in the custody of the Nebraska State Historical Society.

In the Indian Camp

their trail in the snow which the soldiers followed. The council of old men appointed ten young men to go out that night and watch the soldiers. The camp slept feeling secure under the protection of the sentinels. The scouts missed the soldiers in the dark and storm and did not find the trail until the soldiers had attacked the camp.[27] They probably went down the south fork of Otter Creek, instead of the north fork which the soldiers had ascended.

Captain Egan's charge caught the camp wholly by surprise. Most of the warriors were still asleep in their robes. All was confusion. Women screamed and snatched up their children to take them out of harm's way. The old people hobbled off. Most of the warriors helped the women and children in their flight up into the rocks, while others, seeing there were not many soldiers in the camp, pinned Egan's company down with its back to the river. These warriors were outflanked when Mills's company charged in at their backs, and they joined the retreat up the side of the mountain. When the hunting parties and the sentinels returned, the warriors commenced working southward along the mountainside.

At the north end of the village, the river bends to the west, where it almost meets the high bluffs. The Indians ran north from the village to the shelter of the river bottom and then scurried up the large ravine north of the bluffs. Halfway up the mountainside is a little bench or rocky ledge which extends the full length of the mountain. After seeing that the women and children were safe, the warriors filtered back along the mountain taking positions behind the numerous rocks and ravines. There is another large ravine west of the north edge of the village which is covered with rocks, caves, and side gulches. On the south edge of this ravine and about halfway up the side of the mountain is a crest of rocks about fifty yards long facing the southeast, which commands all of the village. It was from here that the Indians delivered their enfilading and plunging fire which compelled Rawolle and Moore to retire under the mesa.[28] The rugged mountainside offered a perfect defensive

---

[27] Marquis, *A Warrior Who Fought Custer*, 164.
[28] Here, buried under rocks and moss, were found the following: Two .50-caliber rimfire Spencer cartridges manufactured by the Sage Ammuni-

position, and it is not surprising that only one or two of the warriors were killed. The little bench enabled them to work around to a point west of and above Rawolle's men without exposing themselves. The terrain protected the Indians while they delivered their fire on the soldiers' line. The towering bluffs south of Thompson Creek afforded positions from which they harassed the troopers retreating along the river bottom. It is remarkable that the Indians recovered from the complete surprise on the cold winter morning when life was at low ebb. While the terrain played an important part in the Indians' stouthearted defense, it was their own high courage and valor which turned back the soldiers.

Woodenleg reported that he, Two Moon, and Bear Walks on a Ridge attacked a soldier. After Two Moon missed with his repeating rifle, Bear Walks on a Ridge fired his muzzle-loading rifle and hit the soldier in the back of the head. They rushed upon the man and beat and stabbed him to death, taking his rifle, blue coat, and other possessions. This soldier was probably Captain Moore's Private McCannon, whose body was never found. Woodenleg claimed that one Cheyenne was killed in the engagement and another had his forearm badly shattered.[29] Lieutenant Ruhlen stated in his report that when the Indians returned to the village they found dead four soldiers, two Indian men, and one Indian woman.[30] The

---

tion Works for the government during the Civil War. These had the initials "SAW" imprinted on the head.

Three .50–70 Springfield cartridges manufactured by the Union Metallic Cartridge Company, with Berdan type primer of early manufacture, and probably containing paper patch lead bullets. These were used in Springfield and Sharps rifles.

One .50–70 Springfield cartridge made by either the U.S. Cartridge Company or the Lowell Cartridge Company. This brass case was shattered, indicating that it had been reloaded several times.

One .45–70 Springfield 1873 Winchester cartridge with outside primed brass case, which was also shattered.

Five .44-caliber Winchester cartridges with raised *H* head stamp, also called the .44 Henry flat, which were used in 1866 Winchester and Henry rifles.

Although I spent many days covering the mountainside from Rawolle's ridge on the south, to the large escape ravine on the north, with a metal detector, I was unable to find anything more. While there must have been many empty cartridge cases after the battle, the chipped shale and rocks which covered the mountainside did not prevent them from being washed down the gullies during cloudbursts.

[29] Marquis, *A Warrior Who Fought Custer*, 167.

In the Indian Camp

wounded Indian woman was found safely ensconced in her tipi, which had been left intact. John Stands-In-Timber, the historian of the Northern Cheyenne tribe, told the author that a Cheyenne warrior named Eagle Chief was killed while riding his horse on the mountainside. This was probably the same Indian Lieutenant Morton saw fall from his horse on the bluff previously occupied by Lieutenant Rawolle's company. Lieutenant Bourke stated in his diary that although the soldiers had captured no bodies, they believed that they had killed and wounded many of the enemy.

From the rocks, the Indians watched the destruction of their village. Occasionally there would be a large explosion when the fires reached a powder keg, and lodgepoles and hides would fly through the air. One can imagine their dismay in surveying the burnt debris and rubble which were once their homes.

Early settlers in the area found no traces of the dead bodies except for a skull on the battlefield and a boot with the foot still in it on the side of a butte east of the river. It was a common practice of the Indians to cut off the feet of dead soldiers after a battle in order to secure the leather in the boots and to facilitate the removal of their clothing. It was probable that the bodies of the soldiers were dismembered and dragged all over the landscape by the wolves and other wild animals. The Sioux believed that some Cheyennes ate the flesh of one trooper.[31]

After returning to the village, the Indians gathered up what they could and started walking northeast to the Oglala camp of Crazy Horse. As all the accounts state the Indians made the journey on foot, one wonders why they did not ride the ponies which were not captured by the troops. It may have been that the ponies were too weak to ride, their cottonwood bark having been burned with the tipis. They were probably gathered up and herded along later by the warriors since they were too valuable to be abandoned. The green buffalo meat which had not burned was probably taken

---

[30] Report of Lieutenant Ruhlen to Acting Adjutant General, Department of Dakota, AGO Records in Mil. Div. of Mo., Doc. Files, Box 169, Special, Sitting Bull Band.

[31] Stanley Vestal, *Warpath*, 180 ff.

along by the refugees to sustain them during the long trip ahead. Most of the warriors stayed behind to recapture the pony herd from the soldiers and to guard against another attack. After a three-day march in the cold and deep snow the band reached the camp of Crazy Horse in the Blue Earth country, far up a creek east of Powder River. It is said that their trail was marked by blood on the snow and the bodies of women and children who perished in the terrible ordeal.

Crazy Horse received the refugees hospitably and gave them food and shelter. Then the old men of the two bands assembled in council. The Cheyennes pleaded for help against the soldiers who were making war upon them. There were only a few Cheyennes, but many Sioux. The bands would soon be increased by people coming out from the agencies to join in the hunting; all of them together might be able to scare the soldiers away. The Oglalas agreed to help, on condition that the two bands would go together to the Hunkpapas, who had Sitting Bull as their leader and who outnumbered the combined Cheyennes and Oglalas. There would be a feeling of greater confidence if they could persuade this tribe to form an alliance with them. There was no more talk of going back to the agencies.

They found the camp of Sitting Bull east of Chalk Buttes on Beaver Creek, near the present Ekalaka, Montana. This band, after staying away from the reservations for several years and avoiding all contact with white people, had refused to come in to Standing Rock Agency in response to the message brought by the couriers. Although Sitting Bull[32] had been an honored warrior dur-

[32] Sitting Bull, a Hunkpapa Sioux, was born on Willow Creek near Fort Pierre about 1838. At the time of the Reynolds campaign he was a heavy-set, muscular man about five feet, eight inches tall. He had been the political leader of the hostile Indians since 1868 and had developed into a prophet, strategist, and medicine man. All through his life he fomented hatred and discontent among the Indians. He had an immense following and was the acknowledged leader of those who were in open revolt against the government. After the Sioux wars, he settled down on the reservation and remained at peace until he was killed by Indian police on December 15, 1890, during the Ghost Dance craze. He was first buried at Fort Yates, North Dakota, but his body now lies under the huge monument of himself in the Black Hills on the Missouri River, west of Mobridge, South Dakota. See Stanley Vestal, *Sitting Bull* (Norman, University of Oklahoma Press, 1957).

In the Indian Camp

ing his younger days, as he grew older he developed into a spiritual leader and philosopher among the Indians. He fomented hatred against the white man and was the acknowledged leader of those Indians of all northern tribes who were hostile to the government.

The Hunkpapas received the aggrieved Cheyennes and their Oglala backers hospitably and rehabilitated the destitute Cheyennes with profuse gifts of food, horses, and skins. As they were prosperous, they deliberated several days before deciding to help the Cheyennes resist what was believed to be a determined effort to wipe out the Cheyenne tribe. However, since they were the least desirous of going to war, it was understood that they would be the last to go into actual conflict; in token of this, in their movements from place to place the Cheyennes would always go ahead as the principals involved, while the Hunkpapas would follow last. It was the prerogative of the Cheyennes to choose the direction of travel and places of camping, the supporting Indians following their leadership. Because the first need was to go where there would be the earliest grass for the ponies, the three bands set off northwest toward Powder River. When they arrived there two or three weeks later, they were joined by the Sans Arc Sioux, the Minneconjoux Sioux, and the Blackfeet Sioux, who had been told by runners of the unprovoked attack upon the Cheyennes. An alliance was formed among the six tribes, and the Sioux agreed to fight the soldiers if they came to attack the Cheyennes. In appreciation of their support, the latter agreed to share with the Sioux the grass and game animals in their own hunting country, and led the way to the Rosebud and the Little Big Horn valleys. Thus was the stage set for the bloody conflicts with the soldiers at the Rosebud and the Little Big Horn.[33]

[33] Marquis, "Forcing of Tribe From Black Hills Country Provoked Trouble," *Billings* (Montana) *Gazette,* July 17, 1932.

Chapter 8 THE RETREAT TO LODGEPOLE CREEK

WHEN the soldiers started to retreat, Major Stanton went to Hospital Rock, where the pony herd was being held by a few scouts and some of Noyes's men, and remained there as the troops filed by. He sent an orderly to Colonel Reynolds for orders concerning the disposition of the pony herd. Upon returning, the orderly reported that Major Stanton could kill as many of the ponies as he pleased. There were only five of the scouts there, and the men had only ten rounds of ammunition each, so it was determined to take the herd along with the command. By this time the Indians were closing up and firing at the troops, most of whom had passed by. Stanton claimed that sometimes the herd was close to the command and sometimes far in the rear.

Colonel Reynolds stated later that the orderly was instructed to tell Stanton to bring the herd along and that he was at liberty to shoot as many horses as could not keep up. Prior to that time he had issued orders for the scouts to bring in the herd. There was further conflict in the reports concerning the position the pony herd occupied in the retreating column, Lieutenant Rawolle stating that his company, as rear guard, was behind the herd at all times except at a bend of the river near the Lodgepole camp that night.

Captain Egan left the village in front of Noyes's skirmish line, moved across the river, and formed a line alongside where Captain Noyes's horses were unsaddled, remaining there until the last of the company was saddled up. Upon being relieved by Captain

The Retreat to Lodgepole Creek

Egan, Lieutenant Rawolle informed Captain Noyes that, as rear guard, his company would move on slowly, and Noyes's battalion could take its place in the column passing by. Since forty to fifty Indians followed the retreating men, Lieutenant Rawolle formed a small skirmish line about three-quarters of a mile south of Hospital Rock and repelled a feeble effort by the Indians to molest the retreat. Lieutenant Rawolle was sure that the pony herd left the bend of the river at Hospital Rock before his company since the ponies did not pass through his skirmish line. This is borne out by the statements of Captain Moore and Captain Egan, who overtook the pony herd during the march.

It took quite a while for Captain Noyes to prepare his company for the march. After marching back to their camp, each man had to catch his horse, remove the hobbles, pull up the picket pin, and wind up the lariat. Then he had to pick out his saddle and saddle his horse—a difficult operation because the horses were nervous from the prevailing excitement. The Indians were becoming bolder, and a number could be seen among the trees and ravines along the sidehills. The troopers then led their horses to the line where they would prepare to mount and follow the column. Although protected by Egan's skirmish line, Noyes was chagrined at being left behind by the rear guard. He had been assured by Colonel Reynolds that his men would be covered by skirmishers while saddling up, but there was only Captain Egan's company to protect them from the annoying fire from the Indians. They were so hurried that Lieutenant Hall was obliged to saddle his own horse, his groom having been on the line with him. Captain Noyes's company was finally ready and moved out followed by Captain Egan's company. It was now two o'clock. The battle had lasted five hours.

After Noyes's and Egan's troops had passed the rear guard, they hurried to catch up with the column. Captain Moore fell in behind them, and Lieutenant Rawolle, in command of the rear guard, dismounted two sets of fours and a non-commissioned officer as a skirmish line to protect the retreat.

I left the men dismounted, Rawolle testified, as long as I thought the

Indians might follow us. One Indian did follow us and my men fired on him. I thought at first he was a scout, but they were sure he was an Indian and allowed them to fire. I kept them dismounted I don't know how long. I remember the men were getting tired and I allowed them to mount, and then kept up a mounted skirmish line until later in the day, when no one was following us. The only one that did follow us I suppose was a medicine man, and he fell from his saddle: I don't know whether he was hit or not. The men claimed that he was hit. I had the men form in column of twos and kept them as a rear guard, probably 100 or 150 yards in the rear of the command. The pony herd was ahead of me and at times some of the colts would run through my company. We kept in the rear of them until we struck a bend in the stream where they seemed to take a short cut. It was then getting to be dark. Dark at that time came at six o'clock.... *Q.* What time did you get into camp that night. *A.* I think it was eight or half past: it was some time after dark.

Sergeant Land, who was with the rear guard, said that during the march his company was three to four hundred yards in rear of the whole command. At one time, a travois which was carrying a wounded man broke down and had to be fixed, causing a delay. A skirmish line was thrown out, and an Indian came up close. Land fired at him and did not see him any more; he thought he killed him.

The head of the column moved south-southwest up Powder River at a brisk walk. The scout Grouard led the men over the route which was easiest to follow: sometimes they marched on the east side of the river, sometimes on the west side. After going eight to ten miles, Grouard showed Colonel Reynolds a trail coming in from the northwest over which General Crook might arrive from Otter Creek. Since the area around the mouth of Lodgepole Creek, which came in from the southwest, did not offer suitable camping ground, the command kept on several miles farther south and found a better campsite in a bend of the river on the east side. The total distance marched was about twenty-two miles. Captain Mills's company arrived there at sundown, or about six o'clock, and the other companies came straggling in from time to time. It was very cold, with several inches of snow on the ground.

The Retreat to Lodgepole Creek

Captain Moore testified that during the march he overtook Major Stanton, with whom he talked over the action of the day:

> He [Stanton] seemed pleased with the success of the day, and the first thing he said to me was, "Won't I send a flaming dispatch to the Tribune about this business," and the next thing was "When we get into camp I will give you the best drink of brandy you ever had." *Q.* Where did he say he was going to get it from. *A.* From the pack train when Gen Crook came in. We rode side by side for a while when he said he was tired and could not ride any farther, and asked me to halt my battalion and stay with him and the ponies under a bluff. I said no, I was going into camp with Col Reynolds. *Q.* How far were you from Col Reynolds' command when he proposed to go into camp there. *A.* Probably eight or ten miles.

The ponies moved very slowly since some would stray off into ravines and it was difficult to herd them along. They were overtaken by Captain Egan, who rode along and talked with Major Stanton. The latter said he did not believe he would be able to bring the herd of ponies along because he did not have enough men. Captain Egan told him he would stay and help him. They travelled together until they came within sight of the fires of the camp, when Egan went forward and encamped under the direction of Captain Noyes. When the ponies arrived at the camp about nine o'clock, Stanton was ordered to drive them alongside the camp on the south. It was dark, and he thought it was Lieutenant Drew the quartermaster who gave the order, but Drew later denied that he had done so.

Colonel Reynolds had burned all the meat and supplies in the village in the belief that he would meet General Crook at the appointed rendezvous at Lodgepole Creek that night, where they could get their blankets and food from the pack train and grain for their jaded horses. At his trial Reynolds told about the march and their disappointment at not meeting General Crook:

> The march from the village to Lodgepole was very fatiguing and proved longer than expected, our guides' idea of miles being very vague.

The Reynolds Campaign on Powder River

During the wearisome march our spirits were buoyed up with the hope and fervent expectation of finding at its termination the other column, also the pack train with our blankets and rations. For two long hours we looked every moment for the signs of the encampment of our comrades and when at sundown we reached the long looked for mouth of Lodgepole and found that our friends were not there, our hearts sank within us, we were weary and hungry and had a cold night before us without supper or blankets.

The limit of human endurance had been reached. We were all, men and horses, completely worn out. Orders might be given and men might be posted as sentinels, but the demands of nature would assert themselves and sleep would take possession of every one regardless of orders or anything else. Under the circumstances I sought to make such dispositions as would enable the men to get some rest—what is called a running guard was established, relieving the men much more frequently than usual so as to have some one moving around nearly all the time.

Lieutenant Bourke described in his diary the discomforts of the new camp:

Had plenty of water, or ice, a sufficiency of wood, but very little grass for our large herd of animals.

Officers and men were very uncomfortable from want of adequate clothing, altho today has been warmer than yesterday. Have no rations, not even for our poor wounded men. Occasionally an officer will be found with a small quantity of cracker crumbs in his saddle pouches, another one has carried away a small quantity of buffalo meat from the rancheria, and a third, mayhap, has a spoonful of tea or coffee. We make miserable apologies for supper: a piece or two of buffalo meat, roasted in the ashes, goes around among 5 or 6, each getting a mouthful only: and a cup of coffee is supped like the pipe of peace at an Indian council. Our slumbers are sound, despite the cold, as we have marched between 68 and 75 miles since yesterday morning, besides fighting 5 hours today.

Our men are, of course, very tired: guard duty is done by "running tours" of the whole company, but we feel almost satisfied with our day's work which has been praiseworthy and brilliant enough when we take into regard the disadvantages we had to contend against to gain any success at all. . . . The men named this "Camp Inhospitality," a name well deserved and a name well bestowed. . . . Mr. Strahorn and I had made a couch out of a worn out saddle blanket, covering ourselves with a large, untanned buffalo robe I had brought out of the village. It was so stiff we might just as well have employed a board for a blanket.

The cavalry horses were hobbled and lariated for the night. They had had nothing to eat since leaving General Crook except what they could pick off the ground. In the river bottoms they were able to nibble the grass through the snow, but there was not much of it.

When the captured pony herd arrived about nine o'clock, Major Stanton turned it over to some unknown person claiming the authority, went to a campfire, and went to sleep. Colonel Reynolds consulted with Frank Grouard as to where the herd should be kept for the night. Grouard assured him that he knew many of the ponies, that they were accustomed to graze along that valley, and that they would be found in the morning up beyond the camp since he knew of no trails by which they could get back toward the village except the one running down the valley where they were camped. The herd was then driven up to a point beyond and adjoining camp and guarded by the pickets, who from sheer exhaustion probably slept when they should have watched.

Grouard claimed that Colonel Reynolds left the herd unguarded on his own responsibility without asking his advice, but his testimony on this point was evasive. According to John Shangrau, the scouts asked Reynolds if they should night-herd the ponies, and Reynolds replied, "No, drive them up the river about a mile from the camp and turn them loose."[1]

Lieutenant George A. Drew said he overheard Grouard state to Colonel Reynolds, motioning his hand up Powder River, that that would be a safe point for the ponies and that there would be no danger from Indians because they had all they could do to attend to their families that night. Regardless of where the responsibility lay, the fact remains that the Indian ponies were driven up the river south of the camp and left unattended.

It was very cold that night, and the men, having only saddle

[1] Ricker, "Narrative of John Shangrau," *Interviews,* Tablet 27, 76.

blankets, threw themselves on the ground with insufficient shelter, and as a consequence arose in the morning stiff, sore, and very little refreshed from sleep; some of them woke up early because of the cold. It is probable that Captain Mills' men suffered severely since they did not even have their overcoats.

There were no rations for breakfast. Lieutenant Bourke found two biscuits and gave one of them to one of the men, who traded it for coffee. Lieutenant Rawolle had brought along some hard bread, but it was stolen, and he had to get a few crumbs from Captain Noyes.

About daybreak Colonel Reynolds awakened Frank Grouard and had some conversation with him about renewing the search for General Crook and about the safety of the pony herd. Grouard reported the pony herd "all right," and Reynolds directed him to get up a party of scouts and start out at once to find General Crook. Louis Shangrau, Jack Russell, John Shangrau, and Baptiste Garnier[2] volunteered to accompany Grouard, but at eight o'clock, just before they started out, it was discovered that the pony herd was missing. Reynolds instructed the party to send back information

[2] Baptiste Garnier, commonly known as "Little Bat," lived as a small boy with his mother and father in the little settlement at Richaud's Bridge. His father worked for Richaud, but he was killed by Indians one Saturday as he was bringing home a deer on his back. The widow moved to Fort Laramie with her only son and her three daughters. Five or six years later, she and two of her daughters were burned to death, and a man named Whitcomb took the two orphans, Little Bat and his remaining sister, to live with him in his home at Fort Russell. He got Bat a small rifle with which to hunt chickens and rabbits, but Bat became such an expert shot that he was soon hunting larger game. He soon went to Fort Laramie as a professional hunter and sold game to the soldiers at the fort. In 1868 or 1869, Bat married Julia, a daughter of Magliore Mousseau, and went to the Chug, and then to Box Elder Creek, where he engaged in hunting and in selling the meat his gun brought down. In 1876 he was employed as a scout by General Crook and performed such valuable services during the Indian wars that on the recommendation of the general he was given the position as scout for the army at $100 per month for as long as he lived. He was stationed at Fort McKinney for a short time but went to Fort Robinson after his first-born son was scalded to death. There he lived near the fort with his father-in-law. Little Bat had eight sons, all except one of whom died in his lifetime, and six daughters, all of whom survived him. When fifty years of age, he was shot and killed by a bartender in Detrich's saloon in Crawford, Nebraska. Although it was a cowardly and cold-blooded murder, the bartender was acquitted. Little Bat was buried in the post cemetery at Fort Robinson. See Ricker, "Narrative of Mr. Mousseau," *Interviews*, Tablet 28, 51 ff.

The Retreat to Lodgepole Creek

about the herd, since the ponies would probably be encountered while being driven back past the camp toward the village.

The circumstances attending the loss of the pony herd were told by Captain Noyes in his testimony:

> It was definitely known the Indians had got the herd between 8 and 9 o'clock.... I knew they were gone as I told the scouts I wanted them to get me two nice ponies, and the men had told me that as soon as they threw the lariat over their heads they bolted to the middle of the herd, and they could not get them until we got into camp. When they got into camp the men were tired out and had layed [sic] down. That night I told those men I wanted them to be up at the very crack of day, and get those ponies out. I was up myself at the very crack of day, and stirred those people out. They started out and the men came back and said they could not find the ponies, that they had scattered a good deal during the night. I told them to go out and tell the scouts that I would send more men out to find them, and I did send out two more men. In a half or three quarters of an hour the men came back and said a large part of the herd had strayed up the river. I told them to go out and stay out until they found out where they were. About a half an hour later the scout himself came in and said he was positive the pony stock had been driven off. He came in about half past seven and he started right out again and about eight o'clock he and another scout came in and said they had followed the trail until it turned into a canyon and they were certain the Indians had the stock.... At nine o'clock they were reported right opposite the camp, behind some bluffs. The tops of the bluffs were 2 or 3 miles away. How far beyond they were I do not know.

When word came in that the Indians had captured the ponies, Major Stanton reported the fact to Colonel Reynolds, who refused to permit any pursuit of them. Captain Mills tried to prevail upon Reynolds to send a detachment to recapture the ponies, saying that if he let the herd get away it would mean he had lost the battle. Reynolds replied that the ponies were of no use to the troops and that he would rather have one company of horses than all the ponies there. Mills urged that General Crook would rather lose all the horses in the Third cavalry than the pony herd because the army could buy more horses, while the Indians could not obtain more ponies. When asked if he thought his horses were in a condition to capture the ponies, Mills said that they could capture a large herd of ponies because the latter could not travel very fast, but he suggested the best way would be to make a detail of ten men from each company for the pursuit. Major Stanton came up about this time, and the same conversation took place between him and Colonel Reynolds, who declined to allow pursuit of the herd.

General Crook claimed later that the campaign was a failure because of the loss of the pony herd, and this was one of the charges brought against Colonel Reynolds in the court martial proceedings. Reynolds claimed that the man who had returned from Grouard's party about nine o'clock brought only very indefinite information. He said he had not seen either Indians or ponies, but estimated from the trail and signs of dragging ropes that there were 30 ponies and 4 or 5 Indians, who were, when he started back, from one-half mile to three miles from camp and entirely out of sight. The location of the bulk of the missing herd was not known, and in view of the service that was in store for the men and animals in returning to Fort Fetterman, an uncertain chase over the hills after the ponies was wholly inexpedient. The country was unknown to the soldiers, and the reliable scouts were searching for General Crook. About 180 ponies remained of the captured herd.

It would seem that the value of the pony herd was overestimated, since the evidence was overwhelming that it consisted mostly of colts, yearlings, and brood mares. This loss would not be a severe blow to the Indians because they still had their war ponies. Some of the officers thought it wise to let the pony herd go because the soldiers and their horses were in poor shape. They argued that if a party had been sent out to recapture them, there would not have been enough troopers left to guard the camp.

Meanwhile, Grouard's party took the back trail of the night before. There were two trails leading to the camp at Otter Creek, one leading northward, the other following the river towards the northeast for twelve miles and then branching off toward the northwest. Since the first one was shorter and more direct, Grouard, who

Library of Congress

AWAY THE LED HORSES.
From a painting by Frederic Remington.

Library of Congress

CHARGE.
From a painting by Charles Schreyvogel.

The Retreat to Lodgepole Creek

thought that General Crook would take that route, decided to follow it. On the way the little party met two Indians driving sixty to seventy ponies which they had recaptured. The scouts took the ponies and drove them along with them to a point about halfway to Otter Creek where it became apparent that they would not meet General Crook. Upon returning to the camp of the night before, it was discovered that the troops had moved farther up the river. Grouard knew that Crook had joined Reynolds because he could see the tracks of the pack mules. After following the broad trail for two miles through the driving snow, the scouts came upon the tracks of an Indian war party following the troops. Abandoning the ponies, they followed behind the Indians until their trail turned off into the river bottom near the cavalry camp. Upon rejoining the command, the scouts were given a hearty welcome by General Crook, who had returned by the other route. That night, some Indians charged on the camp but did no harm.[3]

After the scouts had left, Colonel Reynolds consulted with his officers concerning the next move his command should make. General Crook had not been heard from, the men were without blankets and rations, and the cavalry horses were without forage. Something had to be done. Colonel Reynolds determined to move southward in the direction of Fort Reno in the event General Crook did

[3] Ricker, "Narrative of John Shangrau," *Interviews,* Tablet 27, 76–81. This account is used because it is believed to be more factual than that of Frank Grouard as given in *Life and Adventures of Frank Grouard.* According to the Grouard account, the trip to locate General Crook was a running battle with the Indians, and Little Bat's horse was shot, instead of giving out. In reading this biography, one gets the impression that events are embroidered so as to glorify Grouard and to make a more exciting tale. Whether this was the fault of Grouard or his biographer is not clear, but the narrative of F. E. Server throws some light on this: "Mr. Server says that he was thoroughly acquainted with Frank Gruard, that Frank could not write his name, that he was not to blame for DeBarthe's lies, that DeBarthe told lies in the Gruard book to give it savor, that he heard DeBarthe admit this fact in a quarrel that Gruard had with his historian. When Gruard complained because of the story of his visit to the Custer Battlefield, DeBarthe said he put it in fictitiously. Gruard accused DeBarthe of other falsehoods. Server says that DeBarthe lied when he stated that he had almost superhuman difficulty to induce Gruard to submit to being written up. He says that Gruard died a practical pauper and was buried in Potter's Field." Ricker, "Narrative of F. E. Server," *Interviews,* Tablet 7, 35.

not arrive. The accounts are conflicting as to the hour at which the movement was to commence.

Lieutenant Morton said that he was directed to notify the company commanders to get ready to move by either twelve or one and that it was then about three-quarters of an hour till time to start. Mr. Strahorn testified that Colonel Reynolds told him that he was going to move whether General Crook came or not and that he would continue on moving if it were necessary to do so. Major Stanton said that Reynolds told him that if General Crook did not arrive by two o'clock the command would move without him and that he must go toward the wagons. The hour was later changed to one o'clock, and orders were sent around to have the horses watered and saddled so as to be ready to move. Captain Mills, who was officer of the day, said the first order was given by Lieutenant Morton at Colonel Reynolds' fire, and that it was that they should move at eleven o'clock if General Crook did not come by that time. About twelve or twelve-thirty, Lieutenant Morton came to Mills's campfire and said that Reynolds had directed that his company saddle up and that the command would move at half-past one. Captain Mills went to Colonel Reynolds and they discussed the failure of Crook to arrive as he had engaged. Mills said there was nothing strange, as there was some good reason why he did not come. Some of the officers said that General Crook would never come, that he had gone straight on for the wagons. Mills hooted at the idea, saying that no court-martial in the world would acquit him for doing a thing of that kind. Colonel Reynolds did very little talking while the arrangements were made by Captain Moore and Lieutenant Rawolle to move the command southward. Mills urged Reynolds not to move, but he said he did not know what else to do. General Crook had made arrangements to meet them and had not done so. The command could not stay there, but had to do something to save themselves. Some officers assented to this, while others condemned it. Lieutenant Morton was very much displeased because he thought they should wait for General Crook. Captain Mills said it did not matter because Crook would be there before

The Retreat to Lodgepole Creek

half-past one; he took his field glasses, got on a hill, and saw Crook's command approaching in the distance.

Colonel Reynolds was later accused of abandoning General Crook in the belief that the latter had been attacked by the Indians and "worsted." Colonel Reynolds stated at his trial that he issued orders to march up Powder River at one o'clock and that he was obliged to move camp to procure grass for his horses. He had sent the scouts to find Crook, and he had no intention of marching any considerable distance. In going southward he would have been moving in the direction of the wagon train at Fort Reno toward which all were marching.

Thus the tired, hungry, and shivering little band anxiously awaited the arrival of General Crook and the pack train.

Chapter 9   THE RETURN
TO FORT FETTERMAN

AFTER the command had been divided on the evening of March 16, General Crook remained on the headwaters of Otter Creek with the four cavalry companies and the pack train. They went into camp for the night as the last of Colonel Reynolds' column vanished into the dusk. According to the guides, the mouth of Lodgepole Creek was only eighteen to twenty miles to the south and could be easily reached by the next morning. There were two trails by which the command could go there. One led from camp southward and struck Powder River five miles south of the mouth of Lodgepole, while the other went eastward along the trail Reynolds had taken and came out at Powder River about twelve miles north of the mouth of Lodgepole.

By seven o'clock the next morning, at the same time that Reynolds' men were on the mountain overlooking the village, General Crook's column was on the march, following the route taken by Reynolds. This was a little longer, but it would be easier marching and would sooner reach the river, where water could be found for man and beast. General Crook and his head scout Louis Richaud[1]

---

[1] Louis Richaud (Reshaw, Richard), a son of John Richaud, Sr., grew up in the vicinity of Richaud's Bridge (near the present site of Evansville, Wyoming), which was owned and operated by his father. He was scout and interpreter for General Crook in 1876. While the Richaud family was described as a "hard lot," Louis Richaud was said to have been a fine man and well respected. He claimed that President Grant sent for him through John S. Collins, the post trader at Fort Laramie, to come to Washington to act as interpreter. A special train took him to Washing-

The Return to Fort Fetterman

led the way. At the head of the column was Company A, Third Cavalry. It was under command of Lieutenant Joseph Lawson since the captain of the company, William Hawley, was acting as battalion commander. Next in line was Company D, Third Cavalry, under Lieutenant W. W. Robinson.[2] Captain Thomas B. Dewees was commander of the rear battalion led by Company B, Second Cavalry, under Captain James T. Peale and Lieutenant Frank U. Robinson.[3] Next came the pack train, followed by Company A, Second Cavalry, as rear guard. This company was commanded by Lieutenant Daniel C. Pearson[4] since the captain of the company, Dewees, was battalion commander.

The march was leisurely, the first ten miles taking four hours. Then the trail turned farther toward the south, while Reynolds' trail continued on eastward. It was already eleven o'clock; General Crook must have decided that the pace was too slow since the march then became more rapid. When the column came within half a mile of Powder River, General Crook halted the command

ton, where he spent a month. He further claimed that he received a check signed by President Grant for $1600 one year later in recognition of his services. These pretensions were received with reserve by his friends and acquaintances. He died one Fourth of July on Lake Creek, twenty-five miles northwest of Cody, Wyoming.

[2] Lieutenant William Wallace Robinson, Jr., from Wisconsin, served as a private in the Wisconsin Infantry until 1865, when he was appointed to the Military Academy. Graduating in the class of 1869, he was commissioned a second lieutenant in the Third Cavalry in which he served on the frontier until his transfer to the Seventh Cavalry on June 26, 1876. During 1875 he was in command of Troop D at Camp Robinson and in the Black Hills. He had a long and successful army career and eventually became a general officer. He died March 23, 1917, at Walter Reed Hospital, Washington, D. C., at the age of seventy-one.

[3] Lieutenant Frank U. Robinson was born in New York and was appointed second lieutenant in the Forty-first Infantry on October 1, 1864. After being mustered out in December, 1867, he was commissioned second lieutenant in the Nineteenth Infantry in March, 1868, and was assigned to the Second Cavalry on July 14, 1869. He was promoted to first lieutenant on March 31, 1878, to captain on December 28, 1888, and to major on February 2, 1901.

[4] Lieutenant Daniel Crosby Pearson, born in Massachusetts, graduated from the Military Academy in the class of 1870, when he was appointed to the Second Cavalry. He served as lieutenant, captain, and major in that regiment in Montana, Idaho, Nebraska, Wyoming, and Arizona. He died August 25, 1920, at Cambridge, Massachusetts, at the age of seventy-five.

He wrote an article entitled "Military Notes, 1876," in the September, 1899, issue of the *U. S. Cavalry Journal,* covering the campaigns of General Crook in 1876.

and stood perfectly still a few minutes. When Captain Hawley rode up and wanted to know what the delay was, General Crook told him he had seen an Indian going up Powder River and supposed there was a village near. Because he wanted to keep out of sight of the Indians, General Crook ordered the column to countermarch, and they went into camp a few minutes after five o'clock about a mile and a half back, where the animals had been watered.

Lieutenant Lawson,[5] who was in charge of the pickets that night, while on a hill looking for a position, heard two shots a few miles southeast up Powder River. When he got back to camp, several scouts came in and reported they had seen two Indians. No attempt was made to locate Reynolds' command. The campsite was on the south side of a little tributary of the Powder and, according to Lieutenant Lawson as stated in his testimony, was a "tolerably fair camping ground." It was apparent that the scouts had misled General Crook about the distance to Lodgepole, since the column had marched nearly thirty miles and had not yet even reached Powder River. Crook said later that the scouts had only vague ideas of the meaning of a mile, the distance to the mouth of Lodgepole being forty-five miles.

The night passed without incident. At seven o'clock the next morning the column was on the march with Captain Dewees' company in the lead and Lieutenant Lawson's company as rear guard.

[5] Lieutenant Joseph Lawson was born in Ireland but moved to Kentucky, where he was the proprietor of a grocery store. When the Civil War broke out, he entered the service at the age of forty as a second lieutenant in the Eleventh Kentucky Cavalry and became a captain November 28, 1862. He served through the rebellion and was mustered out July 17, 1865. He entered the regular army February 23, 1866, as a second lieutenant in the Third Cavalry, was promoted to first lieutenant July 28, 1866, and to captain September 25, 1876.

Lawson was described by John F. Finerty, the newspaper correspondent for the *Chicago Times,* as an eccentric old gentleman who had many peculiarities. When they had nothing else to do, his brother officers would quiz him and badger him to the amusement of all. He bore it all with supreme good nature, and at the Rosebud battle and the Milk River fight "showed the whole brigade that an officer need not always hail from West Point in order to gain that place in the affections of his soldiers which dauntless courage alone can win." Finerty, *Warpath and Bivouac,* 200.

Captain Lawson died on a Sunday night, January 30, 1881, at Fort Fred Steele, Wyoming, of paralysis. Thus passed a gallant old gentleman who had served his country long and well. A tribute to Captain Lawson upon his death appeared in the *Army and Navy Journal,* Vol. XVIII, (February 5, 1881), 543.

The Return to Fort Fetterman

The head scout Louis Richaud rode in front of the column by himself. After passing down a long canyon for about two miles, the troops struck Powder River and saw Colonel Reynolds' trail with the prints of the shod horses on the west side of the river. The trail spread across the valley, in some places being one to two hundred yards wide. Soon after the column turned south along the river, Louis Richaud saw seven or eight Indians approaching about half a mile away, driving back to the village seventy-five to eighty ponies they had just captured from Reynolds' camp. Richaud returned to General Crook, and the two men got off their horses, went up the side of the hill, and fired at the Indians, who escaped into the bluffs on the east side of the river. According to Lieutenant Bourke's diary, "The General himself got a very good sight on a savage upon whom he fired. The pony saddle, buffalo robe and blanket of the buck fell into our hands, but he was carried off by his retreating comrades." The scouts took charge of the ponies and drove them along with the column. Some were horses which General Crook recognized as belonging to Reynolds' command. Lieutenant Lawson saw the excitement in advance of the column and the troops moving up rapidly. He led his company forward, but was disappointed to find only twenty-five to thirty ponies which had been captured. This incident did not delay the column very long, and it moved on ten or fifteen miles up the river to Colonel Reynolds' camp, which was getting ready to move up Powder River. It was now about noon.

One can imagine the joy with which Reynolds' frozen and hungry men beheld the approach of General Crook and the pack train. Here were the warm blankets and food which had been so sorely needed since Otter Creek. With the arrival of the four fresh companies there was nothing more to fear from Indian attacks.

Colonel Reynolds immediately made a concise report to General Crook of all that had occurred since their separation at Otter Creek. Within a few minutes, Crook had heard about the capture of the village, the destruction of the supplies, the leaving of the dead upon the field, and the loss of the pony herd, but said nothing about it at the time. Then going over to the campfire of Captain

Noyes and Captain Egan, he congratulated them on the part they had played in the engagement. He found Egan's company saddled up and ready to move. Deciding that it was too late to try to recapture the pony herd, he ordered the command to move up Powder River to find better forage for the horses. The command moved southward eight miles and camped on the west side of the river, where there was plenty of wood, water, and grass for the horses. The men had a good warm supper and spent a comfortable night, although it began snowing at sundown and became very cold.

Before the campfire, Mr. Strahorn wrote his dispatch of March 18 to his newspaper, and Lieutenant Bourke brought his diary up to date. Both condemned Colonel Reynolds for the mistakes during the battle and especially for permitting the Indian herd to be recaptured. His failure to send a detachment out after the pony herd that morning was the last straw, and Bourke was highly critical, as appears from the entry of that date in his diary.

The theft [of the pony herd] was promptly reported to General Reynolds and one of our guides told him the animals were still in plain sight going over the ridge nearest camp three or four miles distant. To the surprise of all, General Reynolds declined sending any detachments to attempt their recapture. Great dissatisfaction now arose among all: several of the officers vented their ill feeling in splenetic criticism and openly charged Reynolds with incapacity. This exhibition of incompetency was the last link needed to fasten the chain of popular obloquy to the reputation of our commanding officer. It was remembered that no guard had been placed over the cattle herd the Sioux had stampeded near Fort Fetterman: that our vedette system had been neglected until General Crook had interfered and had caused it to be instituted; that in yesterday's fight our troops had been badly handled, the heights overlooking the enemy's position not seized upon as a single glance of the eye would have suggested: that our men were now suffering for food and covering while everything they could desire had been consumed before their eyes in the village and what was the worst shame and disgrace of all, our dead and dying had been abandoned like carrion to the torture and mutilation of the Indian scalping knives. The favorable impression General Reynolds' affable manners had made upon his subordinates had been very rudely and completely effaced. I cannot use a better term than

The Return to Fort Fetterman

to say we look upon him as a sort of General Braddock, good enough to follow out instructions in a plan of battle conducted according to stereotyped rules, but having nothing of that originality of thought, fertility of conception, and promptness of execution which is characteristic of great military men. Reynolds' imbecility is a painful revelation to many of us.

The pony herd was driven to the new camp by Lieutenant Drew. The Indians had failed to recapture about 180 ponies, and the herd was augmented by the 40 to 50 which were driven in by Crook's scouts. Because of the difficulty of driving and herding them at night, Colonel Reynolds ordered that all of them be killed except those needed by the scouts and as cavalry remounts. He stated in his official report that 110 ponies were killed, while 96 were taken along with the column. Four or five Indians made an attack on the camp about midnight, but the pickets of Captain Noyes's company fired and drove them back.

The Indians hung round our camps every night [wrote Bourke], occasionally firing a shot at our fires, but more anxious to steal back their ponies than to fight. To remove all excuse of their presence Crook ordered that the throats of the captured ponies be cut, and this was done on two different nights: first, some fifty being knocked in the head with axes, or having their throats cut with the sharp knives of the scouts, and again, another "bunch" of fifty being shot before sun-down. The throat-cutting was determined upon when the enemy began firing in upon camp, and was the only means of killing the ponies without danger to our own people. It was pathetic to hear the dismal trumpeting (I can find no other word to express my meaning) of the dying creatures, as the breath of life rushed through severed windpipes. The Indians in the bluffs recognized the cry, and were aware of what we were doing, because with one yell of defiance and a parting volley, they left us alone for the rest of the night.

Steaks were cut from the slaughtered ponies and broiled in the ashes by the scouts; many of the officers and soldiers imitated their example. Prejudice to one side, the meat is sweet and nourishing, not inferior to much of the stringy beef that used to find its way to our markets.[6]

[6] Bourke, *On the Border with Crook*, 281.

The Reynolds Campaign on Powder River

The next morning, the nineteenth, the command breakfasted by the light of the stars between three and four o'clock. Bourke noted in his diary that they shot forty Indian colts and brood mares that morning.[7] They marched twenty-one miles south-southwest up Powder River just above the mouth of Crazy Woman's Fork. The rations were getting low. Bourke grumbled that in such cold weather and with such arduous service, the amount of daily ration should have been doubled, with an allowance of twenty ounces of hard bread, one pound of bacon, and beans and sugar increased in proportion. This was a good camping ground with plenty of wood, water, and grass. It snowed all night.

On the twentieth the command started at seven o'clock, marching over a muddy trail in the snowstorm for twenty-two miles. The weather was warmer, and the ice in the river was getting so weak that it would barely support the horses, which were beginning to give out. A note was sent ahead by Buckskin Jack Russell and Tom Reed to Captain Coates, Fourth Infantry, commanding camp at Fort Reno, to move the wagons and supplies over to the Fetterman (south) side of the river, to go into camp there, and to be ready to march without delay.

The next day the command got an early start and marched ten

[7] This occurred on the east side of Powder River on a little flat one mile south of Joe Creek. When an early settler, George Linn, came to this country he found forty to fifty horse skulls near the river opposite Linn Draw. As no iron horseshoes were found, these may have been the skulls of the Indian ponies which were killed here. A mile to the north the river makes a bend to the west, and since it is heavily wooded it is possible that this was the campsite, although Mr. Linn never saw evidence of a camp having been located here. The distances check with the accounts, and Lieutenant Morton's map shows the camp to have been at or near this place. I believe I have been very fortunate in pin-pointing the Linn Draw site and am indebted to Evan Watt of Arvada, Wyoming, for obtaining this information for me. We carefully went over the place where the horse skulls were found but did not find anything. The big flood of 1923, when the river rose twenty feet, had washed everything away.

Local residents at the mouth of Lodgepole Creek (now known as Clear Creek) have not found any evidence of a campsite. There is a treeless flat opposite the mouth, while bluffs run southeastward along the river for several miles. The soldiers probably went along the bluffs until they came to the wooded river bottom on the east side of the river and made camp there. No evidence of the campsite at the mouth of Crazy Woman has been found, although there are many Indian campsites in the vicinity.

and one-half hours over a rough slippery road and arrived at old Fort Reno at 4:00 P.M. The wagon train and infantry guard were all encamped on the south side of the river and were in good condition. The exhausted column received a royal welcome from Major Coates, Major Ferris,[8] and Lieutenant Colonel Mason,[9] and a good warm supper of coffee, bacon, and beans was prepared for every one of the columns, commissioned and enlisted alike. The animals were fed on grain and carefully tended.

During the grueling march, Dr. Munn had cheered his patients with promises of the comforts awaiting them at the field hospital at Fort Reno. All were disappointed to find that no preparations had been made for them.

I found only the hospital tent pitched [complained Dr. Munn in his official report], its interior wet, no fire in or about it, and no bed save one on which lay poor Wright whom I scarcely recognized, so much was he changed by disease and, as I believe, by neglect. I found Dr. Ridgley and asked why so little preparation when he had been informed of our coming by a scout and in the light of my instructions. His replies aroused my indignation and amounted to "I didn't or I couldn't." I soon procured a stove and sent to the different companies for food and after two or three hour's hard work made my patients comfortable. I believe that nearly all the hours not spent in sleep at camp at Reno by this old gentleman were utilized in garrulous controversies with superior or inferior

[8] Major Samuel P. Ferris was appointed from Connecticut to the Military Academy, from which he graduated in the class of 1861. While serving in the Civil War, he was brevetted captain on June 14, 1863, for gallant service in the campaign against Port Hudson, Louisiana, and major on October 28, 1864, for such services at the battle of Hatcher's Run, Virginia. By the end of the war he was colonel of the Twenty-eighth Connecticut Infantry. After many years on the western frontier he died on February 4, 1882.

[9] Lieutenant Colonel John Sanford Mason was appointed to the Military Academy from Ohio and upon his graduation in 1847 was commissioned second lieutenant of artillery. He served through the Civil War and was captain of the Eleventh U. S. Infantry and later major of the Seventeenth U. S. Infantry. He was brevetted major for gallant services at the battle of Antietam, Maryland, September 17, 1862; lieutenant colonel, December 3, 1862, for such services at the battle of Fredericksburg, Virginia; brevet colonel on March 13, 1865, and brevet brigadier general on March 13, 1865. From 1873 to 1883 he served as lieutenant colonel in the Fourth Infantry on the western frontier. He was promoted to colonel of the Ninth Infantry in 1883 and died November 29, 1897.

associates and that by the infirmities of age he is incapacitated for army field duty and by his infirmity of disposition from real usefulness at permanent posts.

The command remained in camp on March 22 to rest the horses. General Crook sent a mounted party in advance to Fort Fetterman with dispatches, among them the following to General Sheridan, U. S. Army, Chicago, Illinois:

> Western Union Telegraph Co, March 22nd
> Dated in the field OLD FORT RENO, WYO. T. 1876
> Received at FORT FETTERMAN the 23rd.

TO GENERAL SHERIDAN, CHICAGO.

Cut loose from wagon train on 7th instant scouted Tongue and Rosebud rivers until satisfied there were no Indians upon them then struck across country towards Powder River Gen Reynolds with a part of command was pushed forward on a trail leading to village of Crazy Horse near mouth of Little Powder River this he attacked and destroyed on the morning of the 17th finding it a perfect magazine of ammunition war material and general supplies Crazy Horse had with him the Northern Cheyennes and some of the Minneconjous probably in all one half of the Indians off the reservation every evidence was found to prove these Indians to be in partnership with those at the Red Cloud and Spotted Tail Agencies and that the proceeds of their raids upon the settlements have been taken into those agencies and supplies brought out in return in this connection I would again urgently recommend the immediate transfer of the Indians of those agencies to the Missouri River am satisfied if Sitting Bull is on this side of the Yellowstone that he camped at mouth of Powder but did not go near there for reasons to be given by letter. Had terribly severe weather during absence from wagon train snowed every day but one and the mercurial thermometer on several occasions failed to register will be at Fetterman 26th inst. and if you desire me to move these Indians please have instructions for me there by that date or else I shall return cavalry to railroad at once for recuperation.

GEORGE CROOK, Brig Gen

The Return to Fort Fetterman

The wounded were taken off the travois and placed in the ambulances. The pack mules were unloaded, and everything possible was put in the wagons so as to ease the loads. On March 23 the whole command took up line of march to return to Fort Fetterman and moved fifteen miles to the head of the Dry Fork of the Powder River. The next day it rained from time to time, and the road was soft and sticky. Camp was made twenty-one miles farther on at the head of Wind River.

Several days after the battle, Colonel Reynolds had issued verbal orders to all company commanders to make a written report of the fight and the part each company took in it. By the time the command reached Fort Reno, all reports were in except those of Lieutenant Johnson and Captain Mills. At the Wind River camp, Reynolds' tent faced General Crook's headquarters, which were shared with Major Stanton. Reynolds saw Major Stanton talking to Mills and Johnson in front of headquarters, and in a few minutes Mills and Johnson came over to Reynolds' tent. Captain Mills told him that he would like to include in his report only his list of casualties and nothing else, that he had asked Major Stanton whether he said anything about him [Mills] in any of his letters, and Stanton had assured him that he had not. Reynolds asked Mills what objection he would have to making a memorandum report, and Mills replied that if he did so he would be obliged to reflect upon the conduct of Captain Moore, and that Reynolds, for his own protection, should take notice of Moore's conduct. Reynolds laughed this off and said he did not need any extraordinary protection but he wanted the report filed. This was the first word he had received which reflected upon the conduct of Captain Moore. Captain Mills's report was filed after the command reached Fort Fetterman. Lieutenant Johnson first filed a very brief report showing only casualties in his company, but Captain Mills required him to submit a second report which included material damaging to Colonel Reynolds and Captain Moore.

On the road the snow was from three to five inches deep, and the sticky mud made the march difficult for the animals. All along the road the cavalry horses and pack mules were giving out and had to be abandoned and shot. During the march from the village, fifty-eight cavalry horses and thirty-two mules were killed or abandoned from exhaustion. According to Private Phineas S. Towne, who was wounded in the summer campaign against these Indians at the Battle of the Rosebud on June 17, 1876, and was awarded the Order of the Purple Heart,

> On this expedition I rode four extra horses and one Indian pony, besides the horse which had been issued to me at Ft. Russell when the expedition started out. These horses were completely played out and had to be killed as they were too weak to travel because we had used up all our forage and there was no grazing for them on account of the deep snow. The troops themselves had nearly run out of rations. First we were put on half rations and then on quarter rations and we were very fortunate to get back to Fort Russell before running out of rations entirely.[10]

On March 25 the command covered twenty miles along the Bozeman Road to the South Cheyenne River, where camp was made. The horses were "balling" terribly. The sticky, gumbo mud clung to their hooves so that they were covered with large balls of mud. The next day, after a march of twenty-seven miles through the snow and mud, the head of the column reached Fort Fetterman about noon, while the wagon train and mules arrived between three and four o'clock. John Hunton was at the post when the expedition arrived. He reported much drinking and talk about officers being court-martialed for failure of the campaign. While the military brass cast about for scapegoats, the enlisted men got drunk. The Hog Ranch did a thriving business.

The wounded were glad to leave the springless ambulances and to be placed in the post hospital. Dr. Munn, upon being advised that the hospital had received cases of erysipelas and that gunshot wounds had not done well in it, determined to remove all his patients except Wright, who had but little hope of recovery. Dr. Munn accompanied Droege and Eagan to Fort Laramie, where their companies were to be stationed, while Dr. Stevens took Sergeant Kaminsky and Corporal Lang to Fort Russell.

[10] "Letter of Phineas Towne," *Winners of the West* (February, 1926).

The Return to Fort Fetterman

General Sheridan telegraphed General Crook to make what dispositions he found necessary to recuperate the command's horses and then to resume the campaign against the hostiles.

On March 27, Colonel Reynolds issued orders dissolving the expedition. One company of cavalry and the two infantry companies remained at Fort Fetterman, the two companies from Fort Laramie left for that post on the twenty-eighth, and the other seven companies of cavalry left on the twenty-ninth for Fort Russell. After encountering a heavy snowstorm, they reached that post on April 6. The captured ponies were distributed among the scouts who had conducted themselves with gallantry and the soldiers of the ten cavalry companies. The ten scouts under Louis Richaud returned to Fort Robinson, Big Bat was sent to Fort Laramie as a guide, and Frank Grouard and Speed Stagner were stationed as guides at Fort Fetterman. The pack train returned to its base at Camp Carlin.

The army was not satisfied with the results of the expedition and planned new operations against the hostile Indians. General W. T. Sherman expressed the opinion of the War Department in his report of November 10, 1876:

> This expedition was not conclusive or satisfactory. Therefore, General Sheridan determined to proceed more systematically by concentric movements, similar to those which in 1874–'75 had proved so successful at the south against the hostile Comanches, Kiowas, and Cheyennes. He ordered three distinct columns to be prepared to move to a common center, where the hostiles were supposed to be, from Montana, from Dakota, and from the Platte. The two former fell under the command of the Department Commander, General Terry, and the latter under General Crook. These movements were to be simultaneous, so that Indians avoiding one column might be encountered by another....[11]

General Crook was disappointed that the expedition had failed to round up all of the hostile Indians and believed that, measured by the yardstick of his previous successes against other Indians, it

[11] Report of the Secretary of War, 44th Cong., 2 sess., 1876. Report of the General of the Army, 29.

was a failure. Because this was his first encounter with the fierce Sioux and Cheyennes, he did not yet realize that they were the best light cavalry in the world and, man for man, superior to his own troopers. At the time, he and most of his officers firmly believed that the Indians in the village should have been rounded up and captured, although that had never been done before and was not to be done after. He believed that in staying away from Colonel Reynolds' column near Powder River he was giving Reynolds his big chance to distinguish himself. The failure of the campaign was attributed to poor leadership and cowardice rather than to the fighting qualities of the enemy. This contempt for the Indians was carried into the next campaign and was the real reason for Crook's defeat at the Rosebud. Custer had the same disdain for the Indians at the Little Big Horn and boldly rode into the trap from which he never returned.

The Indians were not damaged much by the battle. One warrior was killed, and probably many were wounded. Some Indian women and children died in the snow and cold during the long journey back to the next camp. The Indians regained all but about three hundred of their ponies. The hardest blow was the loss of their tipis and food supplies, but these were soon replenished in the spring from the huge herds of buffalo.

Because the failures of the campaign were believed to be the result of mismanagement, cowardice, and negligence, General Crook filed a series of charges against Colonel Reynolds the day he reached Fort Fetterman. These were tried by a general court-martial at Cheyenne, Wyoming, from January 6, 1877, to January 23, 1877. After the filing of the charges against him, Colonel Reynolds in turn filed charges against Captain Noyes for negligence in unsaddling his company during the engagement, charges which were tried by a general court-martial at Fort D. A. Russell from April 24, 1876, to April 29, 1876. Later, after some investigation, Reynolds filed charges against Captain Alexander Moore for neglect of duty. These were later withdrawn and replaced by more serious charges signed by General Crook, charges tried immediately after the trial of Colonel Reynolds and by the same court.

The Return to Fort Fetterman

Ever since the battle, the camp had seethed with charges and countercharges. Every movement and phase of the campaign was analyzed and criticized over the campfires; imagination magnified and distorted every error. Even as Captain Egan was withdrawing from the village, he complained to Major Stanton about the lack of support and the fact that Captain Moore had failed to take the position thought to have been assigned him. That night and the next morning, at Captain Noyes's campfire at Lodgepole, Captain Egan and Major Stanton discussed at great length Captain Moore's culpability. Major Stanton urged Egan to take some action against Moore, while Captain Noyes tried to dissuade him.

Camp gossip and rumor were on every tongue. Why did Captain Moore fail to cover the north end of the village? Why did he stay behind that ridge one thousand yards away from the village? Why did his line retreat down under the sagebrush mesa? Captain Noyes was charged with hiding behind Hospital Rock and eating lunch while the battle raged. Why did Colonel Reynolds burn all the meat and supplies which were so badly needed? Why did he retreat from the village after he had won the battle? Why did he leave the dead and wounded on the field to be scalped and mutilated by the Indians? Why did he fail to guard the pony herd? Why did he not try to recapture the pony herd? Why did he not send to General Crook for help? These questions were asked by every trooper. Captain Mills was criticized for excitedly sending for reinforcements all through the engagement and for the loss of the overcoats of his company. Colonel Reynolds blamed the company commanders for not removing their dead and wounded and for failing to obey his orders.

The result of the controversy was that the officers became divided into two groups, one supporting General Crook, and the other favoring Colonel Reynolds. Comrade turned against comrade and lifetime friendships were forgotten. General Crook, who shared his tent with Major Stanton, was undoubtedly influenced by his aide Lieutenant Bourke, and by Lieutenant Drew, Captain Mills, Captain Egan, Lieutenant Johnson, Lieutenant Paul, and Mr. Strahorn. On the other side, upholding Colonel Reynolds, were

Captain Noyes, Captain Moore, Lieutenant Rawolle, Lieutenant Hall, Lieutenant Morton, and his son, Lieutenant Bainbridge Reynolds.[12] In later years, Captain Mills summed up the campaign:

> Owing to the age and feebleness of Colonel Reynolds, and the bitter feud that existed in our regiment (similar to that in the 7th Cavalry between Colonel Sturgis and his friends and Colonel Custer and his friends, that proved so disastrous at the Little Big Horn), this attack on the village on Powder River proved a lamentable failure. Reynolds disobeyed Crook's order to hold the village until his arrival, abandoning the field and retiring in the direction of Fetterman.[13]

By the time the column reached Fort Fetterman the controversy had been fanned to a white heat. Lieutenant Bourke stated in his diary that in his opinion Lieutenant Morton had done much to embroil and precipitate matters by ill-judged criticisms upon Mr. Strahorn, the correspondent of the *Denver News,* who boldly averred that he was going to publish the truth in spite of all the Reynoldses and Mortons in the army. His conclusion was that General Crook had no other remedy but to probe the matter to the quick in a general court-martial.

Captain Egan signed a series of charges against Colonel Reynolds which had been written by Major Stanton and sent them to General Crook. The latter had concluded that Reynolds should be held responsible for the mismanagement of the attack upon the Indian village, especially in view of his neglect to investigate the behavior of Captain Moore, who was believed by most of the officers to be

---

[12] Lieutenant Bainbridge Reynolds was born September 15, 1849, at West Point, where his father, Colonel Joseph J. Reynolds, was on trial from his regiment as assistant professor. He graduated from the Military Academy number nineteen in the class of 1873, and was assigned to the Third Cavalry.

His company was in disgrace after the fight on Powder River and fought with reckless abandon at the Rosebud field the following June to redeem the good name of the "Old Third." Many years after this engagement Reynolds was tendered a brevet for his gallantry in the Rosebud battle.

"B," as he was fondly called by his family and friends, never married, but died at his mother's residence in Washington, D. C., on July 10, 1901, at the age of fifty-two after a protracted illness due to cancer. See *Annual Reunion Association of Graduates of the United States Military Academy,* 1901.

[13] Mills, *My Story,* 166.

The Return to Fort Fetterman

guilty of cowardice. General Crook drew up his own charges and sent a copy by Lieutenant Morton to Colonel Reynolds on the evening of March 26th. General Crook had rooms in the quarters of Major Alexander Chambers,[14] Fourth Infantry, Commandant of the Post, and, anticipating a visit from Colonel Reynolds, requested Chambers to be present. Shortly after breakfast the next morning, Colonel Reynolds came to see General Crook. Major Chambers described the interview in his testimony:

Col Reynolds said I am very much surprised to get this paper. I have thought I have done my whole duty and am perfectly surprised to have such a paper as this and I would like to have it withdrawn. I am an old man, and this is the first time in my life in the military service, that I have ever been charged with anything. Gen Crook said he would not withdraw those charges, and went on to say that the expedition had been a failure, and it was through his misconduct that it had been a failure; that he had disobeyed his order: that he had burned the saddles, he had ordered him to keep, and he burned the meat that he had been ordered to save. That he disliked very much to put charges against him that he would rather go through six battles than to prefer the charges, yet he thought it was his duty to do so and he would not withdraw them. Gen Crook said I understand one of our companies went into camp and went to cooking coffee during the battle. Col. Reynolds said Yes Major Noyes company did so. Gen Crook said I also understand one of your officers failed to perform his duty in that battle. I think Col Reynolds said he did not know anything about that. That is my recollection of it. Besides that Gen Crook said I have understood it was your intentions after the battle was over to take your command and go straight to Reno, leaving me with four companies the impedimenta of the command while you were going to Fort Reno. Gen Reynolds replied that such an idea never en-

[14] Major Alexander Chambers graduated from West Point in 1853 and was a classmate of General Crook. Serving with infantry during the Civil War, he was brevetted for gallant services at the battles of Shiloh, Tennessee, Iuka, Mississippi, Vicksburg, Mississippi, Champion Hills, Mississippi, and Meridian, Mississippi. He was commissioned major of the Twenty-second Infantry in March, 1867, transferred to the Tenth Infantry in 1869, assigned to the Fourth Infantry in 1870, and promoted to lieutenant colonel of the Twenty-first Infantry in October, 1876. He served at many different army posts along the western frontier. He died at the early age of fifty-five at San Antonio, Texas, on January 2, 1888, while colonel of the Seventeenth Infantry.

tered his head, and that he would have put his hand in the fire and burned it off before thinking of such a thing. . . . As Col Reynolds stood in the hall he asked Gen Crook if he would withhold the charges for a few days or for a time and General Crook said he would.

According to General Crook's version of the interview, Reynolds asked that the charges be withdrawn because it was wiping away the record of a lifetime to have them held against him. Crook told him it was a very painful duty for him but that he could not withdraw them since the fruits of the whole expedition had been lost by allowing the escape of the pony herd. He did not propose to assume the responsibility for the loss of the animals. The camp rumor was that there had been a great deal of mismanagement, no investigation had been made of it, and it was the duty of General Crook to prefer charges against Reynolds. Reynolds said that he had only heard the rumors the day before and wanted time in which to investigate them and that he had done his duty in good faith all the way through. General Crook replied that there was no use trying to hush up the mismanagement since word was bound to get all over the country, and that Reynolds had taken no notice of it, and it was an idle statement to say he had done his duty. Colonel Reynolds said he was going to make an investigation into the talk in camp and the whole subject—the loss of the animals and everything. General Crook said that there seemed to be a manifest disposition to hush the matter up but that he might as well try to smother Vesuvius as smother this matter up, that the feeling in the command was such that it was bound to spread all over the country, and that the investigation, if not commenced there, would commence from Washington. General Crook told him that the worst part of it was that after he had done so much for Reynolds, the latter was going to skip out leaving him to his fate, thinking that Crook had had the worst of it in a battle with the Indians. Colonel Reynolds called upon God to witness that this was not true.

General Crook referred him to Captain Mills, Major Stanton, and Lieutenant Bourke for evidence as to the misbehavior of Noyes and Moore. Colonel Reynolds did not deny the above conversation, except to say that Crook ordered him to file charges against Noyes and Moore, promising that if he did so the charges against him would be dropped. Crook was impatient and accused Reynolds of making Moore his adviser and of trying to hush up the rumors prejudicial to Moore which ran through the camp.

On the next morning, March 27, at six o'clock, General Crook and Lieutenant Bourke went to Cheyenne via the cutoff, and thence to Omaha, where plans were started for the summer campaign.

Chapter 10   THE COURT-MARTIAL PROCEEDINGS

ON March 28, Colonel Reynolds applied to the War Department for a court of inquiry for the purpose of examining his conduct of the battle and clearing his name. On April 5 he formally applied to the Adjutant General for a court of inquiry, but none was ever called. He then preferred charges against Major Stanton, which were never brought to trial.

Since Captain Noyes had, at all times, freely admitted that his company had unsaddled and made coffee, Reynolds filed charges against him immediately. The two men remained on the best of terms; and while Reynolds claimed that he was ordered to file the charges by General Crook, it is probable that he remembered his vexation when it took Noyes an hour to respond to the call to the village one-half mile distant, while Mills was frantically calling for reinforcements. On April 13, General Crook ordered a general court-martial to convene on April 24 at Fort D. A. Russell for the trial of "such prisoners as may come before it." Captain Noyes, having been put under arrest, was the first "prisoner" to come to trial. While Colonel Reynolds was in Omaha the middle of April, the judge advocate changed the charge against Captain Noyes from neglect to the more serious one of neglect of duty before the enemy. The proceedings were much publicized in the newspapers, and the engagement of March 17 was facetiously referred to as "the St. Patrick's Day Celebration on the Powder."

The court, appointed by General Crook, consisted of Colonel

The Court-martial Proceedings

John E. Smith, president; Colonel Franklin F. Flint; Lieutenant Colonel Luther P. Bradley; Major Nathan A. M. Dudley; Major Alexander Chambers; Major Andrew W. Evans; Major Edwin F. Townsend; Major Alexander J. Dallas; Captain John J. Coppinger; Captain George H. Brady; and Captain William L. Collier. Major Nathan A. M. Dudley was later excused. Major Horace B. Burnham,[1] judge advocate, prosecuted the case for the government, while Captain Noyes acted as his own counsel. The charge was conduct to the prejudice of good order and military discipline, and the one specification alleged that Captain Noyes "did order the horses of his company to be unsaddled, and they were unsaddled, thus rendering him in a degree unable to respond promptly to the order which might at any moment be expected for his Company to move at once, and also endangering to an unwarranted and wholly unnecessary degree the safety of his horses from a dash of the enemy to stampede them, or recover the captured herd."

Captain Noyes pleaded not guilty, and the trial commenced. Colonel Reynolds, who had signed the charge, was the first witness. He tried to excuse Noyes on the ground that while he should not have unsaddled and had lunch during the battle, it did no harm because the company was ordered to the line dismounted. He also claimed that the charges were not filed by him voluntarily but on order of General Crook who was actually the accuser. Captain Noyes then moved to dismiss the trial as the court appointed by General Crook had no jurisdiction. Technically, General Crook could not be the accuser in the case and be permitted to pick the personnel of the court, so the first question to be decided was whether the court had jurisdiction. General Crook then took the stand and denied that he had ordered or even suggested that charges be filed by Reynolds against Noyes. This testimony, being supported by the witness to the conversation, Major Chambers, convinced the court that Reynolds was the real accuser, which gave the court jurisdiction of the case. While deliberating on the ques-

---

[1] Judge Advocate Horace B. Burnham was born in New York but was appointed to the army from Pennsylvania. During the Civil War he served with the Sixty-seventh Pennsylvania Volunteers until 1864 when he was appointed judge advocate.

tion of jurisdiction, the court received a note from the post commandant that a suitable enlisted man could not be found to act as clerk of the court-martial. "Cook [the stenographer] will be at your service if sober. In case Cook's spree continues, and to save time, the General thinks it would be well for you to look up a citizen clerk."

Apparently Cook's spree continued, as the court met in Cheyenne on April 29 to proceed with the trial. Lieutenant Christopher T. Hall of Captain Noyes's company was the next and last witness for the government. For the defense, Sergeant Skinner[2] of Noyes's company testified that it was Captain Noyes's practice to rest his men and horses as often as possible and that when he did so on this occasion it did no harm. Captain Noyes did not take the stand, instead submitting a written statement wherein he admitted the unsaddling but claimed that the action was a small skirmish at long range and could not be dignified by the term "battle." He said the soldiers were nervous and fired fifty shots to the Indians' one. His men and horses needed rest and food, and on the march back his company was the freshest of them all.[3]

The court found the accused "guilty as charged except the words 'wholly unnecessary' and of the excepted words 'not guilty.' Of the charge—Guilty. Sentenced to be reprimanded by the Department Commander by general orders."

On May 2, 1876, General Crook, in approving the proceedings and sentence, said:

Referring to the sentence in the foregoing case the Department Commander deems it proper to remark that Capt Noyes' reputation during

[2] First Sergeant William Skinner of Company I, Second Cavalry, had re-enlisted for the five-year term at Fort Laramie on June 17, 1874.

[3] In September, 1958, looking for some evidence of the location of Noyes's campsite on the east side of Powder River, I found an old campsite, which may have been his bivouac, opposite the center of Hospital Bluff and several hundred yards farther south than the site indicated on Noyes's map. There were burned rocks, old tin cans, and other debris scattered about a little flat close to the river. Today, large trees screen the site from the battlefield, but in 1876 there might have been a clear view of the village. The site was not behind a hill and was not so far away from the engagement as to suggest that Captain Noyes was purposely absenting himself from the action.

The Court-martial Proceedings

the late war, supported as it is by the evidence adduced, is ample assurance, that in unsaddling his horses, at the time and place he did, he simply committed an error in judgment, and that he was not actuated by a desire to evade or shirk any duty that he might be called upon to perform. In the opinion of the Department Commander no terms that he can use will add to the punishment of a soldier of Capt Noyes' sensibilities more than that of the opinion of the Court composed of his fellow officers that his error merits their censure as expressed in the sentence.

Captain Noyes did not even cross-examine General Crook, and one gets the impression that all were going through a good-natured farce for public consumption. Noyes later testified for Reynolds, his accuser, in the latter's trial. Even General Crook paid him tribute in affirming the findings of the court. Captain Noyes was immediately released from arrest and returned to duty in time to join the summer expedition of General Crook in which he was given command of a battalion of five companies of the Second Cavalry.

Since General Crook had referred Reynolds to Major Stanton for information about Captain Moore's conduct in the fight, Reynolds requested a written memorandum from him. From this and Captain Mills's official report, he wrote out charges in pencil at Captain Coates's quarters. When Reynolds came to Fort Russell, he gave Moore a copy and sent one to department headquarters in Omaha. In the middle of April, when ordered to Omaha, Colonel Reynolds consulted with the judge advocate, who changed the charges from simple neglect of duty to the more serious charges which were finally signed by General Crook. While in Omaha, Reynolds claimed that General Crook told him that he had ordered trial for Noyes and Moore and that if he could make out a case against them it would be sufficient, and nothing more would be said about the charges preferred against Reynolds. Nobody had seen the charges against Reynolds because they had not yet been filed at division headquarters. All of this was denied by General Crook and Judge Advocate Burnham. Colonel Reynolds steadfastly maintained that the conduct of Noyes and Moore was satisfactory and that he would never have preferred charges of his own motion, but he admitted that he preferred the charges to keep charges from being pressed against himself.

On April 26, Captain Moore filed a request with the court that his case be tried next after that of Captain Noyes. After he was notified to appear for trial, Moore was informed by Reynolds that the court would be unable to try his case because General Crook, who had signed the charges, was the real accuser. Major Burnham, recognizing the validity of the plea, discharged the witnesses and postponed the trial until the next general court-martial. Captain Moore was kept under technical arrest and was not permitted to leave with his company on the Rosebud campaign.

After spending several days in Omaha, Colonel Reynolds returned to Fort D. A. Russell, where he was busily engaged in shipping in supplies and equipment and fitting out ten of his Third Cavalry companies for the next expedition which was scheduled to leave Fort Fetterman the last of May. When all was in readiness, the cavalry companies, with the pack train and wagon train from Camp Carlin, started the march for Fort Fetterman, taking the route by way of Fort Laramie. Here they crossed the North Platte River, which was overflowing its banks, on the new iron bridge and followed the Mormon emigrant trail on the north side of the river. Colonel Reynolds remained behind intending to follow later with one escort company.[4]

Lieutenant Colonel William B. Royall,[5] Third Cavalry, stationed at Omaha, Nebraska, received orders on May 16 to go to Fort Russell and join the expedition. He received a sealed letter, which was the arrest of Colonel Reynolds, and was told that upon his arrival he would receive instructions by telegraph whether to

[4] For a detailed account of Crook's summer campaign, see J. W. Vaughn, *With Crook at the Rosebud*.

[5] Lieutenant Colonel William B. Royall as next in command of the Third Cavalry was the logical successor when Colonel Reynolds was arrested. He had been appointed to the army from Missouri and served all through the Civil War with distinction. He won brevets for gallant action in cavalry fights at Hanover Courthouse, Virginia, and Old Church, Virginia. He served in the west after the Civil War and engaged in many Indian skirmishes. In his personal appearance he was impressive—a tall man of about fifty, with a full gray mustache, heavy eyebrows, and a high forehead on which were several scars inflicted by a rebel saber during one of his engagements before Richmond.

The Court-martial Proceedings

deliver the arrest or to return it by mail to department headquarters. Royall arrived on the freight train about twelve or one o'clock and received a dispatch from the assistant adjutant general of the department to deliver the arrest to Colonel Reynolds, assume command of the regiment, and join General Crook at Fort Fetterman. He went up to the post and met Colonel Reynolds on his way to town. After delivering the order of arrest, he returned with Reynolds to Fort Russell. The boundaries of the post were the limits of the arrest, so Reynolds was not permitted to accompany the column which he had helped to equip and outfit. One wonders if the decision to arrest Colonel Reynolds was influenced by his statements which resulted in the postponement of Captain Moore's trial.

Lieutenant Colonel Royall apparently resented this treatment of his superior and the slur on the Third Cavalry, as he and R. B. Davenport,[6] a newspaper correspondent attached to his staff, were later at odds with General Crook for many years. This conflict came to a head in Omaha in 1886, when each blamed the other for the loss of the Rosebud battle.[7] Colonel Reynolds had many friends with the new expedition, including his son Lieutenant Bainbridge Reynolds, who commanded his company in place of Captain Moore. With this background it is easy to understand the lack of co-operation between Royall and Crook which nearly proved disastrous for them both on the Rosebud field.

Having distinguished themselves for bravery during the Civil War, Colonel Reynolds and Captain Moore were humiliated by this

[6] R. B. Davenport was a newspaper correspondent for the *New York Herald* and accompanied the June and September campaigns of General Crook against the hostile Indians. He was entirely unused to the rough life on the frontier and was the target for practical jokes and bantering from his fellow correspondents and some young officers. He apparently did not relish this since in writing up the campaigns for his newspaper he reflected upon the conduct of his tormentors. During the Rosebud campaign he was attached to Royall's command and became very critical of General Crook. This was the beginning of a feud of long duration between Davenport and his newspaper and General Crook. It may be that this ill-feeling arose from Davenport's hearing resentment expressed by Third Cavalry officers over the court-martial proceedings. See Charles King, *Campaigning with Crook* (New York, Harper and Brothers, 1890); and Vaughn, *With Crook at the Rosebud*.

[7] Vaughn, *With Crook at the Rosebud*, 166.

first blemish on their long records of service. Confined to the limits of their posts, they planned their defenses against the charges. By the time the general court-martial convened on January 6, 1877, they had already been severely punished. Besides the disgrace, they had suffered the wound of seeing their comrades leave for the front without them. The battles of the Rosebud, Slim Buttes, and Dull Knife village were now history. The power of the Indian tribes had been broken and many had returned to the reservations. Those still defiant toward the government were scattered in small bands, starving, harassed, and seeking only to evade capture.

The court met at the Inter-Ocean Hotel in Cheyenne, Wyoming, and J. W. Jenkins, E. P. Johnson, and First Lieutenant Christopher T. Hall, Second Cavalry, appeared as counsel for Reynolds. The members of the court appointed by President Grant were Brigadier General John Pope, Colonel John H. King, Colonel John Gibbon, Colonel Jefferson C. Davis, Colonel John E. Smith, Colonel George Sykes, Colonel Franklin F. Flint, Colonel Alfred Sully (later excused and not present), Lieutenant Colonel Luther P. Bradley, Lieutenant Colonel Pinkney Lugenbeel, Lieutenant Colonel Daniel Huston, Jr., Lieutenant Colonel Amos Beckwith, and Major George D. Ruggles. Major David G. Swaim[8] was judge advocate of the court. These distinguished officers were contemporaries of Colonel Reynolds, and many of them had held high command during the Civil War.

The charges filed by Captain Egan being ignored, those signed by General Crook were read to Reynolds, who pleaded "not guilty" to all of them. The charges and specifications covered five printed pages. Each charge of misconduct was supported by one or more sets of facts or specifications which were relied upon by the government to prove the charge.

The first charge was for disobedience of orders. The first specification was that Reynolds issued orders to march away from the Lodgepole Creek camp in order to prevent the junction with Gen-

[8] Judge Advocate David G. Swaim was born in Ohio and was appointed to the army from that state. He served with the Sixty-fifth Ohio Volunteers all through the Civil War and after that conflict was appointed judge advocate in 1869.

eral Crook. The second specification was for burning the saddles, meat, and equipment in the village in violation of orders. The second charge was that Reynolds misbehaved before the enemy in running away and abandoning the dead and wounded on the field. The third charge was for conduct to the prejudice of good order and military discipline. The first specification was that Reynolds negligently permitted the capture of the pony herd, while the second was that he negligently failed to recapture the pony herd. The third specification was that he failed to support Captain Egan's charge and permitted Noyes's company to unsaddle while it was needed on the line. The fourth specification was that Reynolds falsely declared under oath that he was neither the accuser nor the prosecutor of Captain Noyes, while the fifth specification was that he had falsely declared under oath that the conduct of Noyes did not merit the filing of charges against him. The fourth charge was for conduct unbecoming an officer and gentleman. The first specification was for falsely testifying at the Noyes trial that General Crook had ordered Reynolds to file charges against Noyes. The second specification was that Reynolds falsely stated to General Crook at the Lodgepole camp that he did not intend to march to Fort Reno but intended only to move up the river for grass for the animals.

In sharp contrast to the Noyes trial, the Reynolds trial was a bitter struggle. Colonel Reynolds, confident in his innocence, cross-examined the witnesses himself and engaged in many acrimonious exchanges during the course of the trial. He claimed that Crook was well satisfied with the campaign until the controversy threatened to reach the newspapers. He added that Crook then attempted to forestall personal criticism by bringing charges against him and making him the scapegoat. In his final statement he launched a stinging attack on Crook for dividing the command and for failing to co-operate with him.

General Crook was the first witness for the government. His main testimony was that he gave Reynolds definite orders at Otter Creek to save saddles, equipment, and meat for the use of the troops and to capture the Indian ponies in order to put the Indians on foot. Contrary to orders, Reynolds had destroyed everything and had permitted the Indians to recapture the pony herd. Crook admitted that he had agreed to meet Reynolds at Lodgepole Creek on the night of the seventeenth, but "barring accidents." Crook claimed that he was anxious that Reynolds keep any captured food and provisions so that the command might go farther down Powder River and surprise other Indian villages. This statement must have sounded rather hollow to the court, since the evidence showed that it was all the command could do to get back to its base.

Major Stanton was the next witness, followed by Major Chambers, Lieutenant Bourke, Frank Grouard, Captain Mills, Lieutenant Morton, Robert E. Strahorn, Captain James Egan, and Captain Noyes. Privates Michael Himmelsbaugh[9] and George Maitland[10] of Egan's company and Private Jeremiah Murphy and Blacksmith Albert Glavinski of Mills's company were called to testify to the leaving of the dead and the one wounded man in the hands of the Indians. At this point the government rested its case.

On January 12, Colonel Reynolds put on his defense and called as his first witness Lieutenant William C. Rawolle. Two sergeants of Rawolle's company, William Land and Lewis Gilbert, were then called, and they were followed by Captain Noyes, Lieutenant Morton, Dr. C. E. Munn, General Crook, Lieutenant George A. Drew, Captain Mills, Captain Joseph Lawson, Captain T. B. Dewees, Captain James T. Peale, Sergeant Jeremiah Foley[11] of Lieutenant Johnson's company, Corporal Dennis Giles[12] of Captain Moore's company, and Lieutenant J. B. Johnson. Louis Richaud, the scout with Crook's column, and Major Stanton, Major Chambers, and Lieutenant Colonel William B. Royall were also called. In order to discredit Captain Mills, Reynolds introduced into evidence a

---

[9] Private Michael Himmelsbaugh of Company K, Second Cavalry, had re-enlisted in Omaha, Nebraska, on March 12, 1875, and was entitled to the $2.00 a month extra pay for his five years' continuous service.

[10] Private George H. Maitland of Company K, Second Cavalry, had enlisted in Chicago, Illinois, on November 25, 1873.

[11] First Sergeant Jeremiah Foley of Company E, Third Cavalry, had re-enlisted at Fort Sanders on January 6, 1873, for the five-year term.

[12] Corporal Dennis Giles of Company F, Third Cavalry, had enlisted in Cincinnati, Ohio, on February 23, 1875.

The Court-martial Proceedings

copy of charges on which Mills had been tried by a general court-martial at Camp McDowell, Arizona Territory, in October, 1871, and a copy of the findings of the court whereby Mills was found guilty of many of the charges and was suspended from rank and command for sixty days and reprimanded by the department commander, who happened to be General Crook. The main charges were that Mills had acted as a newspaper correspondent while in command of an expedition against hostile Indians and, after publishing the account of the affair under an assumed name, then denied he had done so. Most of the charges were for petty personal grievances which had arisen between him and other soldiers at the camp.[13] Captain Moore was one of the last witnesses called by the defense. He claimed that while behind the ridge before Egan charged, he had sent Sergeant Warfield ahead with fifteen men, and that this party had entered the village within five or six minutes after the charge. He denied having had any conversation with Stanton on the ridge. These statements were not borne out by any other witnesses. Both Rawolle and Moore said the ridge was only four hundred yards from the village, but all other witnesses said it was one thousand yards to three-quarters of a mile from it. Captain Peale[14] testified that General Crook was the actual commander of the expedition inasmuch as he issued the orders. At Crazy

[13] It was inevitable that men of strong personalities would clash when cooped up within the narrow confines of the frontier posts. Officers spent much of their time sitting as judges during trials of court-martial proceedings. Often three or more families would live in the same house under very primitive conditions, which gave rise to many petty conflicts. There are many cases of officers being discharged or forced to resign because of personal spite and jealousy. I have been told by retired army officers that there are but few career officers who have not at some time been tried by court-martial for some petty offense. The charges against Captain Mills were not of a serious nature and were no reflection on his character. The phrase "conduct unbecoming an officer and a gentleman" covered a wide variety of real or fancied sins. The rigid moral code of personal conduct during the period made it possible for the most innocent act to be misconstrued, and the small garrisons were hotbeds of gossip, talebearing, and personal feuds.

[14] Captain James T. Peale of the Second Cavalry was born in Pennsylvania and was appointed to the army from that state. He served with the Fourth Pennsylvania Cavalry through the Civil War and was brevetted lieutenant colonel of volunteers on March 13, 1865, for gallant and meritorious service in the engagement at Wyatt's Farm, Virginia. After serving in the Second Cavalry on the border, he left the service on December 20, 1880.

Woman, the officers had been instructed by him as to fitting out the men for the march and had been given a lengthy talk on equipment, supplies, and conduct during the ensuing march. General Crook denied issuing orders directly to the command except those given in disciplinary matters. Colonel Reynolds did not take the stand but prepared and filed his written statement of defense, which was followed by the filing of the judge advocate's reply.

Colonel Reynolds' statement was a strongly worded document wherein he vigorously defended his actions and criticized General Crook for dividing the command:

> There was no reason whatsoever for dividing the command and it should not have been divided. The pack mules had at that time very light loads; they made a night march, very heavily laden, the first night out from the wagons over a much rougher country. The mules were rough shod and in the best condition it was possible to have them. They could go any place that a horse could go and with much more facility. This is a fact well known to every officer of experience and to every man who has had anything to do with horses and mules. With four more companies, the whole command instead of three-fifths of it at the village, the result might have been more satisfactory to Gen Crook, who did not participate in the action and information with reference to which, he has procured principally from irresponsible noncombatants, hangers-on to the expedition. . . .
>
> When Gen Crook joined me at Lodgepole about noon of the 18th, I immediately reported to him concisely all that had occurred since our separation, including an account of the escape of the ponies, our sad disappointment at not meeting him there, my efforts to find him, a party being then sent out, etc. Not a word of displeasure or disapprobation escaped him: on the contrary he rode right to the campfire of Capt Noyes' battalion and congratulated him and Egan upon the operation in which they had participated.
>
> The afterthought which subsequently grew into such proportions as to result in the assembling of this Court, had not then taken form and shape.

Reynolds said that he never received specific orders from General Crook of any kind, that he was left to his own discretion and

South Dakota Historical Society

Captain James Egan with Company K, Second Cavalry, at Custer City, South Dakota, in September, 1876.

Sketch map of the battle area, made by Captain Henry E. Noyes.

judgment. He could not, with his force, bring away the saddles, meat, and provisions under the circumstances, so he destroyed them. Catching and loading the ponies was impracticable, since he could not spare men from the skirmish line to do it. He had never given orders to leave the dead on the field. The company commanders were supposed to look after their own dead; Mills tried to shift responsibility on to him for leaving Ayers on the field. There was no co-operation contemplated between the two commands, since General Crook went to Lodgepole Creek by a different route from that agreed upon.

Colonel Reynolds spent a good deal of time with Moore's battalion because he messed with Moore and his son Lieutenant Reynolds, who was in Moore's company. It was not intended this way, but the arrangements for messing with the pack train had fallen through just as they were leaving the wagons, and Moore had offered him a place in his mess.

Many searching questions were asked by Colonel Reynolds in his statement to the court. If Crook wanted the provisions hauled away from the village, why did he not furnish some pack mules? If Crook wanted the ponies recaptured on the eighteenth, why did he not do it when he arrived at Lodgepole with fresh troops? Why did General Crook countermarch when within half a mile of Powder River? Why did he not take the trail agreed upon in going to Lodgepole Creek? Why did he abandon Reynolds' trail to turn south to Lodgepole? When Crook arrived at Lodgepole, he selected a suitable grazing place for the animals—as Reynolds had proposed to do before he came!

Reynolds was especially bitter against Major Stanton.

The United States Army is entitled to know whether a non-combatant paymaster can be taken from his legitimate duties, to act as a newspaper correspondent on an Indian campaign, and giving strength to his statements by his official position, can, under the smiles and encouragement of the Dept Commander denounce in public print, as cowards and imbeciles his fellow officers, both his superiors and inferiors in rank, and not even have his conduct inquired into. Nay more, he has been openly and defiantly continued on a duty out of his proper sphere and for which he is not qualified.

The findings of the court were that Reynolds was guilty of burning the saddles, meat, and equipment in violation of orders and guilty of the second charge of abandoning the dead on the field, except for the words "misbehaved himself before the said hostile Indians, enemies as aforesaid, and ran away with his said command" and "and wounded." He was found guilty of negligently failing to recapture the pony herd. Although there was no criminality attached, he was found guilty of falsely declaring under oath that he was not the accuser of Captain Noyes and of declaring under oath that the conduct of Noyes did not merit filing of charges against him. The court found him guilty of all other charges and specifications and sentenced him to be suspended from rank and command for the period of one year.

The findings were approved by the secretary of war, except for that of burning the saddles, meat, and equipment in violation of orders. However, "in view of the long distinguished and faithful service of Col Reynolds the President has been pleased to remit the sentence."

Colonel Reynolds won a partial victory in that the court reprimanded General Crook for permitting Major Stanton to accompany the expedition as a newspaper correspondent in violation of longstanding orders and regulations. The findings of the court included the statement that "this Court cannot but regard such a practice as pernicious in the extreme and condemns it as unsoldierly and detrimental to the efficiency and best interests of the service."

The approval of most of the findings by the secretary of war placed a stigma on Colonel Reynolds from which he never recovered. President Grant's remission of the sentence on the grounds of long faithful service was itself a confirmation of guilt. Disgraced and dishonored in the eyes of the public, he retired from the army on account of disability on June 25, 1877. History has stamped him as the man who foolishly burned up meat and provisions which were badly needed by his troops, and who supinely stood by as the Indians retook the pony herd. Major Stanton received the honor of being commissioned lieutenant colonel on February 27, 1890, for "gallant service against the Indians under Crazy Horse on Powder River, Montana, March 17, 1876."

Reynolds was undoubtedly guilty of leaving the two dead men on the bluff, because they could have been lashed to horses and taken along with the column. While it is impossible to assess accurately the merits of the other charges against him, which are now obscured by time and controversy, there are undisputed facts which place him in a more favorable light. In the first place, his plan of attack was based upon faulty information given him by the scouts about the location of the village. This resulted in the attack being made only from the south and southwest, instead of from the south and north as intended. Because the village was farther away than was thought, the led horses were left too far from the scene of action. It was a miracle that they were not stampeded by the Indians, and their rescue is a tribute to Reynolds' skillful juggling of his forces. In ordering the horse-holders to tie their led horses to trees in the river bottom and dash up on the mesa and drive back the Indians, he adroitly met the emergency at hand. According to all estimates, the warriors numbered between 200 and 225, approximately the same as the number of soldiers on the line. On the morning of the eighteenth, at Lodgepole, the men and horses were exhausted and were without food and forage. The pony herd, which had just been recaptured by the Indians, was of little military value, being composed of colts, yearlings, and less valuable animals. The charges relating to the giving of oral orders depended upon one man's word against another's. During the stress and strain of the campaign there was every possibility of misunderstanding. It would seem that if Colonel Reynolds committed any errors, they were errors of judgment which were made during the heat of battle, when instant decisions were required.

In his biography, Frank Grouard claimed that Louis Richaud was jealous of his influence with General Crook and that he turned some of the officers against Grouard by saying that Frank was still friendly to the Indians.[15] He also intimated that Colonel Reynolds withdrew from "Crazy Horse Village" because of fear that Grouard had set a trap for him there. While there may have been a personal feud between Richaud and Grouard, it is unlikely that it had any effect upon the conduct of the battle. If it had, it would surely have come out at the trials as an excuse for the withdrawal from the village. When the command was divided at Otter Creek, Louis Richaud remained with General Crook and was not even present at the engagement.

Robert A. Strahorn, the correspondent for the Denver *Rocky Mountain News,* had justified Reynolds in withdrawing from the village in his dispatch of March 18:

> The Indians, severely punished . . . took refuge in the mountains thus unguarded . . . and had a positive advantage over the troops. Scattered over this almost impregnable mountainside, and secreted behind the numerous walls of rock, they could pick off our men without running the slightest risk of losing their own lives.Therefore the more the engagement was prolonged, after the prime object of the expedition was accomplished, the more serious and useless were our losses. Realizing this, General Reynolds . . . ordered the command to abandon its position and to at once proceed toward the mouth of Lodgepole.

Yet after the hue and cry had been raised, Strahorn was one of the most outspoken witnesses against Colonel Reynolds.

In his telegram of March 22 to General Sheridan from Fort Reno, Crook jubilantly announced that Reynolds had "attacked and destroyed" the village, "finding it a perfect magazine of ammunition war material and general supplies. . . ." The note of triumph was repeated in his telegram of March 23 to General Sheridan at Fort Laramie, Wyoming: "We succeeded in breaking up Crazy Horse's band of Cheyenne and Minneconjous, killing more than one hundred Indians and burning their village on Little Powder River. An immense quantity of ammunition, arms and dried meats were stored in their lodges, all of which we destroyed. Our loss was four men killed and eight wounded." In this message

---

[15] DeBarthe, *Life and Adventures of Frank Grouard,* 104–106.

he sought to share in the credit for the victory through phrases such as *"We* succeeded," *"We* destroyed," and *"Our* loss."

In his official report of May 7, after the affair had been aired in the newspapers, General Crook was careful to enumerate the "failures" of the expedition, and he stated that he had almost come to believe that operations were impossible in the rigors of the climate during the winter and that he wished to demonstrate by personal experience whether this was true. He did not accompany the attacking column but "remained with the train to the end that the command might not be embarrassed by any division or appearance of such on the field, and the commander himself might feel free from all embarrassment that he might otherwise feel if the Department Commander were present."

In his official report of May 7, he further said:

My instructions being to take the horses and ponies which I was certain they should capture and from them remount my command, and with the supplies captured push on and find whatever other force there might be.

The failure therefore to properly secure the captured horses rendered a further prosecution of the campaign at this time abortive and the expedition returned reaching Fort Fetterman on the 26th of March.

It is difficult to accept this statement, because while the battle was being fought, and the next day, General Crook's column was headed southward toward the wagons at Fort Reno. Horses and men were in such pitiful condition after the long campaign that it was all they could do to get back to their base. The report has a defensive tone and seems to be an effort to escape personal responsibility and to disassociate himself from the engagement. He had been ordered to head the expedition and in his report of September 25, 1876, declared, "I took the field, with Fort Fetterman as the base." It is surprising that he "had almost come to believe, that operations against Indians were impossible in the rigors of the climate during winter and early spring," because he says in the same report, "I believe that the most successful campaign . . . would be that prosecuted in winter, or, at least, in the early spring months." When the expedition was first considered, Crook was of the opinion that operations could have been undertaken at any time. In the following November he was still of that opinion as he headed another expedition into northern Wyoming which attacked and destroyed the Cheyenne village of Dull Knife under adverse winter conditions. It was probable that the decisions to attack during winter weather were influenced by public clamor to start hostilities against the Indians immediately because they were barring the road to "civilization."[16]

While it has been freely conceded that Reynolds surprised the Indians in their village, destroying all of their lodges, supplies, and equipment, and was able to withdraw his command with only a small loss, yet historians have unanimously condemned him for not holding the village after it had been captured and for failing to recapture the pony herd. Upon close analysis, these criticisms are not justified. It has not been explained what possible benefit could have accrued to the soldiers from camping on the site of the destroyed village on the night of the battle. Had they done so, the command would have been subject to the constant plunging fire from the warriors in the rocks on the mountainside. There would have been more casualties, and the men would have lost their much-needed rest. It seems clear that Reynolds' horses were too jaded to attempt the pursuit of the pony herd. If General Crook was so anxious to have it recovered, he could have gone after it with his four troops of fresh cavalry, since it had been gone only a few hours when he arrived.

In appraising the results of this highly controversial campaign, the objectives of General Crook and Colonel Reynolds should be considered. According to General Crook, the purpose was to capture the Indians, or all of their ponies, and to destroy all property which could not be used by the troops. Neither the Indians nor all of the ponies were captured, so therefore the campaign was a failure. Colonel Reynolds claimed that his instructions were to

---

[16] This opinion has been developed at length by Charles Edmund DeLand in his article "The Sioux Wars," *South Dakota Historical Collections,* Vol. XV (1930), 304–308.

The Court-martial Proceedings

damage the enemy as much as possible and then get away. It would seem that Reynolds' objective was the most feasible, since this was all that was accomplished during similar attacks at the Washita, Summit Springs, Dull Knife village, Lame Deer village, and Slim Buttes. Although these engagements followed the same pattern as the Reynolds campaign, they were hailed as great victories for the soldiers. In each, an Indian village was destroyed and a few warriors killed, but in none were the Indians rounded up and captured en masse. In most of these encounters the pony herds were captured, but the warriors always seemed to procure other mounts with which to continue the unequal struggle. The army, waging a war of attrition by the constant pursuit and harassment of the Indians, eventually forced them to surrender after they had lost their lodges, food, supplies, and equipment. The Reynolds campaign, the first blow struck in the series of expeditions against the Indians, was as effective in this kind of warfare as the more spectacular successes.

The controversy which later developed was, as Captain Mills said, the result of the ill-feeling between the two cliques in the command. The private feud assumed such proportions that the newspapers took it up. Then it was every man for himself. There was so much criticism and ridicule that in the eyes of the public the expedition was a failure. The politic course for Reynolds to have taken would have been to join Crook in condemning Noyes and Moore and in making them the goats, but instead he tried to protect them. In so doing he brought it all down on his own head. It would seem that the findings of the court, exclusive of that regarding the abandonment of the two dead men on the field, were cruelly unjust to Colonel Reynolds.

On January 16 the court started taking testimony in the trial of Captain Moore, before the decision was reached in the Reynolds case. Moore introduced J. J. Jenkins, Captain Payne, Fifth Cavalry, and Lieutenant Rawolle, Third Cavalry, as his counsel. Major David G. Swaim was judge advocate of the court. The first charge was for disobedience to the lawful command of his superior officer in failing to co-operate or attack the village as ordered. The second charge was for violation of the forty-second article of war in misbehaving before the enemy. The first specification was that he did "tardily, timorously (and cowardly fail to) cooperate in said attack ordered and instructed, and did remain so far from said point of attack . . . as to render the service of his command of little or no service. . . ." The second specification was for withdrawing his command from the mountainside to a position down under the mesa and for failing to resume his former position when ordered by Captain Mills.

After Moore pleaded not guilty to all charges, which had been signed by General Crook, the trial commenced. The first witness called for the government was Colonel Reynolds. He testified that from his position on the mountain he ordered Moore to get as near the village as possible without revealing himself to the Indians and that the precise position to be occupied by his battalion was necessarily left to him. Moore's conduct was entirely satisfactory. Reynolds had previously brought similar charges against Moore, but claimed he did it under orders from General Crook and not of his own volition. Major Stanton, Lieutenant Augustus C. Paul, Lieutenant F. W. Sibley, Lieutenant Charles Morton, Captain Mills, Frank Grouard, Robert E. Strahorn, and Dr. C. E. Munn were called to the stand in rapid succession. They testified that the orders given by Reynolds to Moore were to take his battalion to the mountainside near the north edge of the village and to kill or capture the Indians as they ran up into the ravines, but that instead of doing this, Moore stopped on the ridge one thousand yards from the village and waited there for the attack. Captain Mills and Lieutenant Paul described the withdrawal of Moore's men down under the mesa after they had been outflanked by the Indians. The government rested its case, and Colonel Reynolds was recalled for the defense. Captain Noyes and Lieutenant Bainbridge Reynolds testified that the ridge on which Moore's battalion took position was only four hundred yards from the village and that the men got to the village within five or six minutes. Captain Frederick Van Vliet,[17] Third Cavalry, said that Major Stanton had

The Court-martial Proceedings

told him that if Moore had moved his command into the position assigned him, the Indians would not have escaped from the village and that he had urged him to take the position but he would not do it. During the conversation he had called Captain Moore a "God Damned Coward." Sergeant Jeremiah Foley of Company E, Third Cavalry, Lieutenant Sibley, and Lieutenant Johnson were called for the defense.

On rebuttal, General Crook took the stand and stated that the charges signed by Reynolds were not brought on his order, direction, or suggestion. Captain Moore did not take the stand and did not file the usual statement for the defense. The court had already heard his version of the matter and apparently did not believe it. He must have felt that the court was against him, since instead of trying to defend himself he filed testimonials concerning his bravery during the Civil War. A number of letters signed by General Phil Kearny, General J. Hooker, General George Meade, Rufus Ingalls, General Pleasanton, and General H. G. Berry attested to his high courage and valor during that conflict. An extract from a field order signed by General Sherman was introduced. In it an attack made on an Apache Indian camp in the Hatchet Mountains, New Mexico, August 27, 1868, by a detachment of infantry under Captain Moore was favorably mentioned.

The court found Moore not guilty of disobeying orders and of withdrawing his command after the flank attack by the Indians. He was found guilty of conduct to the prejudice of good order and military discipline in failing to co-operate fully in the attack, but not guilty of misconduct before the enemy and "cowardly failing to" co-operate. He was sentenced to be suspended from command for six months and to be confined to the limits of his post for the same period. The findings and sentence were approved by President Grant but were remitted in view of his previous record.

Lieutenant Bourke and Mr. Strahorn were very outspoken

---

[17] Captain Frederick Van Vliet, Third Cavalry, was described as "tall, thin and good-looking." Finerty, *Warpath and Bivouac*, 75.

Having been appointed to the army from New York, he served all through the Civil War and was brevetted for gallant services in the campaign from the Rapidan to Petersburg and in the siege of Mobile, Alabama.

against Moore and repeatedly denounced him for cowardice. However, there is one bit of testimony by Major Stanton, who was openly hostile to Moore, which throws some doubt on his guilt. Major Stanton and Sergeant Gilbert both testified that when the small party of five men advanced to the little point ahead of the line, they had to stay hidden for five minutes in order to escape being seen by an Indian herding the ponies. If five men had to be that careful, the three companies of 150 men would have had difficulty in advancing over the same ground without escaping the sharp eyes of the herders. It is possible that Moore was right in claiming that he got as close to the village as he could without being discovered. He was undoubtedly justified in withdrawing his men when the Indians came around above him because the flank was literally "up in the air." He was also blameless in failing to go to a point on the mountainside opposite the north end of the village where he would be in plain sight of the Indians. To have reached there by going around the west side of the mountain would have required three or four hours. It is probable that the court found him guilty because of his rather obvious misstatement before it that the ridge was only 400 yards from the village, when he had told Captain Mills that it was only 150 yards from the village. His statements that he sent Sergeant Warfield ahead with fifteen men and that he had no conversation with Stanton on the ridge were not confirmed by other testimony. If he had confined himself to the truth, he might have been cleared. The fact that he failed to submit a statement of defense was probably taken as an admission of guilt by the court. During the summer he had signed an official report of the battle written up by Major Stanton in which he had implicated himself. Guilty or not, Moore's army career was ruined under these circumstances, and he resigned his commission on August 10, 1879.

In those days little was known about proper diet: Napoleon had made the statement that an army travels on its stomach, but this maxim had not yet been adopted by the U. S. Army. The ordinary rations of bacon, beans, hardtack, and coffee seem scanty enough, but when these were cut in half during a march for many days in cold weather over rough country, the minds and bodies of the men were inadequately nourished. This could have accounted for the many mistakes made during the campaign. The outspoken, excitable Mills was at fault in leaving the overcoats of his company on the mountain and was at least partly to blame for leaving Private Ayers in the hands of the Indians. The old battle-scarred war horse, Captain Egan, failed to keep his men on the line after the initial charge. The aggressive Major Stanton got tired and wanted to stop eight or ten miles short of camp. The stern and impassive Crook failed to reach the Lodgepole camp at the time agreed upon. The scholarly Bourke was one of the first to reach the Lodgepole camp and, when other officers arrived, was roasting buffalo meat. Everyone was anxious to get away from that village, and even the rear guard, under the Prussian officer Lieutenant Rawolle, failed to wait until all had left. Captain Noyes's men saddled up so quickly that Lieutenant Hall had to attend to his own horse.

It seems that the forced night march and the early morning attack were too much for the men, who had been on half rations for days and whose physical and mental capacities were at a low ebb. Probably the real explanation for the defeat, if it was a defeat, was the tenacity and daring of the warriors. The flanking attacks on the mountainside and in the brush along the river bent the line back at both ends so that all the troopers were subject to enfilading fire. When the Indians countercharged, they got up so close that troopers began to fall before the well-directed fire. This broke the spirit of the weary men. Reynolds had decided to withdraw before the countercharge was made, but the movement was delayed for two hours because of the difficulty in getting the led horses down from the mountain. It is clear that he could not have held the village if he had wanted to. General Crook attributed the failure of the campaign to mismanagement by Reynolds, although by the time of the trial, he had been made aware of the bravery and valor of the Sioux and Cheyennes.[18]

---

[18] After the Rosebud and Slim Buttes campaigns in 1876 against the Sioux and Cheyennes, General Crook became fully aware of the fighting qualities of his enemies. In his report of September 25, 1876, he stated, "Of the difficulties with which we

The warriors, fortified by the consciousness of right, were fighting for their homes and families on land set apart for them by the treaty of 1868. Treaties of the United States, made by the president with the concurrence of two-thirds of the senators present, were the "supreme law of the land."[19] The solemn treaty with the Indian tribes certainly could not have been revoked by a mere departmental order of the Indian Bureau directing them to return to the reservations. The Indians had a right to ignore it. Neither did the army have the right to send the expedition against the roving tribes, because the power to declare war was vested in Congress, which had not acted. The whole campaign was a violation of the treaty and of the Constitution of the United States. There was no more legal right to attack this village than there was to attack a Canadian village across the border. While the troopers were simply acting under orders, the campaign had been carefully planned and executed under the direction of General Sheridan and General Sherman, with the blessings of President Grant. This flagrant action reflected the temper of the American people, who were incensed with the failure of the Indian tribes to surrender

---

have to contend, it may be well to remark that when the Sioux Indian was armed with a bow and arrow he was more formidable, fighting as he does most of the time on horseback, than when he got the old fashioned muzzle-loading rifle. But when he came into possession of the breech-loader and metallic cartridge, which allows him to load and fire from his horse with perfect ease, he became at once ten thousand times more formidable.

"With the improved arms, I have seen our friendly Indians, riding at full speed, shoot and kill a wolf, also on the run, while it is a rare thing that our troops can hit an Indian on horseback, though the soldier may be on his feet at the time. The Sioux is a cavalry soldier from the time he has intelligence enough to ride a horse or fire a gun. If he wishes to dismount, his hardy pony, educated by long usage, will graze around near where he has been left, ready when his master wants to mount either to move forward or escape.

"Even with their lodges and families, they can move at the rate of fifty miles per day. They are perfectly familiar with the country; have their spies and hunting parties out all the time at distances of from twenty to fifty miles each way from their village; know the number and movements of all the troops that may be operating against them, just about what they can probably do, and hence can choose their own times and places of conflict, or avoid it altogether." Report of the Secretary of War, 44 Cong., 2 sess., 1876, Vol. 1, 498.

[19] See J. P. Dunn, *Massacres of the Mountains* (New York, Harper and Brothers, 1886. Reprint edition, New York, Archer House, Inc., 1958), 21.

The Court-martial Proceedings

the Black Hills. The only regret was that the little band had not been completely annihilated.

The net result of the campaign was the Sioux war. The Indians were enraged at the unprovoked attack. They had withdrawn far from the most advanced white settlements. The Cheyennes had long been at peace with the Great White Father, but now they joined with the Sioux tribes under Sitting Bull and the war chief, Crazy Horse, for mutual protection against the soldiers.

Column after column was thrown against them. General Crook led a force of over 1325 soldiers and allied Indians northward from Fort Fetterman, but was surprised and turned back by a part of the warriors from the hostile encampment at Rosebud Creek, in Montana, on the following June 17. The Custer disaster occurred eight days later on the Little Big Horn.[20] These two victories for the Indians demonstrated the "prowess of the Sioux" and finally convinced the army that it had an opponent worthy of an all out effort. From this time on, however, the power of the tribes waned because they were unable to obtain ammunition and supplies necessary to carry on the war. Valor alone was not enough.

The third expedition of the year, known as the "starvation march" or the "mud march" and composed of several thousand men under General Crook, surprised a small village of thirty-five tipis at Slim Buttes on September 9 and killed and captured a few squaws and warriors. In the cold of an early November morning, General Mackenzie struck the Cheyenne village of Dull Knife, nestled in the Big Horn Mountains of Wyoming. Many warriors were killed, and women and children perished in the snow. The war of attrition continued, and the country was shocked by the news of the Lame Deer fight, in which General Miles made a surprise attack on a small village one mile south of the present site of Lame Deer, Montana. In the battle of Wolf Mountain, an Indian force under Crazy Horse was driven from mountain heights along Tongue River by the use of small cannon, of which the Indians were afraid. After this the small bands scattered and most

---

[20] For the most complete and accurate account of this epic campaign the reader is referred to the scholarly work of Edgar I. Stewart, *Custer's Luck*.

of them surrendered, unable to keep up the unequal contest. With the exception of small uprisings, there was no more action until 1890, when the band of Big Foot was almost annihilated by the vengeful Seventh Cavalry in the tension-filled atmosphere at Wounded Knee Creek. While it was probable that a big showdown between the whites and the hostile Sioux and Cheyennes was inevitable, it was undoubtedly triggered by the Reynolds fight on Powder River.

Appendix A NAMES OF TROOPS IN THE CAMPAIGN

THE names of the troops who were in the Reynolds fight on Powder River are taken from the faded scrip of the company muster rolls, which were filed on April 30, 1876, by the company commanders. The enlisted men who belonged to these organizations but who for various reasons were not in the campaign are omitted. Some of these were on detached service, others in hospitals or in confinement. There were very few desertions prior to the battle, most of them occurring after the men had returned to their posts. The excuse given was that they did not care to serve under officers who would permit their dead and wounded to fall into the hands of the enemy. After the campaign the companies of Captain Noyes and Captain Egan returned to Fort Laramie, while the companies commanded by Lieutenant Rawolle, Lieutenant Johnson, Captain Moore, and Captain Mills returned to Fort D. A. Russell.

The muster rolls give the dates of enlistment together with the extra pay to which each soldier was entitled. The privates having over five years' service received an extra $2.00 per month, while those with over ten years' service received an extra $3.00 per month. From this data it is possible to determine the number of raw recruits in each company, many of whom had enlisted only a few months before the campaign.

COMPANY E, SECOND CAVALRY

William C. Rawolle, First Lieutenant
Frederick W. Sibley, Second Lieutenant

William Land, First Lieutenant
Louis Gilbert, Sergeant
William P. Cooper, Sergeant (sick in hospital)

George S. Howard, Sergeant
Lewis Shaucer, Sergeant
Harvey Dollmair, Sergeant
Samuel Gilmore, Corporal
John Lang, Corporal
   (wounded—sick in hospital)
Peter Haag, Bugler
Michael Cahill, Farrier
Joseph Barles, Blacksmith
Joseph F. Long, Saddler
Jackson B. Burke, Private
George Blass, Private
   (sick in hospital)
Nicholas Burback, Private
William Croley, Private
John Curley, Private
William I. Dougherty, Private
George E. Douglas, Private
William P. Englehorn, Private
Thomas Edwards, Private
Joseph W. Foyer, Private
Gabriel Damon, Private
George S. Gage, Private
John Glancey, Private
Jacob R. Herd, Private
Heinrich Holzechuler, Private

David L. Hogg, Private
John Hipp, Private
John Hollenbacher, Private
Charles Jones, Private
William C. Kingsley, Private
Benjamin Mason, Private
Montgomery McCormich, Private
Samuel McWalters, Private
William McWalters, Private
William C. Murry, Private
Gustav Martini, Private
Isaac Nichols, Private
John P. Nolan, Private
Lindon B. Perry, Private
Richard Parrington, Private
Valentine Rufus, Private
Orson M. Smith, Private
James A. Scott, Private
Frank H. Soule, Private
Charles Tauscher, Private
William Volmer, Private
James Vane, Private
John T. Welch, Private
   (sick in hospital)
Hugo Wagner, Private

The total of officers and men in the campaign was fifty-three. Captain Elijah R. Wells, the captain of the company, was sick, and First Lieutenant William C. Rawolle was attached to the company temporarily at Fort Sanders on February 16, 1876. First Lieutenant Randolph Norwood was also sick and not in the campaign. Four privates were absent for various reasons. Corporal John Lang was the only casualty reported in the company as a result of the fight, and he was still in the hospital on April 30, the date of the muster roll. Privates Benjamin Mason, Samuel McWalters, and William McWalters deserted in April, 1876. Thirty-one horses were reported serviceable, and twenty were reported unserviceable. Private Isaac Nichols was discharged on April 20 on a surgeon's certificate of disability. On April 30 four men were still sick in the hospital, probably the result of the extreme hardships they had undergone. Twenty of the men in the campaign had less than one year's service.

COMPANY I, SECOND CAVALRY

Henry E. Noyes, Captain
Christopher T. Hall, First
   Lieutenant
William Skinner, First
   Sergeant
William Taylor, Sergeant
Hugh K. McGrath, Sergeant
Eli I. Bennett, Sergeant
George Cooper, Sergeant
Thomas Meagher, Corporal
Amos Black, Corporal
Thomas C. Marrion, Corporal
John P. Slough, Corporal
John I. Donovan, Trumpeter
John Raynor, Trumpeter
George Fisher, Farrier
Henry Knapper, Saddler
Michael Gavan, Blacksmith
Henry Wilson, Waggoner
   (sick in hospital)
Phillipp Bennett, Private
William A. Blyler, Private
John E. Collins, Private
Charles R. Craft, Private
Daniel Donahue, Private
Henry Doyle, Private
Charles Emmons, Private
John F. Fitzgerald, Private
Charles G. Graham, Private
John B. Hall, Private

Daniel Hanesworth, Private
William G. Henno, Private
Frank E. Joy, Private
Robert Johnson, Private
William H. Keenright, Private
Walter B. Keenright, Private
Thomas Kennedy, Private
Michael Kiley, Private
Andrew W. Kinross, Private
George H. Liddle, Private
Martin Maher, Private
Charles Minarcik, Private
John Moran, Private
Charles Morrison, Private
Hugh Nicholl, Private
Gustav Ohm, Private
Ashley L. Parker, Private
James H. Ray, Private
John Reynolds, Private
William Riley, Private
Gottlieb Ruf, Private
John Russell, Private
John M. Stevenson, Private
William Schroder, Private
Zachary Taylor, Private
Elle Ubben, Private
Patrick H. Wall, Private
   (sick in quarters)
Daniel Walsh, Private
George Watts, Private

The total of officers and men in the campaign was fifty-six. No casualties were reported, but seven horses were abandoned as unserviceable

The Reynolds Campaign on Powder River

and unable to keep up with the column. The total of serviceable horses was thirty-nine and nine were reported as unserviceable. There were twenty-five certificates of disability issued during the two-month period. Captain Noyes reported the part that his company had performed in the battle: "The duty assigned the company at the attack on the Indian village was to capture, run off and guard the Indian herd of ponies, which was successfully performed—the herd numbering 600 or 700 animals. One hour before the troops left the ruins of the village, the company was relieved from duty over the pony herd and ordered to cover the withdrawal of the other troops from the field of action, which was done." Only five men in the company had seen less than one year's service.

COMPANY K, SECOND CAVALRY

James Egan, Captain
John McGregor, First Sergeant
Charles Fisher, Sergeant
John Gleuson, Sergeant
Charles Dahlgreen, Sergeant
Thomas J. Kelly, Sergeant
Andrew Cullin, Corporal
Joseph Parker, Corporal
 (sick since 3/31)
James Truka, Corporal
Patrick Norton, Corporal
Augustus E. Bellows, Trumpeter
Patrick Goings, Farrier
Vernon Droninburg, Blacksmith
Edward H. Droege, Saddler
John Burke, Private
William Bethon, Private
William J. Brown, Private
Joseph Benson, Private
James H. Bennett, Private
James Carney, Private
Paul Crowley, Private
George Dresden, Private

John Droege, Private
 (sick in hospital since 3/31)
Edward Eagan, Private (sick)
Frank Fergargreen, Private
Charles Fersch, Private
Thomas Fillinger, Private
John M. Fluschman, Private
Norman Fielder, Private
Howard Fuller, Private
Henry Griefield, Private
Theodore Gouget, Private
William Holland, Private
William E. Hood, Private
Henry W. Hulin, Private
Michael Himmelsbaugh, Private
Thomas Hamilton, Private
James Jameison, Private
Edward Kelly, Private
John Kelly, Private
Edward Langley, Private
William Ludlow, Private
Henry Luhring, Private
George H. Maitland, Private

Names of Troops in the Campaign

Andrew Mulaskey, Private
Paul Newport, Private
George Odbert, Private
August Richert, Private
George Schneider, Private (killed)
James Smith, Private
Robert B. Selfridge, Private
William Studley, Private
Jonathan R. Southwick, Private
Warren C. Tasker, Private
Frank N. Taylor, Private
William F. White, Private

The total of officers and men in the campaign was fifty-six. Colon Auger, first lieutenant of the company, and James N. Allison, second lieutenant of the company, were absent on detached service. Five enlisted men were also on detached service. Captain Egan noted that "the company lost as follows, Killed Private George Schneider, Wounded, Farrier Patrick Goings, Private John Droege and Private Edward Egan. Horses killed 2 wounded 7." Six of the wounded horses were abandoned and shot by order on the return march to Fort Fetterman. The company marched for Fort Laramie by way of La Bonte and Horseshoe creeks. Privates Edward N. Langley and James Smith were discharged April 1, 1876, on surgeon's certificate of disability. Private Howard Fuller deserted at Fort Laramie on April 17, and Private Frank N. Taylor deserted at Cheyenne while on a seven-day pass. Thirty-five horses were reported serviceable, and eight horses were unserviceable. Forty-six certificates of disability were issued during the two-month period, and the three men reported sick on April 30 included the two wounded privates, John Droege and Edward Eagan. Seventeen men had enlisted less than one year before the battle.

COMPANY E, THIRD CAVALRY

J. B. Johnson, First Lieutenant
Jeremiah Foley, First Sergeant
Edward Glass, Sergeant
Alexander Reardon, Sergeant
Frank P. Secrist, Sergeant
Morgan B. Hawks, Sergeant
Graefe Neurohr, Sergeant
James Montgomery, Corporal
Edward McKiernan, Corporal
William Miller, Corporal
Evan S. Worthy, Trumpeter
George Hapstetter, Trumpeter (sick)
Samuel Stanley, Farrier
George Hauerwas, Blacksmith
Peter Jansen, Saddler
Christopher Ayers, Private
Edwin F. Ambrose, Private
Daniel Akley, Private
John Beatts, Private

Henry Burton, Private
Michael Brannon, Private
Joseph Budka, Private
Joseph Carley, Private
James Conway, Private
William H. Clark, Private
Henry Collins, Private
Charles Cunningham, Private
Andrew Dolfer, Private
Patrick J. Dowling, Private
Richard Dillon, Private
John S. Davis, Private (sick)
Malachi Dillon, Private
James Devine, Private
Peter Dowdy, Private
   (killed March 17, 1876)
Orlando H. Duren, Private
George D. Damon, Private
John Foley, Private
Thomas Ferguson, Private
Louis S. Grigsby, Private
Michael Glannon, Private
Patrick Hennessy, Private
Patrick Hallahan, Private
Henry Harold, Private (sick)
Marcus Hansen, Private (sick)

William G. Hill, Private
Bernard Kelly, Private
Thomas Lloyd, Private
Edward Lavelli, Private
Allen Lupton, Private
William C. C. Lewis, Private
John Langan, Private
Thomas McNamara, Private
Thomas Nolan, Private
Robert Naughton, Private
Joseph Patterson, Private
Henry Perkins, Private
William Pease, Private
James H. O'Neil, Private (sick)
James Quinn, Private
William Rice, Private
Daniel C. Rass, Private
John J. Ready, Private
William Schubert, Private
Patrick Scully, Private
Alexander Shore, Private
Benjamin Slater, Private
Daniel Timmey, Private
John Tomamichael, Private
Charles N. E. Williams, Private

The total of officers and men in the campaign was sixty-nine. Captain Alexander Sutorius was under arrest for excessive drinking. First Lieutenant George E. Ford was absent on sick leave, and Second Lieutenant Henry R. Lemly was on leave of absence. No wounded were listed in the company, but there were five men sick at the date of the report, and twenty-two certificates of disability had been issued. Privates Patrick Hallahan, Charles Cunningham, and Benjamin F. Slater all deserted in April. There were fifty-one serviceable horses and six unserviceable horses reported. Lieutenant Johnson gave a summary of the campaign: "Private Peter Dowdy was shot through the head and killed instantly. One public horse . . . dropped dead from exhaustion on march near Clear Creek WT March 8th. One public horse . . . had to be abandoned and was

Names of Troops in the Campaign

ordered to be shot on account of exhaustion on march near mouth of Crazy Woman's fork and Powder River WT March 19, 1876. One public horse . . . had to be abandoned and was ordered to be shot near Sage Creek WT March 26th 1876, said horse having utterly given out and unable to proceed any further. One public horse . . . had to be abandoned and was ordered to be shot on march between Sage Creek and Fort Fetterman March 26th, 1876, on account of exhaustion. One public horse . . . died at picket line of the company during the night of March 26th, 1876, near Fort Fetterman WT on account of exhaustion." Twelve men had enlisted in the company during the past year.

COMPANY F, THIRD CAVALRY

Alexander Moore, Captain and Brevet Major
Bainbridge Reynolds, Second Lieutenant
Michael A. McGann, First Sergeant
Thomas Hackett, Sergeant
David Marshall, Sergeant
John Warfield, Sergeant
Robert Emmet, Sergeant
Frank Rugg, Sergeant
John Gross, Corporal
Dennis Giles, Corporal
John Kohn, Corporal
John Fry, Corporal
Arthur N. Chamberlin, Trumpeter
Richard O'Grady, Farrier
Avirus D. Varney, Blacksmith
Jeremiah Murphy, Saddler
Fred Adams, Private
Spencer Bates, Private
John Berry, Private
Otto Brodersen, Private
Henry Carson, Private
William Chambers, Private (sick in hospital)
Thomas S. Clougher, Private
David Cochran, Private (sick in Fetterman hospital)
Thomas Cramer, Private
Samuel Cupp, Private
Charles T. Decker, Private
Charles Dennis, Private
Peter Dyke, Private
Michael T. Donahue, Private
Frank W. Estabrook, Private
William Featherly, Private
Edward Glasheen, Private
Joseph A. Gould, Private
John Hecker, Private
Frederick Hershler, Private
Julius Jansen, Private
Peter Jones, Private
John W. Jordan, Private
Henry Kett, Private
John Lannen, Private
David Lindsay, Private (sick)
Robert Livingston, Private

Richard Lynch, Private
Patrick Lynch (sick in hospital)
Michael I. McCannon, Private
  (killed in action Mar 17th)
Oliver Meservey, Private
John Meyer, Private
Jay Mohr, Private (sick in hospital)
James Moran, Private
William Mulry, Private
James T. Murphy, Private
John Murphy, Private
Michael McGraine, Private
Frank McNeal, Private

Alexander Noteman, Private
Gerald J. O'Grady, Private
Michael O'Hearne, Private
Charles E. Richards, Private
Gilbert Roe, Private
Ferdinand Rutten, Private
Albert Salice, Private
John Semple, Private
John Staley, Private
John Tischer, Private
Phineas Towne, Private
Charles R. West, Private
Francis Woltering, Private

The total number of officers and men in the campaign was sixty-eight. First Lieutenant A. D. Bache Smead was absent on leave. Five men were sick in the hospital at the date of the muster roll. No wounded were reported, but fourteen certificates of disability had been issued during the two-month period. Forty-two horses were serviceable, but eight were reported unserviceable. This company with sixty-eight men must have lost many horses during the campaign as it had a total of only fifty on April 30. Twenty-nine men, almost half of the company, had seen service for less than one year.

COMPANY M, THIRD CAVALRY

Anson Mills, Captain
Augustus C. Paul, First Lieutenant
Frank S. Rittel, First Sergeant
Charles Kaminsky, Sergeant
  (sick in quarters)
Frank V. Erhard, Sergeant
Henry Prescott, Sergeant
Franklin B. Robinson, Sergeant
Alexander B. Ballard, Sergeant
John A. Kirkwood, Corporal
John H. Boyce, Corporal
Elmer A. Snow, Trumpeter
  (sick in hospital)

Frank Serfas, Trumpeter
Albert Glavinski, Blacksmith
Charles H. Sindenberg, Saddler
Lorenzo Ayers, Private
Ernest Bliss, Private
Myron P. Boyce, Private
Henry Badgery, Private
Bernard F. Cullen, Private
Charles S. Chamberlin, Private
Henry E. Curley, Private
Isaac H. Drake, Private
Dennis I. Duggan, Private
George W. Delmar, Private

Names of Troops in the Campaign

William Dillon, Private
  (sick in hospital)
Bernard Deringer, Private
John E. Douglas, Private
Henry I. Emptage, Private
Gilbert Exford, Private
George Foster, Private
John A. Foster, Private
Joseph Gilmore, Private
Matthew Grappenstetter, Private
Peter S. Hogeboom, Private
James Hopkins, Private
Charles S. Hicks, Private
Isaac S. J. Kelton, Private
Edward Larkin, Private
Dennis M. Larkin, Private
Hugh H. Massy, Private
Patrick McGuire, Private
Timothy McCarthy, Private
Jeremiah Murphy, Private
Albert Merganthaler, Private
William McGinnis, Private
Joseph W. Morgan, Private
James B. Miller, Private

Charles O'Donnell, Private
Thomas I. O'Keefe, Private
Adam Pringle, Private
William H. Reynolds, Private
George Raab, Private
Isaac C. Renear, Private
Fred Shuttle, Private
Blasius Schmalz, Private
Joseph Schmidt, Private
James Shavely, Private
George Sheehan, Private
  (sick in hospital)
Robert Smith, Private
William Scarlett, Private
John M. Singer, Private
Thomas Sheridan, Private
John I. Stevenson, Private
John Sweeney, Private
Robert C. Thornhill, Private
  (sick in hospital)
Charles E. Tredick, Private
Soren O. Very, Private
Joseph Walzer, Private

There were sixty-eight officers and men in the campaign. Second Lieutenant Fred Schwatka was absent on leave. Private Lorenzo Ayers was killed, and Sergeant Charles Kaminski was wounded above the right knee joint. Private Ernest Bliss was given a medical discharge April 11. Ten certificates of disability had been issued during the two-month period. Fifty-four horses were listed as serviceable, and five were unserviceable. Five men were still sick by the date of the report, but their illnesses may not have resulted from the campaign. Twenty men had enlisted less than a year prior to the campaign.

Appendix B OFFICIAL REPORTS OF THE BATTLE

THIS appendix includes copies of all of the official reports of this battle on Powder River, except lengthy ones by Dr. C. E. Munn, which are now in the files of the National Archives. The telegraphic report by General Crook from old Fort Reno on March 22 appears elsewhere in this book, but his official report of May 7, 1876, is included below. Colonel Reynolds' report is followed by those of Captain Anson Mills and Lieutenant J. B. Johnson. Captain Henry E. Noyes made a report on behalf of his company, but no report by Captain Egan has been found in the National Archives. He is the only company commander whose official report is missing. Paymaster T. H. Stanton filed a report and enclosed with it the reports of Captain Alexander Moore and Lieutenant William Rawolle. After the controversy developed, Lieutenant Rawolle filed another supplementary report dated April 19, 1876, and Captain Moore filed his report of April 29, 1876, pursuant to order of General Crook. These reports as set forth here are exact copies of the originals.

OFFICIAL REPORT OF GENERAL GEORGE CROOK

Headquarters Department of the Platte

May 7, 1876

To the Assistant Adjutant General,
Military Division of the Missouri,
CHICAGO, ILLINOIS,
SIR:

For a long time it has been the opinion of well informed men that the principal source of all the depredations committed by Indians along the

Official Reports of the Battle

line of the Union Pacific Railroad, has been in the camp of certain hostile bands of renegade Sioux, Cheyennes, and the other tribes who have roamed over the section known as the Powder, Big Horn and Yellowstone country.

Having the run and many of the privileges of the reservations where those of these tribes, who are supposed to be at peace, are located, and enjoying immunity from any restraint upon their movements, they have been able to procure arms and ammunition, and whenever any important raid was contemplated, reinforcements from the restless young warriors on these reservations, thus inflicting incalculable damages to the settlements upon which their raids have fallen.

To correct this and remove the principal cause, the Interior Department caused these hostile bands to be notified that they must come in upon the reservation set apart for them by a certain date, January 31st, current year, or thereafter be considered and treated as hostiles.

The date of which they were allowed to accomplish this movement having arrived and the bands notified having treated the summons with the utmost contempt; acting under the instructions of the Lt. Gen. Commanding, I commenced operations against them in March, with a detachment of troops known as the Big Horn Expedition.

The object of this expedition was to move during the inclement season by forced marches, carrying, by pack animals, the most urgent supplies, secretly and expeditiously surprise the hostile bands and if possible chastise them before spring fairly opened, and they could receive as they could always do in summer, reinforcements from the reservations. The number of hostiles being largely augmented in summer, while in winter the number is comparatively small.

The campaign was up to the moment our troops entered the large camp on the Powder River, on the 17th of March, a perfect success, the Indians were surprised, the troops had their camp and about 1000 ponies, before the Indians were aware of their presence, or even proximity. Of the mismanagement, if not worse, that characterizes the actions of portions of the command during the skirmish that followed, and its movements for the following 24 hours, it is unnecessary to speak, as they have been made the subject of serious charges against several officers notably the immediate commander of the troops, Col. J. J. Reynolds, 3rd Cavalry.

The failures however may be summed up thus, first, a failure on the part of portions of the command to properly support the first attack.

Second, a failure to make a vigorous and persistent attack with the whole command. Third, a failure to secure the provisions that were captured for the use of all the troops instead of destroying them. Fourth, and most disastrous of all, a failure to properly secure and take care of the horses and ponies captured nearby all of which again fell into the hands of the Indians the following morning. The success may be summed up thus: 1st a complete surprise of the Indians and second the entire destruction of their village, with their camp equippage and large quantities of ammunition. The undersigned accompanied the expedition, not as its immediate commander, but in his capacity as Department Commander, for several reasons, chief of which may be mentioned, that it had been impressed upon him and he had almost come to believe that operations against these Indians were impossible in the rigors of this climate during the winter and early spring and he wished to demonstrate, by personal experience, whether this was so or not.

When the attacking column was sent to surprise the village, the Department Commander having given the immediate commander ample instructions as to his wishes, did not accompany it, but remained with the train to guard to the end that the command might not be embarrassed by any division or appearance of such on the field, and the commander himself might feel free from all embarrassment that he might otherwise feel if the Department Commander were present.

My instructions being to take the horses and ponies which I was certain they should capture and from them remount my command, and with the supplies recaptured push on and find whatever other force there might be.

The failure therefore to properly secure the captured horses rendered a further prosecution of the campaign at this time abortive and the expedition returned reaching Fort Fetterman on the 26th of March. Attention is respectfully invited to copies of the report of Col Reynolds commanding the expedition, with sub reports and accompanying papers delays in receipt of which have caused my delay in forwarding this. I am, sir,

      Very Respectfully your obedient servant,
         GEORGE CROOK,
         Brig Gen Commanding

Official Reports of the Battle

OFFICIAL REPORT OF COLONEL JOSEPH J. REYNOLDS

FORT D. A. RUSSELL, WY TY.
April 15, 1876.

Assistant Adjutant-General,
Department of the Platte,
OMAHA, NEB'.
SIR:

I have the honor to submit the following report of the operations of the "Big Horn Expedition" which left Fort Fetterman on the 1st March and returned to the same point on the 26th March, 1876.

The expedition was commanded by the Department Commander Brigadier-General George Crook, immediate command of the troops being assigned to the undersigned. The command consisted of 10 Companies of Cavalry 2 Companies of Infantry organized into six battalions as follows:

Battalion	Co'	Regiment	Commanders	Pack Train
1st	M	3rd	Captain A. Mills	
	E	Cavalry	3' Cavalry	McAuliff.
2nd	A	3rd	Capt Wm Hawley.	
	D	Cavalry	3' Cavalry	Closter.
3rd	I	2nd	Capt' H. E. Noyes	
	K	Cavalry	2' Cavalry	Foster.
4th	A	2nd	Capt' T. B. Dewees	
	B	Cavalry	2' Cavalry	Young.
5th	F	3rd Cavalry	Captain Alex Moore,	
	E	2nd Cavalry	3' Cavalry	Delaney.
6th	C	4th	Captain E. M. Coates,	
	I	Infantry	4th Infantry	

Assistant Surgeon, C. E. Munn, U. S. A.
Acting Assistant Surgeon C. R. Stephens.
Acting Assistant Surgeon John Ridgely.
1st Lieutenant G. A. Drew, 3rd Cavalry, A.A.Q.M. and A.C.S.
2' Lieutenant C. Morton, 3rd Cavalry, Adjutant
2' Lieutenant J. G. Bourke, 3' Cavalry, Aide-de-Camp, accompanying General Crook.

32 Scouts and Guides and 3 Herders.

Mr. R. E. Strahorn of Denver accompanied the command as Correspondent of the *Rocky Mountain News,* newspaper of Denver Col.' At Fort Fetterman before starting out the Department Commander organized the scouts with Major T. H. Stanton, Paymaster, U.S.A. as Chief of Scouts.

Making a total of

Commissioned	30
Enlisted	662
Scouts, Guides and Herders	35
5 pack trains, Chief Packer and employees	62
Wagon Train employees	89
Ambulance employees	5
Aggregate	883

The command left Fort Fetterman with the above aggregate of persons and Wagons, all kinds, including ambulances — 85

Public Horses — 656

Public mules, including pack mules and mounts of employe's Scouts and Guides — 892

rationed for forty days; meat two thirds beef on the hoof one third bacon and 200,000 pounds of grain.

Miles (By Odometer)

March 1	The command made Sage Creek and encamped, water in detached pools, no wood but sage brush General Course N W	16
March 2	Made South Cheyenne, wood and water abundant, one of the cattle herders was shot here by two Indians during the night and his horse captured. The horse was subsequently recaptured at Crazy Horse's Village. The Cattle stampeded towards Fetterman and were not recovered. General Course nearly N.	13
March 3	Made N Cheyenne or Wind River. Wood and water. Water not very good and wood not abundant. Course nearly N. Slightly W.	20
March 4	Made dry fork of Powder River. Wood and water the latter in holes and about the same quality as at last Camp Course N.W.	23

Official Reports of the Battle

March 5	Made Powder River and camped in bottom on right bank opposite old Fort Reno, Course N.W. Command fired into by Indians soon after dark one non commissioned officer of Company C, 4th Infantry slightly wounded in jaw. Intention of Indians apparently was to stampede some of our animals, but failing in an opportunity to do so, after exchanging many shots with our guards and pickets they retired. Number of Indians unknown. Total distance from Fort Fetterman to Powder River opposite Old Fort Reno by odometer. General Course N. W.	17 89
March 6	Made Crazy Woman's Fork of Powder River by odometer [27] wood and water, latter by far the best since leaving the North Platte. Course N. W.	27
March 7	The ten cavalry companies and mule pack train preparing for night march. Left Crazy Woman's at dark for Clear Fork of Powder River with pack trains, 15 days rations ½ rations of bacon. Marched all night by Indian trails over a very rough country reached Clear Fork at 5 A.M. on 8th. Course nearly N. Wagon train left at Crazy Woman's with Infantry battalion to return on 9th to Old Fort Reno and there await the return to that point of the remainder of the force.	35
March 8	Rested until 10 A.M. and made down Clear Fork and encamped. Course N. E. Stormy and very cold from 5 A.M. through the previous night march	5
March 9	Marched in snow storm at 10 A.M. over rough country by trail to Prairie Dog Creek. Very slippery and hard on animals. Course N. W.	14
March 10	Marched at 9 A.M. snow most of the day and chilly wind in our faces over rough country by Indian trail. Camped on Prairie Dog Creek near its junction with Tongue River. Fatiguing day on animals and men, crossed many bad arroyas, very slippery, and dangerous for men and horses. One accident reported, Corporal Moore, Co' D, 3rd Cavalry, horse fell on him. He was transported the remainder of the campaign on travois. Thermometer at 8 P.M. 13° below Zero. Course N. W.	22

March 11	Thermometer at 8 A.M. 23° below zero. Marched at 10 A.M. to Tongue River moved down that river and after crossing five times on the ice camped on left bank. Cut through ice two feet thick to reach water which was very fine. Course N.	8
March 12	At 8 A.M. thermometer 26° below zero and the end of graduation, mercury in bulb. Marched at 9:30 A.M. Down the valley of Tongue River crossing it eighteen times and making course N. E. Camp not good. Wood plenty. Grass indifferent and scarce. No wood from last camp for about fifteen miles	20
March 13	Marched at 9:30 A.M. and camped on Tongue River having made [12] Scouts picked up an Indian mule. Crossed Tongue River seven times. Scouts killed an old buffalo which the men cut to pieces with avidity. Old Indian camps along march today. Course N. W.	12
March 14	Marched at 9 A.M. very disagreeable cold wind and slight snow camped at 12:30 P.M. N. E.	10
	On left bank of Tongue River about ten miles above the mouth of Otter Creek and opposite the mouth of Red Clay Creek a dry fork of Tongue River from the east side. Crossed Tongue River three times. Scouts sent out towards Rose Bud and Yellowstone. Large Indian Camps today.	
March 15	Thermometer 10° below zero at sunrise. Command lay in camp today awaiting return of scouts who came in at 2:30 P.M. and reported no signs of Indians.	
March 16	Marched at 8 A.M. crossed to N. E. of Tongue River and moved up valley of Red Clay Creek over a high dividing ridge and down into the valley of Otter Creek, which was reached about 2:30 P.M. Course E slightly S	18
	The scouts in advance discovered on Otter Creek two Indians and gave chase but did not overtake them. It is believed that these two Indians did not see the command except the scouting party which was some distance in advance of the column.	

Official Reports of the Battle

CRAZY HORSE VILLAGE

General Crook was with the scouting party in advance on arriving in camp he informed me of the discovery of the two Indians and expressed the belief or probability that to follow back the trail by which those two Indians had come would lead to the discovery of other Indians or possibly a village. The General ordered that the command be divided into two parts, three battalions, six companies, to pursue by a night march, and the other two battalions, four companies, and all the pack trains, to remain in camp on Otter Creek over that night and follow on to Powder River the next day by a different route. I was to move with the six companies and the General to remain with the four and the train the column for the night march to take no supplies except a days rations of hard bread. The 1st, 3rd and 5th battalions were detailed for the night march. A portion of the guides and scouts including the principal guide Frank Gruard accompanied my column, the remainder staying with the General and trains. Major T. H. Stanton, Chief of Scouts, Lieutenant Bourke, Aide-de-Camp to General Crook and Mr Strahorn, Correspondent moved with the scouts. Assistant Surgeon C. E. Munn, U.S.A. moved with the column as Medical Officer. At 5 o'clock P.M. we marched under the guidance of Frank Gruard a separate guide being also assigned to each battalion to enable it to follow the trail of the scouts or preceding battalion in case they should become separated in traversing the rough country in our night march. The General's portion of the command was to unite with mine at the mouth of Lodge Pole Creek on Powder River the following evening. The night was favorable for such a march being cloudy, hazy, damp and cold; the moon not being above the horizon until very late and then giving but little light. The guides were obliged frequently to dismount and light matches in order to ascertain whether we were on the trail or to recover it when lost.

March 17. About 4 o'clock A.M. of the 17th we were within a few miles of Powder River. The command was then concealed in a ravine or arroya and the scouts were sent out to look for Indian signs. While waiting here for two hours the men suffered intensely from cold, the officers of the command being obliged to move about among their men and prevent them from falling asleep in which case they would almost certainly have been frozen to death as the ground was covered with several inches of snow and the weather very cold. At the dawn of day Frank Gruard returned and reported that a large Indian trail had been discovered. The other guides were to follow it up while he returned to report. The command at once moved forward after marching probably five miles, the sun being now some distance above the horizon, the party of scouts was seen ahead, the column halted and Frank sent ahead to ascertain whether anything had been discovered. He soon returned and announced the discovery of a large Indian Village on the left bank of the Powder River under or against a large mountain bluff separated from that on which we found ourselves by a ravine widening towards the River. This ravine was cut by irregular gulleys rendering the approach to the village after descending from the mountains very difficult. After getting an imperfect view of the village and questioning Frank Gruard as to the best mode of approaching it, I immediately made disposition for attack. Company K, 2nd Cavalry, Captain Egan, was selected to charge the village mounted using his pistols. Company I, 2nd Cavalry, Captain Noyes, mounted, was to drive off the animals that were seen grazing in the vicinity of the village. In this work the scouts under Major T. H. Stanton were to assist and retain general charge of the captured herd. Moore's battalion dismounted was to approach as near the village as possible without discovering themselves to the Indians and hold themselves in readiness to promptly and vigorously follow up the charge. The dismounted force was soon afterwards increased by Company M, 3rd Cavalry, Captain Mills, with orders to support Moore and co-operate in taking and holding the village. The nature of the ground over which these troops had to approach the village was wholly unknown and could not be ascertained with any degree of accuracy from the top of the mountain 1000 feet high, where we were and where directions in general terms had to be given. Mills was the Senior Captain in the command and my first intention was to hold his Battalion "M" and "E" 3rd Cavalry in hand and descend the mountain with it. I afterwards decided to increase the dismounted force and hence the order to Mills to dismount his own company and approach the village.

It was not possible to designate any precise positions for the dismounted troops to occupy. This was necessarily left entirely to their commanders with the general direction to conceal their men until the cavalry charge and then render their co-operation the greatest possible. Captain Mills descended the mountain, overtook Moore, passed to his right and approached as near the village as practicable without discovering his command to the Indians and all the dismounted men concealed awaited the cavalry charge. I succeeded in descending the mountain with the only remaining company, Johnson's, who experienced great difficulty in leading their horses down. I was then under the impression that we had been discovered by the Indians as I saw men in the small ravine or dry creek near the village and thought they were Indians. They proved to be our own dismounted men however who were concealing themselves in this ravine and beyond it behind a ridge awaiting the cavalry charge. Being assured then that we had not been discovered I signaled to Egan and Noyes to go ahead. They had been previously halted under the momentary impression that we had been discovered and would probably have to make new dispositions for attack. The surprise seemed to be complete. Egan charged that portion of the village towards the river using his pistols and there dismounted near the river bank and used his carbines.

As Egan struck the village, Moore fired a volley from his own company. Mills rushed into the village and at once opened fire. Moore's battalion also moved promptly into the village and took position therein with his left occupying the sandy bench overlooking the village and commenced firing. The Indians fled from the village and assumed positions behind rocks, trees etc and opened fire upon our line making it necessary that our position just taken should be strongly held by our troops to prevent the Indians from recapturing the village. Johnson's company was sent in temporarily to cut out ponies and having driven some 200 to the rear was halted and reformed. I rode forward to survey the ground and inspect the village more closely and was fully convinced from my inspection and the extent of the ground to be occupied that to hold the skirmish line until the village could be destroyed, would be for my force a heavy undertaking but I resolved to try it. Johnson was ordered to dismount, make a detail to destroy lodges and re-inforce Mills, who had already asked for him. This disposed of every available man, the horse holders holding eight horses and not a man was left as a reserve or for an unseen emergency. I determined to destroy the village and then resume the march for the mouth of Lodge Pole twenty miles distant up the river where I was to meet General Crook with the other portion of the command. Instructions to this effect were given to Mills and Moore and also to Egan who was about this time ordered to re-inforce Mills on the right with his available dismounted men.

Noyes and the scouts had dashed between the herds and the village and thence toward and across the river and cut out the animals that were grazing in that vicinity and driven them across the large ravine securing them on a plateau on the side of the mountain to our rear. Besides the herds thus cut out there were other herds of ponies which we saw from the mountain grazing beyond the village. The animals captured did not include more than half the number seen by us. Noyes was guarding the captured herd and I directed it to be moved into the river bottom behind a promontory and tending up the river believing I would have to call upon Noyes' company before we could get away from the village. I gave verbal orders in general terms to destroy the lodges by burning, and with them everything of value to the Indians. I found great difficulty in preventing the men from pilfering. They delayed the firing of the lodges to bring out robes and meat. I required them to throw these things down where they were and ordered that the destruction of the village be promptly made. I permitted the men who were at this work to retain a piece of meat when they should find any such amount as could be conveniently carried and directed them to throw the remainder outside the lodges and complete their destruction together with the ammunition etc, that might be found in them. I was most of the time, save one orderly, alone in the supervision and found great difficulty and delay in having my orders executed, the Company Officers being on the skirmish line. There was danger that the Indians now becoming bolder and stronger by creeping among the logs, trees, sage brush, rocks and willows which were found from one end of our line to the other, would pick off our men from concealed positions and where our return fire would not be as effective as theirs. After the lodges were destroyed our withdrawal was delayed some two hours in consequence of the great difficulty in getting our horses down from the mountain.

    Captain Mills made several appeals to me for reinforcements after I sent Egan to him, but I did not have a man to send I finally ordered Noyes to leave the herd in charge of the horseholders and with the remainder of his men dismounted to hurry to the front. At this time the horses from the mountain were on the flat having crossed the large ravine and were coming toward us. Some Indians discovering this crept along the rocks on the face of the mountain adjoining the village on the side furthest from the river and appeared on the plain attempting to cut off our horses. To prevent this I went in person to the horse holders of Egan's and Johnson's companies and ordered them to tie their held horses to trees, seize their carbines and run up on the plain and fire at the Indians. This was done under the immediate direction of Lieut. Morton and the Indians driven back thus averting what appeared to be great danger of a stampede of the horses of three companies. At this juncture Noyes arrived on the ground with his company dismounted and took a position in rear of the line up to this time held by Mills and Moore. These two battalions then withdrew and mounted and the command at half past one o'clock P.M. started up the Powder River for the mouth of Lodge Pole, Mills leading and Moore as rear guard. Noyes retired after the others and returning to his former position his battalion marched with the column. The captured herd was driven principally by the scouts under the direction of Major Stanton assisted by Rawolle's company which was in the rear. Anticipating difficulty in driving the herd I thought of shooting the animals but feared that I might require the ammunition for other purposes and on that account was deterred from killing them, but gave directions that all animals that were slow or troublesome to drive after the column started should be shot the more the better.

At sundown the head of our column reached the mouth of Lodge Pole the appointed place of meeting the General, the pack trains and fresh troops to guard our stock and give us relief. We had marched fifty four miles and fought four hours during the last 26 hours had no sleep during the previous night and in fact no rest during the previous 36 hours and march of 73 miles from the camp on Tongue River. The General and trains arrived about noon the following day.

Men and animals were completely exhausted. Orders were given the guards should be changed more frequently than usual that the men might get rest. The herd came in after dark; its strength I am unable to state, it was estimated all told 400 to 700 with usual proportion of young colts and mares with foal. Expecting an attack from Indians that night I did not deem it prudent to herd the captured ponies in among the cavalry horses. I consulted Frank Gruard and he assured me that he knew many of the ponies, that they were accustomed to graze along the river in that vicinity and that they would be found in the morning grazing up beyond our horses. Under these circumstances and to spare the men from two consecutive nights without sleep in addition to their other exertions, the herd was guarded only by the picket line which would have been quite sufficient if these guards had been ordinarily vigilant. From sheer exhaustion they were probably not so. During the morning of the 18th it was discovered that most of the ponies were missing. As no Indian was seen or heard by any one during the night the probability is that the ponies strayed away through the inefficiency of our pickets and were picked up by Indians lurking in the hills for an opportunity to recapture them.

There was no definite and reliable information as to the number of ponies or their locality and I deemed it inadvisable in the condition of our horses to attempt a long and doubtful chase after the ponies. In addition to my own judgment on this point I had in mind the repeated views of the Department Commander to the effect that he did not wish the stock broken down on this expedition having other service in view for it this summer.

Early in the morning of the 18th I took the precaution to send a party of scouts under the principal guide Frank to search for General Crook. They did not find the General; he arrived before their return. There were two points at which General Crook might strike the river besides the mouth of Lodge Pole. These points were according to Frank Gruard about ten miles from Lodge Pole, one below which we had passed the previous afternoon and the other above towards Reno. I expected him at any moment but gave orders to march up the river to change camp for grazing at 1 P.M. About 12 o'clock General Crook arrived having struck the river at the point below the mouth of Lodge Pole but not having camped on the river the previous night. His command had captured about sixty ponies. I reported to the Department Commander on his arrival an outline of the occurrences since we had separated from him. Total distance estimated from Crazy Woman's Fork where we left the wagons to the Crazy Horse Village on Powder River, by our route. 179 miles.

Our column followed the Department Commander and marched up Powder River. Encamped. On account of the difficulty and annoyance of driving and herding at night the captured ponies, with the approval of the Department Commander I ordered all in camp to be killed except such as were required for the scouts and a few cavalry remounts or to relieve the weakest horses. Indians were prowling around our camp tonight and fired several shots into us, about midnight but made no other demonstrations.

In all we killed 110 captured ponies and brought into Fetterman 96.

Casualties

Killed.   Private Peter Dowdy, Company E, 3rd Cavalry.
          Private Michael McCannon, Co F, 3rd Cavalry.
          Private L. E. Ayers, Co M, 3rd Cavalry.
          Private George Schneider, Co K, 2nd Cavalry.
Wounded. 1st Lieut' W. C. Rawolle, 2nd Cavalry (contusion on left leg from rifle ball).

Official Reports of the Battle

Sergeant Chas Kaminski, Co M, 3rd Cavalry.
Corporal John Lang, Co E, 2nd Cavalry.
Private John Droege, Co K, 2nd Cavalry.
Private Edward Eagan, Co K, 2nd Cavalry.
Farrier Patrick Goings, Co K, 2nd Cavalry.

Two of the killed Dowdy and Schneider were brought off the field and left on the Hospital ground, there being no available means of burying them or transporting them. The other two McCannon and Ayers, were not brought from the Picket line, nor seen by their Company Commanders at all when or after they were killed. The wounded who could not ride were brought away on travois partly improvised on the ground by the Surgeon and his assistants and partly taken from the village. In this manner they were safely but with great difficulty transported to the ambulance at Reno 101 miles.

The village consisted of 105 lodges or tepees, unusually large and well stocked with military supplies, powder, lead, caps, cartridges, saddles hatchets etc etc which were burned with the lodges. According to information derived from the scouts some of these Indians had quite recently been into the agencies and had there replenished their stock of military supplies. There is no doubt that Indians were killed and wounded but it is not possible to state the number with any certainty. From all the information that I have been able to obtain I believe I am justified in stating that the total destruction of this large and wealthy village of the Chief Crazy Horse is by far the heaviest blow that has ever been inflicted upon the Sioux Indians by our troops. While this report has been in process of preparation several letters have appeared in the newspapers from the correspondents with the expedition. These correspondents had no interviews whatever with me in relation to the things whereof they write. Their letters contain many mistakes and misrepresentations which I cannot go into the public prints to correct.

For my command and myself I invite the most rigid investigation. Under date of March 28, 1876, and April 5, 1876 I made application for a Court of Inquiry and I now respectfully repeat that application.

March 19. Marched at 7 A.M. up Powder River and camped just above the mouth of Crazy Woman's Fork. 21 miles.

March 20. Marched at 7 A.M. in snow storm made and camped on Powder River. Sent note to Captain Coates, 4th Infantry, Commanding

The Reynolds Campaign on Powder River

Camp at Fort Reno to move over to Fetterman side of River, wagons etc etc and go into camp there. 22 miles.

March 21. Marched at 6:30 made 30 miles in ten and a half hours over a very rough slippery road to old Fort Reno and found the wagon train guard etc all encamped on the right bank of the river. All in good condition and had not been disturbed during our absence. Total distance from Crazy Horse Village to old Fort Reno. 101 Miles.

March 22. Lay in camp opposite old Fort Reno to rest animals.

March 23, 24, 25 and 26th. Employed in marching from Powder River to Fort Fetterman over the same route by which we went out, last day marching thro' snow 3 to 5 inches deep and strong N. W. wind. Total distance from Fetterman to same point again by our route. 485 miles.

March 27. The expedition was dissolved; the three companies, 1 cavalry and 2 infantry, belonging to Fetterman reporting for duty there. The two Companies from Fort Laramie left for that post on 28th. The other seven companies of cavalry left on 29th for Fort D. A. Russell, and after encountering a heavy snow storm the last of them reached Fort D. A. Russell on the 6 April.

Recapitulation of Distances.

Fort Fetterman to Fort Reno	(Odometer	89
Fort Reno to Crazy Woman's Fork	(Odometer	27
Crazy Woman's to Crazy Horse Village	(Estimated	179
Village to Reno	(Estimated	101
Fetterman to Fetterman		485

Animals Lost

	Horses	Mules
Killed in action or died of wounds	2	
Killed or abandoned from exhaustion	58	32
	60	32

The accompanying map will exhibit the route passed over by the expedition.

The plan of Crazy Horse Village was drawn by Lieutenant Charles Morton, 3rd Cavalry. It is wholly from memory and pretends to give only a general view without aiming at accuracy.

Official Reports of the Battle

Herewith are submitted Memorandum sub-reports from 1 to 6.

> I am, Sir,
> Very respectfully,
> Your obedient servant
> J. J. REYNOLDS.
> Colonel, 3rd Cavalry.

OFFICIAL REPORT OF CAPTAIN ANSON MILLS

> Hdqrs 1st Battalion
> Big Horn Expedition
> FORT FETTERMAN WY T.
> March 27, 1876

Lt. Morton, Adjt. Big Horn Expedition,
SIR:

I have the honor to report the part taken by my command in the engagement with hostile Sioux Indians under Crazy Horse on the lower Powder River on the 17th Inst.

About seven A.M. being the second Batt in column the adjutant directed me to double up on Capt Moore's then leading, at the same time informing me that the guides had discovered a village of about 100 lodges.

I found the Expedition Commander and Capt Moore in consultation and on reporting for orders was informed that he was going to charge the village with Egan's pistols and take it with Moore's battalion, being second in command I ventured to remonstrate stating that Egan would just scare them and they would get away from us and asked that he let us all dismount and creep in among them, he replied that Egan had confidence in his pistols and that he thought he would wake them up. I then turned to the Adjutant and asked him to try, and persuade him from his course, but the Adjutant replied that he had already done so but would try again.

I returned to the Expedition Commander and asked what I should do, he replied to remain where I was as he should hold me for future developments. Moore's battalion, mounted, took a direction obliquely to the left as shown in the accompanying diagram, which I append for a better explanation, and Noyes continued to the front and when arriving at a deep ravine, at A I was ordered to follow with my own company only when the order was given me to dismount and follow and support

Moore and send back word whether I wanted Johnson and whether mounted or dismounted.

Moore was out of sight but I took the direction in which I had seen him go, directing the men to leave their overcoats en route where I left my own.

I soon saw Moore's battalion in position at B and on approaching him he motioned me not to come further towards him. I halted my men and went up to meet him, told him that I was ordered to support him, and asked him what he was going to do, he replied that he had a position that overlooked the village, within 150 yards of it and that when Egan commenced his charge he intended firing a volley into it, but that it was no use to bring my company up there as there was a deep impassable gorge in his front and it was impossible to get into the village that way.

I then went up to the top of the mountain with him where I had a full view of the village which appeared to me quite a mile distant. I told Capt Moore that it was utter folly to fire from there, that while I had no authority to give him orders it was our business to get into the village and that we should not fire until we were right amongst them, he replied that it was impossible to go around by his left and he had orders in no case to discover himself until Egan began his charge and as I had the same orders I saw nothing to do as we would be in plain sight if we attempted to move forward or to the right. I saw he had no intentions of going any further forward himself and he finally suggested that I take my company down the point of the mountain as far as I could without being discovered and as soon as Egan began his charge to get into the village as soon as possible and he would follow, to this I agreed and he promised me that he would not fire until he got near the village. Egan and Noyes soon appeared at D and Johnson with the Expedition Commander at M and although all were in full view apparently the Indians did not discover them until Egan who was in advance had crossed the creek and reached the mesa where he began his charge and I started double quick by the route as marked and while passing the ravine was astonished to hear Moore fire a volley over our heads.

I could not see Egan nor the village until I reached the middle of the mesa and when I did Egan was on the brink of the river in the willows at K dismounted and firing was going on, the village being still occupied by Indians.

My men commenced firing when the Indians fled precipitously firing wildly and the company deployed, marched through the village and formed on the extreme end from E to F.

Egan came up and formed his company from E to H dismounted and shortly Moore's battalion came up and formed from F to G with I thought a majority of his men on the mesa. On passing from the mesa bluffs to the village about 200 ponies came charging down through our line and were driven to the rear by Johnson.

I saw Gen Reynolds riding up the lower end of the village and met him about its center and reported to him that we had the entire village and that it was a large one, he ordered me to burn the lodges as quickly as possible and move out to a safer camp. I told him that it would take a long time to destroy it effectively especially the meat and there was much that would be valuable to the men and suggested that we make the village our camp, destroying that which was useless to us and carrying off with the pack trains the robes, meat and other valuables to this he assented and said that he would dismount Johnson and send him to report to me and that I could have the property separated and burn that which was useless.

Johnson soon reported and I told him to deploy his men on my company reserving a detail for the separation and destruction of the property calling some of the noncommissioned officers and men about me telling them that it was the purpose to camp there and giving orders about getting secure places behind trees and logs in order to repel a return attack.

There were perhaps 130 lodges great numbers of robes and saddles some lodges having as many as twenty each, some coffee and sugar, quantities of meat and much ammunition fixed and unfixed.

The Indians had taken their squaws and children up the side of the mountain and in the gorge in front and expecting a return attack as soon as they had placed them in security I looked about to see if everything was in order, when to my surprise the men and horses of Egan's company had disappeared except his first sergeant and perhaps eight or ten men who had clustered around a point near E and on looking to the left I saw that men were going to the rear with the robes. Then the Adjutant came with an order to destroy everything as quick as I could and that we would move to another camp. I then changed the order and went along the line ordering the men to remain and reproving those attempting to go to the rear with plunder. Gen Reynolds came again and was very indignant at the men who were plundering and ordered me to stop it. I tried hard and so did Lts. Johnson and Paul but despite ourselves some would slip out.

The General was impatient at the delay in the destruction when I explained the property was difficult to burn and the explosion of ammunition had rendered it dangerous. By this time I observed that a great portion of Moore's men had left their line and were forming a new line from F to L some remaining in the broken edges of the mesa bluffs and that Capt Moore had taken post in a clump of trees at L.

Seeing a Sergeant of his company and some ten or fifteen men going to the rear from near F I called on him not to go when he replied that he had been ordered to go for the horses.

Gen Reynolds then returned near the lower end of the village when I reported to him that Egan and Moore were not treating me right that Egan had entirely left my right and that Moore was falling back on my left, that it would take some time to destroy everything and that they ought to be made to hold their ground and that I had no command over them, he replied that we would talk about that some other time that Egan had done so well in the charge that he did not like to call on him for any more work, but that he would send me Noyes as soon as he could.

The Indians had been firing from the mountains but it was perfectly harmless and up to this time no one was hurt.

I sent Sergeant Kraminski Co M, with two men to destroy some lodges on the river brink near H when he was wounded by a shot from the willows near him, about this time Private Dowdy, Company E, was killed near F and some Indians were seen to come boldly down the mountain from U to G and at the same time Moore's few men that were left on the bluffs on a prolongation of my line and near F and at right angles to it, got up and deliberately fled down the line towards Major Moore. I called out for Gods Sake not to abandon the bluffs and called to Captain Moore that if he would keep the men in the bluffs he could get the Indians sure as they came down they were dancing about conspicuously and fearing that he might not hear me I sent Pvt Shore Co E, 3rd Cav. who returned with a message from Major Moore that he understood it and would attend to it. Seeing they did not go back and the bullets now coming close and low and low down from both flanks, I sent Lt Johnson to tell Gen Reynolds that Moore had fallen back that both our flanks were exposed and that unless I was supported I would have to fall back, at this time I think there was a gap from F towards C of 150 yards entirely unoccupied. Lt. Johnson returned with a message to the effect that Noyes would soon be up to support me, about that time I asked Lts. Morton and Bourke to carry for me the same message but received no answer.

About this time one of Egan's men was mortally wounded near E I ordered some men to carry him to the rear and sent a man for Dr Munn, and seeing Gen Reynolds coming up toward C, I went down to meet him, he saw them carrying him and asked how badly he was hurt. I told him I thought he was mortally wounded, he told me to ascertain if he were dead. I called to the Sergeant who said he was almost dead when the Gen ordered him left where he was.

On my return I went to Major Moore who with I think all his battalion officers and some twenty or thirty of his men were in a clump behind the trees near C. I told him that I thought that there were too many men and officers there that I had no right to give them orders and would not assume it but as a brother officer I asked him to come forward and to sustain my left to which he made no reply. About the same time I met Egan who said Mills if you want more men on your right I will send them. I replied that I certainly did and a short time before we retired eight or ten men came up and joined.

I sent Lt Johnson again with the same message and he returned with a reply that Noyes would soon relieve me and he soon appeared and formed line in rear of the village when I was ordered to retire to my horses near the creek. I was particular to go along the line and cautioned the men that we were going to retire those in front first and every man I thought moved out together. I was then ordered to mount my battalion and take the lead towards the mouth of Lodgepole and just as I had got mounted and was about to cross the river Blacksmith Glavinski came up and reported that Private Ayers was left wounded on the field. I turned to Gen Reynolds who was by me on his horse and reported to him and asked what could be done, he replied that nothing could be done and directed me to proceed. I called out a man and directed him to go with Glavinski to Major Noyes and report the facts to him and ask him in my name to try to recover him.

When about two miles on the march Private Murphy came riding up to me and reported that Ayers was scalped, stating that he, Ayers and Glavinski were near the point E when I ordered the retirement that immediately on rising Ayers was shot through the thigh breaking his leg that they tried to carry him off and while doing so he received another wound in his arm, when Glavinski went for more help but that he, Murphy, stayed with him until 6 Indians came right up on him and shot his carbine in two when he ran and immediately some 30 or 40 Indians arose out of the willows in his front and looking around he last saw Ayers with these six Indians dancing around him. Pvt Sheridan Co M and Sweeney Co E say that Pvt McCann of F Company [Private Michael McCannon] reported killed was left near the point E.

I went into the village about 9:30 A.M. and was relieved at 2:30 P.M. both officers of my battalion remained close with their men all the time and faithfully and courageously assisted me having the greatest opportunity neither brought a vestige of plunder from the field and the men mostly acted well all courageously, but some could not forego the temptation to plunder and carry to the rear which they saw going on all around them notably by the scouts. Some of the soldiers alleged that they had been detailed by officers to carry plunder to the rear and with some I had trouble in enforcing my orders to desist. One corporal in Company K Second Cav accompanied by a trumpeter, while a mortally wounded comrade was being carried to the rear refused to obey my order until I levelled my shotgun on him and threatened to kill him. I think Private Murphy should receive some recognition for his courage in remaining with Ayers. The foregoing is a plain statement of the incidents as they appeared to me I can't say that I have used the exact language of myself or others or represented exactly correct the topography but I have done the best my memory serves me.

I would respectfully call attention to the report of Lt. Johnson, commanding Company E 3rd Cavalry herewith enclosed.

Respectfully Submitted,
ANSON MILLS Capt 3rd Cav
Commanding Battalion

[*Attached to this report was a map of the battle area drawn by Captain Mills and containing the lettered reference points mentioned in the report. The sketch was sufficiently accurate to have been used in the court-martial proceedings against Colonel Reynolds*].

Official Reports of the Battle

OFFICIAL REPORT OF LIEUTENANT J. B. JOHNSON

Company E, 3d Cavalry,
FORT FETTERMAN, W. T.
27th March 1876

Capt. Anson Mills, 3d Cav'y.
Com'dg Bat-Big Horn Expedition
CAPTAIN

In obedience to your order I have the honor to make the following report.

On the morning of the 17th inst. in compliance with the orders of Expedition Commander, Co. "E", 3d Cavalry advanced upon the Indian village and drove therefrom and to the rear about three hundred ponies when I received an order from the Expedition Commander to dismount the Co. leaving one man to hold eight horses and proceed with it and report to you. Col. Reynolds in the meantime called for and received a detail from the Co., which under his direction destroyed lodges on the right side of the village near the willows. The company was distributed along the line occupied by "M" Company, and acted in concert with that Co., under your direction until finally withdrawn, firing at the Indians an average of upwards of sixty rounds of ammunition per man.

When I came on the line, Capt. Egan's Co. of the 2d Cavalry occupied your right and Capt. Moore's Battalion your left, subsequently during the engagement Capt. Egan's horses and apparently men were removed from the right, which point the Indians gained and fired upon us from.

Capt. Moore's command was apparently withdrawn from the original place occupied, for Indians boldly appeared and danced on the sage brush bench which he had occupied. Our line received the Indians fire from the right, front and left.

Twice you sent me with messages to Col. Reynolds the Expedition Commander. The first time you directed me to say to him that the Indians were on three sides of us and ask him for reinforcements—he replied that he had sent for Noyes and he would be up in a few minutes, that he was doing his best to get the horses down and then we would move away or words to that effect.

The second time you directed me to say to Col. Reynolds that Capt. Moore had fallen back that we were being fired on from three sides and that unless reinforced you must retire. I gave him this message, to which he replied in an ejaculatory manner "that isn't so" or "can't be so"—or words to that effect—and—"Here comes Noyes now to reinforce him." Capt. Noyes' Company was then advancing deployed toward the village. Soon after, Colonel Reynolds directed me to tell you to withdraw the battalion to their horses and to tell Capt. Noyes to bring his Co. out after we had withdrawn which I did. During the engagement which lasted about four hours the enlisted men of Co. "E", carried out their orders with coolness and promptness and without exception to my knowledge behaved well under fire.

If the lodges were not destroyed as rapidly as they might have been, the dampness of the material lodge skin and cloth—danger from powder explosions in the lodges and the change of orders in regard to them must account for it.

Private Peter Dowdy of Co. E, was shot through the head and instantly killed.

Very respectfully Your obedient servant
J. B. JOHNSON
1st Lieut. & Adj't. 3d Cav. Com'dg Co. E.

OFFICIAL REPORT OF CAPTAIN HENRY E. NOYES

Camp of Company I 2nd Cavalry,
on POWDER RIVER, March 1876

Lieut. Chas Morton, 3d Cav.
Adjutant Big Horn Expedition
SIR:

I have the honor to respectfully submit the following report of the operations of my company on the 17th instant.

While en route from Otter Creek at about 7 A.M., I was ordered from the rear of the column to the front and informed that we were near a village. On arriving at the head of the column, I was ordered with my company to go with Captain Egan's company, and run off the stock when his company charged the village. We led down through a very rough ravine, my company following (by file) close behind him, and at about 8½ A.M., found ourselves behind a low ridge, from the crest of which the tepees of the village were in plain sight and about 600 yards distant. Here both companies were halted long enough to close up and form column of twos—and twenty minutes or half an hour was spent in examining the ground over which the charges were to be made. (See concluding paragraph). When all was ready, we advanced in parallel columns, close together down a gentle declivity, at the bottom of which was a ravine thirty or forty feet deep, with bluff banks. As crossing it would probably delay us if both companies kept together, I kept to the left of the course taken by Company K which I joined on the opposite side, just as Captain Egan formed into line. I still kept in column of twos, with the head of my column on line with Captain Egan's company. We continued in this order until within a few hundred yards of the nearest tepees, when Company K charged and I turned the head of my column to the right which threw my company in rear of Captain Egan's. The shouting and shots which attended the charge stampeded the greater part of the Indian herd, which we ran up the river bottom half a mile or so above the village, from which point it was driven into the hills by the scouts and half-breeds and part of my Company.

I then sent the company in small squads to gather up straggling ponies. Lieut. Hall with a few men crossed the river and gathered up what was on that side and drove it over with the rest. When all had been collected I drove it into the hills, half a mile back from the river. Just as it was all together, I received an order to take it around a sharp point a mile above the village towards the mouth of Clear Fork. Before I could get it over the river, I received orders to hold it in the bottom just above the point and guard it there. Thinking this a good opportunity for my men to get something to eat, I had all but the guard unsaddle, and the men commenced cooking their coffee, they had hardly done so, when I was ordered to bring my company up dismounted for duty on the line in front of the village. The natural consequence of running off the stock was the scattering of my company, and when I arrived on the line I had only thirty five men, (the guard, nine men, had been left in camp), the rest of my company (six) were straggling but reported on the line within a short time after I arrived there. My company was detailed to relieve the men of the other companies then on the line, which it did; and, in about half an hour, in accordance with orders, we fell back slowly towards our camp.

I had requested and had been assured that my men should be covered by skirmishers, or something else, while saddling up, but on arriving at our camp we found ourselves virtually a rear guard and unsaddled, under an annoying fire from the Indians, a few of whom had followed us from their village. A part of Col Moore's squadron was halted at my camp and I was informed by him that he had been detailed as rear-guard, and that he would move on slowly and that I could get my place by passing him. The presence of Captain Egan's company of my own squadron assured me that although annoyed we could not be hurt much while saddling, we were so hurried out of our camp that Lieutenant Hall was obliged to saddle his own horse, his groom having been on the line with him, and both being among the last to cross the river. My command behaved well and suffered no casualties.

I have omitted to state that while delaying to examine the ground over which we were to pass in reaching the village, I sent Baptiste Pourrier (one of the scouts) to the crest of a bluff overlooking the village and river to satisfy myself as to the course of river above the village, and that he rendered valuable assistance by the manner in which he performed this duty.

I am, Sir,
Very Respectfully,
Your Obedient servant,
HENRY E. NOYES,
Captain, 2d Cavalry.

OFFICIAL REPORT OF PAYMASTER T. H. STANTON

OLD FORT RENO, WYO.
March 22, 1876

To the Adjutant,
The Big Horn Expedition.

SIR:

I have the honor to enclose herewith the reports of Companies "E", 2nd Calavry, and "F", 3rd Cavalry, (constituting the 5th Battalion of the Big Horn Expedition) of the part taken by them in the battle with Crazy Horse's band of Sioux Indians on the Powder River on the 17th of March, 1876.

I have nothing further to add except that every officer and man in the battalion did their duty.

Lieut. Rawolle commanding Co. "E", 2d Cavalry, handled his men with the greatest coolness and judgment, and the conduct of Lieuts. Sibley, Co. "E", 2d Cavalry and Bainbridge Reynolds, Co. "F", 3d Cavalry, was admirable in this their first action.

Official Reports of the Battle

We got in at 9: P.M. having driven the herd twenty miles from the scene of the engagement.

> Very Respectfully,
> Your Obed't serv't
> T. H. STANTON,
> Paymaster, U. S. A.
> Chief of Scouts.

FIRST OFFICIAL REPORT OF CAPTAIN ALEX MOORE

> OLD FORT RENO, WYO.
> March 22, 1876

To the Commanding Officer,
    5th Battalion Big Horn Expedition.
SIR:

I have the honor to submit the following report of the part taken by my company in the action of the 17th inst., on Powder River, with Crazy Horses band of Sioux Indians. My company was dismounted and took position within 400 yards of the village, waiting fully three quarters of an hour, being concealed behind a crest to await the arrival of the mounted companies which had been designated to cut out the ponies.

Believing that to move nearer the entire company might attract the attention of the Indians I detailed Sergeants Warfield and Emmet and six privates in connection with a detail from Co. "E" 2nd Cavalry, to get as near as possible to the village; and they succeeded in getting within 150 yards of it before the cavalry charge was made, about 9 o'clock A.M., and as soon as the mounted company had charged my company fired a volley into the village and charged on it, which compelled the Indians then engaged with the cavalry to retreat precipitately, abandoning their village.

My company then took position on the extreme right of the Battalion holding the Rancheria and destroying the property until 1:30 o'clock P.M., when it was withdrawn.

The Indians after leaving their village took refuge in ravines beyond the point the mounted companies had advanced to, and later in the day returned along the mountain side under the protection of rocks, trees and brush, firing with much effect.

Before my company was withdrawn everything in my vicinity was utterly destroyed. The men of the company did their full duty and displayed wonderful coolness and discretion in the use of their ammunition although exposed to an annoying fire for nearly four hours.

I have to report Private Michael I. McCannon killed.

In addition to the property destroyed in the village I have the honor to report that a number of ponies and mules belonging to the Indians were killed and wounded during the day.

> Very Respectfully,
> Your Obedient servant,
> ALEX MOORE
> Captain 3d Cavalry,
> Commanding Co. "F".

FIRST OFFICIAL REPORT OF LIEUTENANT WILLIAM C. RAWOLLE

OLD FORT RENO, WYO.,
March 22, 1876.

Captain Alexander Moore,
3d Cavalry, Comd'g 5th Battn,
Big Horn Expedition.
CAPTAIN:

In accordance with your verbal instructions to furnish a detailed report of the part taken by the Company I commanded (viz: "E." 2d Cavalry). in the action of the 17th inst., on "Powder River," I have the honor to submit the following. The proximity of a village had been reported by the scouts and you directed me to follow the guide "Frank" to such a point where it would become necessary to dismount, your instructions to me being to wait for a charge by Captain Egan's Company, "K", 2d Cavalry, who was detailed to cut out the pony herd of the Indians, when my Company as part of your Battn was to make the attack (dismounted).

I found that the guide was mistaken as to the exact locality of the village so that it became necessary to advance some distance farther—position was finally taken within 400 yards of the village, the Company concealed behind a crest to await the charge of the mounted company, which had been designated to cut out the ponies. A knoll being about 150 yards still nearer the village, I detailed Sergeant Gilbert with four men to occupy it in connection with a detail of your own company. As soon as the mounted company began the charge I advanced with my company and took position on the extreme left of our line as you had directed.

Official Reports of the Battle

I judge that this was about 9 A.M.

The Indians after leaving their village took refuge in ravines beyond the point the mounted company advanced and returned along the mountain side under the protection of rocks, trees and brush firing with much effect. I held the position indicated until ordered to withdraw, (at about 1 P.M.) at which time the village and stores of the Indians had been utterly destroyed.

During the engagement Corporal Lang of the company was wounded in the ankle, the bone being shattered. A number of ponies were killed by the company, that were clambering up the mountain side, and which it was difficult to overtake. 1st Sergeant Land, Serg't Howard and Private Douglas whom I had detailed for the purpose also cut 15 or 20 ponies under severe fire. The ponies were ultimately driven in.

Lieut. Sibley distinguished himself for his coolness and energy. Where the entire company did well, it is difficult to mention the names of those who are particularly deserving of credit, though I desire to call the attention of the Colonel Commanding to the names of 1st Sergeant Land, Serg't. Gilbert, Serg't. Howard, Corporal Lang and Privates Vane and Douglas.

The Battalion being relieved by Captain Noyes, Company "I" 2d Cavalry, I mounted my company and halted on the east bank of the stream waiting for Captain Noyes to pass beyond the Battalion, when my company became rear guard. I remained back with a small skirmish line. The Indians made a feeble effort to molest us for a very little while without any result.

                              Very respectfully,
                              WILLIAM C. RAWOLLE
                              1st Lieut. 2d Cavalry
                              Commanding Company E.

SECOND OFFICIAL REPORT OF LIEUTENANT WILLIAM C. RAWOLLE

                              In Camp at
                              FORT D. A. RUSSELL, WYO.
                              April 19th 1876.

Colonel J. J. Reynolds

Recently commanding "Big Horn Expedition."

COLONEL:

Having seen a newspaper report published by an officer of the pay department, who accompanied our expedition in the nominal capacity of "Chief of Scouts" which report has been copied in several other papers of the country and reflects upon the battalion to which I belonged, I desire to make this additional report, that the battalion Moores (though I only mean to speak for my portion of it) obeyed the spirit of the order you communicated, as conveyed to me, and I desire to bring to your notice the fact, that I was the only officer of the entire command who was injured by a rifle ball of the enemy. The medical officer desired to put me on his list of injured, but I would not permit it, as the matter was too trifling. I state this fact now, that mention may be made of it in the proper reports, in order to contrast the mischief created in manufacturing public opinion in newspapers. If the Chief of Scouts, paymaster and Tribune Correspondent had wanted Indians he need only have staid with the battalion in question.

Very respectfully your obdt servt
WM C. RAWOLLE
1st Lieut 2nd Cav. Comd'g Co E

1st endorsement FORT D. A. RUSSELL, WYO.
April 20, 1876.

Respectfully forwarded to Col. J. J. Reynolds, 3 Cav. recently commanding Big Horn Expedition.

A. MOORE Capt. 3rd Cav.
Recently comd'g 5 Battalion Big Horn Expedition

SECOND OFFICIAL REPORT OF CAPTAIN ALEX MOORE

CHEYENNE, W. T. April 29, 1876.

Asst. Adjutant General,
        Dept. of the Platte, Omaha, Neb.

SIR:

In accordance with the requirement of your letter of the 25th inst., I have the honor to submit the following report of the part taken by myself in the action of 17th of March, on Powder River, against hostile Indians.

The scouts discovered a village in the valley of Powder River about 7 o'clock on the morning of the 17th and the fact was immediately communicated to General Reynolds, commanding the troops, by myself. Arrangements for attack were made at once, the scouts being detailed to

Official Reports of the Battle

lead the way for the mounted column down through the bluffs towards the river, and to assist Capt. Noyes in cutting out the herd.

Capt. Egan, with his company, was ordered by General Reynolds to charge the village on the right or upper side, and Capt. Moore, with his battalion dismounted, was ordered to proceed along the bluffs to the left or lower side of the village, and obtain a position covering it's rear, opposite that from which Egan was to enter. I dismounted and proceeded with Capt. Moore's battalion, whose course was along the bluffs parallel to the river. When the battalion had reached a point about one thousand yards from the village, still being on the upper side, it halted and took position on the brow of a ridge. I went to Capt Moore and protested that this was no place for his command, that he could do no good there, and that the Indians would all escape if he remained there. He paid no attention to my remonstrance. I then spoke to 1st Lieut. W. C. Rawolle, commanding the other company of the battalion, using somewhat similar language, to which he replied, "I know this is not the place for this battalion, but you see I am not in command."

I then left the battalion, starting in the direction it should have gone. A few steps in front of the command I saw in some bushes, Sergeant Gilbert, of Company E, 2d Cavalry, with four men. I told him to take his men and come with me. He did so, and a few minutes later Lieut. F. W. Sibley, 2d Cavalry, left the battalion and came and joined me. We crossed the ridges in the direction of the position assigned to the battalion, and reached a point from which we could fire on the Indians as they ran out of the village, which they began to do as soon as Egan charged.

At the same time the charge was made we advanced towards the village, and after expending considerable ammunition upon the Indians, as they ran by us, entered it. Moore's battalion, which had come down the bluffs above and to the right of the village, entered it from the same direction with Egan, instead of the opposite.

Some of the scouts went into the charge with Egan, and afterwards helped to destroy the village. About 2 P.M. orders were given by General Reynolds for the command to retire, and proceed as rapidly as possible up Powder River, and the troops began to move accordingly. The captured herd, which consisted of between 700 and 800 ponies, was held by Capt. Noyes, and some of the scouts at a point about a mile above the village. As I saw the command leaving, I inquired if anyone had orders to bring away these animals, but could find no one who knew anything about it. I then sent an orderly to overtake General Reynolds and inquire if he had any orders concerning the herd. The orderly returned with a reply from General R. that I "could kill as many of the animals as I pleased," but he did not direct me to bring it away, neither did he charge anyone else with this duty so far as I could learn. He had also taken several of the scouts with him as guides, and as the whole number consisted of fifteen, I had only six or seven left to help drive the herd. With these, however, I determined to try to get it away, and started it up the river in the direction Gen. R. was going.

Capt. Moore's battalion was ordered to be rear guard. Sometimes I would be able to get the herd ahead of him, and frequently it was behind. Experiencing considerable difficulty in getting it along, I applied to Capt Moore for a detail from his battalion to assist in driving it. He declined to furnish it, however, stating that his men and horses were very tired.

An hour before we reached the point where General Reynolds had camped, the battalion had gone by me, and there was no one behind with the herd except the few men I had with me.

I believe a large number of Indians were killed and wounded, but I only saw two dead Indians myself.

Very respectfully,
Your Obedient servant,
ALEX MOORE,
Captain 3d Cavalry,
Comd'g 5th Battalion.

[*This interesting document was written in the handwriting of Captain Stanton but was signed by Captain Alex Moore. Most of it is the first person narrative of Captain Stanton, but the first part of the "Report" implicates Captain Moore in admitting that he was ordered to proceed along the bluffs to the lower side of the village and obtain a position covering its rear, but that instead of doing this, he halted behind the ridge one thousand yards from the village and refused to proceed farther. One wonders what the circumstances were surrounding the signing of this unusual report by Captain Moore*].

BIBLIOGRAPHY

(Major Sources Only)

1. DIARIES, LETTERS, GENERAL HISTORIES, GOVERNMENT RECORDS

Bent, George. *Letters to George E. Hyde.* Coe Collection, Yale University, New Haven, Connecticut.

Bent, George. *Letters to George E. Hyde,* Western History Department, Public Library, Denver, Colorado.

Beyer, W. F., and O. F. Keydal. *Deeds of Valor.* 2 vols. Detroit, Perrien-Keydal Co., 1903.

Bourke, John G. Diary. United States Military Academy Library, West Point, New York.

——. *On the Border with Crook.* New York, Charles Scribner's Sons, 1891. Reprint Edition, 1950.

Daly, Henry W. *Manual of Instructions in Pack Transportation.* West Point, United States Military Academy Press, 1901.

DeBarthe, Joe. *Life and Adventures of Frank Grouard.* St. Joseph, Combe Printing Co., 1894. Reprint edition, Norman, University of Oklahoma Press, 1958.

Finerty, John F. *Warpath and Bivouac.* Chicago, Donohue and Henneberry, 1890.

Grinnell, George B. *The Fighting Cheyennes.* New York, Charles Scribner's Sons, 1915. Reprint edition, Norman, University of Oklahoma Press, 1956.

Heitman, F. B. *Historical Register and Dictionary of the U. S. Army.* 2 vols. Washington, D. C., Superintendent of Documents, 1903.

Hunton, John. "Diary." Ed. by L. G. Flannery, printed serially in the *Lingle* (Wyoming) *Guide-Review* beginning February 3, 1955.

Hyde, George E. *Red Cloud's Folk*. Norman, University of Oklahoma Press, 1937.

Marquis, Thomas B. *A Warrior Who Fought Custer*. Minneapolis, The Midwest Publishing Co., 1931.

———. *She Watched Custer's Last Battle, Her Story Interpreted in 1927*. Hardin, Montana, privately printed, 1933.

Mills, Anson. *My Story*. Washington, D. C., privately printed, 1918.

Records of the War Department, Office of Judge Advocate General, *Court Martial of Captain Henry E. Noyes*, RG 153, GCM PP 5473.

Records of the War Department, Office of Judge Advocate General, *Court Martial of Colonel Joseph J. Reynolds*, RG 153, GCM QQ 26.

Records of the War Department, Office of Judge Advocate General, *Court Martial of Captain Alexander Moore*, RG 153, GCM QQ 27.

Ricker, Eli S. *Interviews*. Lincoln, Nebraska State Historical Society, 1906, 1907.

Sandoz, Mari. *Crazy Horse*. New York, Alfred A. Knopf, 1942. Reprint edition, 1955.

Schmitt, Martin F. *General George Crook: His Autobiography*. Norman, University of Oklahoma Press, 1946.

South Dakota Historical Collections. Vols. 1, 14, and 15. Pierre, South Dakota.

Stewart, Edgar I. *Custer's Luck*. Norman, University of Oklahoma Press, 1955.

Vaughn, J. W. *With Crook at the Rosebud*. Harrisburg, The Stackpole Company, 1956.

Vestal, Stanley. *Warpath*. Boston and New York, Houghton Mifflin Co., 1934.

2. PERIODICALS

American Legion Monthly.
Annals of Wyoming.
Annuals, Association of Graduates of the U. S. Military Academy.
Army and Navy Journal.
Army and Navy Register.
Billings (Montana) *Gazette*.
Rocky Mountain News (Denver).
Winners of the West Magazine.

INDEX

Ackley (Acton), Pvt. Daniel: 95
Allison, Sen. William B.: 4
Allison commission: viii, 4, 6–7
"Alter Ego": 10, 13
"Apache": 14
Apache Indians: 13, 32, 36, 185
Aparejo: 36–39, 56
Arapahoe Indians: 4, 17, 21, 41
Ayers, Pvt. Lorenzo E.: 116–20, 177 187

Bear Buttes: 126
Bear Springs: 18
Bear Walks On A Ridge: 132
Beaver Creek: 134
Beckwith, Lt. Col. Amos: 172
Bed Tick Creek: 17
Bell mare: 33, 35, 38–39
Bent, George: 129–30
Berry, Gen. H. G.: 185
Big Foot: 190
Big Horn Expedition: 9, 25, 29, 75n.
Big Horn Mountains: 46, 49, 189
Big Horn River: 17, 20n., 124
Black Coal: 17
Black Crow: 42
Black Hills, Dakota Terr.: viii, ix, 3–4, 15–16, 44, 134n., 149n., 189
Black Hills council: 7
Blackfeet Sioux: 135
Black Kettle: viii
Black Twin: 126
Blue Earth country: 128, 134
Bolln, Henry: 23n.

Bordeaux ranch: 9, 18–19
Bourke, Lt. John Gregory: x, 14–15, 17, 19, 35, 40n., 41–42, 48, 51–52, 55–56, 60, 62, 72, 78n., 81, 103–104, 106, 111, 117, 121, 133, 140, 142, 151–54, 161–62, 164–65, 174, 185, 187
Box Elder Creek: 142n.
Bozeman Trail: vii, 9, 21–22, 43–44, 158
Bradley, Lt. Col. Luther P.: 167, 172
Bradley, L. T.: 16
Brady, Capt. George H.: 167
Brannon, Pvt. Michael: 95
Brazeau, Walter (Frank Grouard, "The Grabber"): 58
Brown, Lt. John R.: 44
Brown Springs: 44
Bryan (Bryant) Hosp. Steward W. C.: 27, 82, 122
Bubb, Capt. J. W.: 17
Buffalo Wallow: 46
Bull Bend of the North Platte River: 17
Bull Coming Behind: 129
Bull Eagle: 129
Bullocks' (Six Mile Ranch): 18
Burnham, Maj. Horace B.: 167, 169–70
Burton, Pvt. Henry: 95

Cain, Capt. A. B.: 21, 23–24
Camp Carlin, Wyo. Terr.: 15–16, 29, 30n., 159, 170
"Camp Inhospitality": 140
Camp McDowell, Ariz. Terr.: 175
Capps, Red "Arkansas": 23
Cargador: 33

Carlisle Barracks, Pa.: 14n.
Chadron, Neb.: 64–65
Chalk Buttes: 134
Chambers, Maj. Alexander: 12, 17, 163, 167, 174
Chambers, Mrs. Alexander: 12
Chase, Mr.: 12
Cheyenne Indians: vii, ix, 17, 123, 125–30, 132–35, 160, 180, 187, 189–90
Cheyenne River Agency: 129
Cheyenne village: ix, 123, 128, 182, 189
Cheyenne, Wyo. Terr.: 4–5, 7, 9–11, 15–16, 18, 24, 29, 160, 165, 168, 172
Chicago Times: 150n.
Chivington, Colonel: vii
Chugwater Creek (Chug): 10, 18–19, 80n., 142n.
Chugwater, Wyo.: 18
Cincha: 38–39
Clark, Lt. W. P.: 129
Clarke, Ben: 15, 40
Clear Fork of Powder River (Lodgepole Creek): 51, 61, 112, 154n.
Closter (Kloster), Richard "Uncle Dick": 29, 55–56
Coates, Capt. E. M.: 26, 46–47, 50, 154–55, 169
Coates, Capt. Lewis: 17
Collier, Capt. William L.: 167
Collins, John S.: 148n.
Commissioner of Indian Affairs: 7–8
Congressional Medal of Honor: 118–19
Connor, Gen. Patrick: 41
"Cook" (stenographer): 168
Coppinger, Capt. John J.: 167
Corona: 37, 39
"Crawler": 127
Crazy Horse: ix, 4, 29n., 58, 61, 74, 79, 100, 123, 126–30, 133–34, 179–80, 189
Crazy Horse village: 100, 129, 180
Crazy Woman's Fork of Powder River: 49, 154, 175–76
Crook, Brig. Gen. George: viii, ix, x, 3, 8, 9n., 10–17, 19, 24–26, 29–33, 35, 40n., 41–44, 46–47, 50–51, 58–62, 64–65, 72n. 75n., 80n., 90–91, 96, 99, 111, 138–39, 141–50, 152, 156–57, 159–66, 168–77, 179–85, 187, 189; telegraphic report, 156; official report, 200–202
Crook Crest, Oakland, Md.: 13n.
Cuney, Adolph: 72n.

Cunningham, Pvt. Charles: 95
Custer, Lt. Col. (Bvt. Maj. Gen.) George Armstrong: viii, 3, 32, 160, 162, 189

Daily, Mary Tapscott: 13n.
Dallas, Maj. Alexander J.: 167
Daly, Henry W.: 30n., 32n., 40n.
Davenport, R. B.: 171
Davis, Col. Jefferson C.: 172
Davis Ranch (Nine Mile): 18
DeBarthe, Joe: 58, 145n.
DeLaney, Edward: 30
Department of the Platte: 13, 29
Department of Texas: 25, 60
Dewees, Capt. Thomas B.: 17, 26, 60, 149–50, 174
Dewey, Miss L.: 16
Dirty Moccasins: 125n.
Douglas, Pvt. George E. "Pat": 94, 227
Douglas, Wyo.: 9
Dowdy, Pvt. Peter: 94–95, 116, 119–20
Drew, Lt. George A.: 16, 77, 111–12, 117, 139, 141, 153, 161, 174
Droege, Pvt. John: 120, 158
Dry Fork of Cheyenne River: 44
Dry Fork of Powder River: 46, 157
Dudley, Maj. Nathan A. M.: 167
Dull Knife: 125n., 182, 189
Dull Knife village, battle at: ix, 172, 182–83
Dye, Maj. William McE.: 20

Eagan (Egan), Pvt. Edward: 120, 158
Eagle Chief: 133
Ecofee, Jules: 40, 72n.
Egan, Capt. James "Teddy": 5, 7, 16, 22, 67, 69–70, 72–73, 75, 77–79, 81–90, 92–95, 98, 102, 104, 106, 108–109, 115–16, 122, 131, 136–37, 139, 152, 161–62, 172–76, 187
Ekalaka, Mont. Terr.: 134
Eldridge, Joe: 41
Elkhorn Creek: 11, 17, 22
Elk Warrior Society: 125n.
Emmet, Sgt. Robert: 86
Evans, Maj. Andrew W.: 167

Fagan Ranch: 18
Famished Elk: 125n.
Farnham, John: 41

Index

Ferris, Maj. Samuel P.: 155
Fetterman, Lt. Col. W. J.: 20
Fetterman Massacre:: viii
Finerty, John F.: 34n., 150n.
Flint, Col. Franklin F.: 167, 172
Foley, Sgt. Jeremiah: 95, 174, 185
Ford, Mr.: 16
Fort Abraham Lincoln, Dakota Terr.: 8
Fort Berthold, Dakota Terr.: 124
Fort C. F. Smith, Mont. Terr.: vii, 21, 43, 125
Fort D. A. Russell, Wyo. Terr.: 9, 15–16, 18, 121, 142n., 158–60, 166, 169–71
Fort Fetterman, Wyo. Terr.: viii, ix, 8–10, 15–18, 20–23, 27, 29, 40n., 41, 43–45, 54, 144, 152, 155–60, 162, 170–71, 181, 189
Fort Keogh, Mont. Terr.: 125n.
Fort Laramie, Wyo. Terr.: viii, 9, 12, 15–19, 40–41, 72n., 80n., 142n., 158–59, 170, 180
Fort McKinney, Wyo. Terr.: 58n., 142n.
Fort Phil Kearny, Wyo. Terr.: vii, viii, 21, 43, 125
Fort Reno, Wyo. Terr.: vii, 17, 21, 43, 46–48, 50, 67n., 120, 145, 147, 154–55, 157, 163, 173, 180–81
Fort Robinson, Neb.: 5, 40, 64, 123n., 129, 142n., 149n., 159
Fort Sanders, Wyo. Terr.: 75n.
Fort Yates, Dakota Terr.: 134n.
Foster, Mr.: 29
Fox Warrior Society: 125n.
Frandsen, Lucille: xi
Frandsen, Slim: xi
Fred Schwartz Ranch: 18
Furey, Maj.: J. V.: 29

Gall (Pizi): 124
Garnier, Baptiste (Little Bat): 41, 62, 72, 80n., 142, 145n.
Gibbon, Col. John: 8–9, 172
Gilbert, Sgt. Lewis: 74–75, 88, 174, 186
Giles, Cpl. Dennis: 116–17, 124
Glavinski, Blacksmith Albert: 116–19, 121, 174
Goings, Pvt. Patrick: 120
Goose Creek, Wyo. Terr.: 75n.
Gouget, Pvt. Theodore: 83
Grant, President U. S.: 7, 25, 148n., 149n., 172, 178, 188

Gringos, Louis: 62
Grinnell, George Bird: 123
Grouard (Gruard), Frank (Walter Brazeau): 40n., 41, 58, 62, 64–65, 67–68, 72, 74, 79, 81, 97, 99–101, 117, 127–28, 138, 141–42, 144–45, 159, 174, 179–80, 184

Hall, Lt. Christopher T.: 16, 88, 121, 137, 162, 168, 172, 187
Hamilton, Lt.: 14n.
Hanging Woman's Fork: 49
Hastings, James S.: 126
Hatchet Mountains, N. M.: 185
Hawley, Capt. William: 26, 60, 149–50
He Dog: 123n., 127–30
Henry, John: 23n.
Himmelsbaugh, Pvt. Michael: 174
Hog Ranch, Fort Fetterman, Wyo. Terr.: 22–23, 43, 158
Hooker, Bill: 23
Hooker, Gen. J.: 185
Horse Creek: 18
Horseshoe Creek (Cave Springs): 17
Hospital Point: 81, 86–87, 89, 93, 96–97, 102–103, 105, 109
Hospital Rock (Hospital Bluff): 89, 97, 104, 107–108, 110, 114, 116–17, 120, 136–37, 161, 168n.
Howard, Sgt. George S.: 94
Hunkpapa Indians (Uncpapa): 124, 130, 134–35
Hunter, Colon: 19
Hunton, John: 18–21, 23, 158
Huston, Lt. Col. Daniel, Jr.: 172
Hutchins, James S.: 28n.
Hyde, George E.: 129–30

Indian Bureau: viii, 64n.
Ingalls, Rufus: 185
Interior Department: 8
Inter-Ocean Hotel, Cheyenne, Wyo. Terr.: 15, 172
Iron Hawk: 128

"Jackass Brigade": 31
Jenkins, J. J.: 183
Jenkins, J. W.: 172
Jennesse, Charlie: 41, 72
Joe Creek, Wyo. Terr.: 154n.
Johnson, E. P.: 172

235

Johnson, Lt. John Burgess: 67, 73–74, 77–79, 81, 85–86, 88, 90–93, 95, 103, 105, 107, 117, 157, 161, 174, 185; official report, 221–22

Kaminski, Sgt. Charles: 94, 120, 158
Kate Big Head: 128
Kearny, Gen. Phil.: 26n., 185
Keeley, Joseph C.: 30n.
Kelley, Hi: 80n.
Kent, T. A.: 11
Killdeer Mountain, Battle of: vii, ix
King, Colonel John H.: 172
Kingsley, Pvt. William C.: 74

La Bonte Creek: 17
Lame Deer, Mont. Terr.:, battle at: 189
Land, Sgt. William: 94–96, 100, 113, 115–16, 138, 174
Lang, Cpl. John: 120–21, 158
La Prelle Creek: 12, 24, 43
Laramie City, Wyo. Terr.: 24
Laramie Peak: 44
Laramie River: 11, 20n.
Last Bull: 126
Lawrence, John: 23
Lawson, Lt. Joseph: 149–51, 174
Linn Draw: 154n.
Linn, George: 154n.
Little Big Horn, Battle of the: ix, 123n., 135, 160, 162, 189
Little Big Horn River: 32, 75n., 135
Little Big Man: 7
Little Dog: 22
Little Powder River: 126, 156, 180
Little Wolf: 125, 130
Lodgepole Creek (Clear Fork of Powder River): 18, 61, 91–92, 108, 112, 117, 136, 138–40, 148, 150, 154n., 161, 173–74, 176–77, 179–80, 187
Lugenbeel, Lt. Col. Pinkney: 172

Mackenzie, Gen. Ranald: 189
Maitland, Pvt. George H.: 103, 117–18, 174
Maple Tree (Box Elder, Tree, Brave Wolf, Blind Bull): 125, 129
Markland, Maj. Matthew: 13n.
Mason, Col. John Sanford: 155
McAuliff, Tom: 29

McCannon, Pvt. Michael I.: 107, 119–20, 132
Meade, Gen. George: 185
Meagher, Cpl. Thomas: 113
Mears, "Uncle" Dave: 30n., 31
Medicine Bow, Wyo. Terr.: 24
Medicine Wolf: 126
Middle Fork of Cheyenne River: 46
Miles, Gen. Nelson: 125n., 189
Milk River (White River), Battle of: 150n.
Mills, Capt. Anson: x, 5, 26, 28, 60, 67, 70, 72–73, 76–78, 81, 84–94, 96 100, 102–108, 111, 115–18, 120, 131, 138, 142, 144, 146, 157, 161–62, 164, 166, 169, 174–75, 177, 183–84, 186–87; official report, 215–20
Minneconjou Sioux: 17, 42, 100, 125, 128–29, 135, 156, 180
Missouri River: 6, 134n., 156
Monaz (Maryavale), Joe: 21
Montana Road: 43
Moore, Capt. Alexander: 26, 60, 67–70, 72–78, 81, 85n., 86–89, 91, 94–96, 100–103, 105–109, 114–17, 131–32, 137, 139, 146, 157, 160–62, 164–65, 169–71, 174–75, 177, 183–86; official reports, 225–26, 228–30
Moore, Cpl. (Company E, Third Cavalry): 52
Moore, Tom: 15, 19, 30
Moorehead, Mont.: xi
Moore's ridge: 86n.
Morton, Lt. Charles: 16–17, 44, 67–68, 73, 86–87, 93, 96–98, 103–104, 106, 114, 117, 133, 146, 154n., 162–63, 174, 184
Mosseau, Julia: 142n.
Mousseau, Magliorie A.: 72n., 142n.
"Mud March": 14n., 189
Munn, Asst. Surg. Curtis E.: 16, 27, 60, 93, 96, 103, 113, 116, 122, 155, 158, 174, 184
Murphy, Pvt. Jeremiah J.: 117–19, 174

Nation, Carrie: 30n.
Nebraska State Historical Society: 64–65
New York Herald: 171
New York *Tribune*: 29, 139

Index

Nickerson, Capt. Azor H.: 15, 40
Northern Cheyennes: vii, 4, 100, 129–30, 133, 156
North Fork of Cheyenne River: 46
North Laramie River: 11, 72n.
North Platte River: vii, 9, 12, 16, 18, 42, 159, 170
Noyes, Capt. Henry E.: x, 16, 26, 60, 67, 70, 72–73, 76, 78–81, 88–89, 93, 95–97, 103, 106–108, 110–17, 136–37, 142–43, 152–53, 160–70, 173–74, 176, 178, 184, 187; official report, 222–24

Oglala Sioux: 97, 100, 123, 125–30, 134–35
Old Bear: 124–25, 129
Omaha, Neb.: 15–16, 165–66, 169–71
Order of the Purple Heart: 158
Oregon Trail: vii, 9, 21
Otter Creek: 58–59, 61–62, 66, 70, 111, 126, 130–31, 138, 144–45, 148, 151, 173, 180

Pack guard: 35
Packmaster: 33, 39
Paul, Lt. Augustus C.: 78, 90, 106–107, 161, 184
Payne, Capt.: 183
Peale, Capt. James T.: 17, 19, 149, 174–75
Pearson, Lt. Daniel Crosby: 17, 149
"Phil Kearny massacre": 10
Phillips (Philips), Portugee (Portagese): 10, 16, 18
Phoenix (cowboy): 22–23
Phoenix (scout): 65
Pine Ridge Agency, Dakota Terr.: 58n., 64–65, 80n., 130
Piney Creek: 51
Pitt River Indians: 13
Platte Bridge Station, Battle of: vii
Pleasanton, Gen.: 185
Plenty Of Bears: 41
Pollock, O. C. C.: 121
Pope, Brig. Gen. John: 172
Pourrier, Baptiste (Big Bat): 41, 62, 72, 80, 159
Powder Face: 129–30
Powder River: vii, ix, x, 9, 17, 29, 46, 48–49, 59, 61, 65–66, 113, 126–29, 134–35, 138, 141, 147–52, 154, 156, 160, 162, 168n., 174, 177, 179, 190

Powder River country: 8, 40, 126
Prairie Dog Creek: 51–52
Provost, John: 41
Pumpkin Buttes: 44
Pumpkin Creek (Red Clay Creek): 56–57

Raab (Robb), Pvt. George: 78
Rawolle, Lt. William C.: 17, 67, 74–75, 85–89, 91, 94, 100–101, 106, 108, 111–12, 114–16, 119, 131–33, 136–37, 142, 146, 162, 174–75, 183, 187; official reports, 226–27, 227–28
Rawolle's bluff: 89, 120
Reade, Fanny: 13n.
Red Cloud: 6
Red Cloud Agency, Neb.: 4, 8, 15, 41, 72n., 100, 124, 126–27, 156
Red Dog: 6
Red Feather: 123n.
Reed, Tom: 41, 154
Reid, Whitlaw: 29
Reno, Maj. Marcus: 27–28
Reynolds, Capt., Twentieth Infantry, son of Colonel J. J. Reynolds: 25n.
Reynolds, Lt. U.S. Navy, son of Colonel J. J. Reynolds; 26n.
Reynolds, Lt. Bainbridge: 19, 26n., 101, 162, 171, 177, 184
Reynolds, Col. Joshua: ix, 12, 15–16, 19, 25–26, 29, 48, 60–61, 63, 65–70, 72–74, 76–78, 84, 87, 90–96, 99–104, 106–108, 110–11, 113, 115–17, 119–20, 129–30, 137–39, 141–53, 156–57, 159–67, 169–74, 176–80, 182–85, 190; official report, 203–14
Richard, Charles: 41
Richaud (Richard, Reshaw), John, Jr.: 22, 72n., 80n.
Richaud (Richard, Reshaw), John, Sr.: 72n., 80n., 142n., 148n.
Richaud (Richard, Reshaw), Louis: 4, 40–41, 65, 148, 151, 159, 174, 179–80
Richaud Creek: 80n.
Richaud's Bridge (Casper, Wyo.): 80n., 142n., 148n.
Ricker, Judge Eli S.: 64–65, 97, 128
Ridgely, Dr. John: 27, 50, 155
Roberts, Brig. Gen. Charles D.: x
Robinson, Lt. Frank U.: 17, 149
Robinson, Lt. William Wallace: 52, 149

Rocky Mountain News (Denver, Colorado): 10, 17, 162, 180
Rosebud, Battle of the: ix, 30n., 40n., 72n., 123n., 135, 150n., 158, 160, 162n., 170–72, 189
Rosebud Agency: 130
Rosebud Creek (River): x, 9, 32, 52, 135, 156, 189
Royall, Lt. Col. William B.: 170–71, 174
Ruggles, Maj. George: 172
Ruhlen, Lt.: 129, 132
Russell, Jack (Buckskin Jack): 41, 62, 65–66, 72, 142, 154

Sage Creek: 41, 44, 64
Sand Creek, Battle of: vii, ix
Sanders, Jack: 23
Sandoz, Mari: x, 130
Sans Arc Sioux: 135
Schneider, Pvt. George: 82, 103–104, 116, 119–20
Schubert, Pvt. William: 95
Server, F. E.: 145n.
Shangrau, John: 41, 64–65, 72, 97, 141–42
Shangrau, Louis: 41, 65, 142
Sheridan, Gen. Philip: 7–8, 13n., 24, 40n., 156, 159, 180, 188
Sheridan, Pvt. Thomas: 220
Sherman, Gen. William T.: 159, 185, 188
Shimmeno, Mitch: 41
Shore, Pvt. Alexander: 103
Short Bull: 125n., 130
Short Bull–Hinman interview: 130
Sibley, Lt. Frederick: 17, 75, 107, 184–85
"Sibley Scout": 75n.
Sims, Albert: 23n.
Sioux Indians: vii, viii, ix, 3–4, 7, 13–14, 16–17, 20, 22, 52, 58, 123–26, 128–30, 133–35, 152, 160, 187, 189–90
Sioux nation: 3, 6
Sitting Bull: 4, 7, 17, 58, 74, 100, 124, 126–27, 134, 156, 189
Skinner, Sgt. William: 168
Slater, Pvt. Benjamin F.: 95
Slavey, Cpl., Fourth Infantry: 95
Slaymaker, Kid: 23

Slim Buttes, Battle of: ix, 72n., 113, 172, 183, 189
Smith, Gen.: 41
Smith, Col. John E.: 167, 172
Sobrejalma: 37, 39
South Cheyenne River: 158
Southern Cheyennes: vii
Spotted Tail: 6
Spotted Tail Agency: 15, 156
Spotted Wolf: 126
Stagner, Speed: 41, 159
Standing Rock Agency: 134
Stands In Timber, John: 125n., 128, 133
Stanton, Maj. Thaddeus H.: 12, 15, 17, 28–29, 40–41, 48, 51, 62, 67, 72, 75, 85, 88, 97–98, 104, 111, 136, 139, 141, 143–44, 146, 157, 161–62, 164, 166, 169, 174–75, 177–79, 184, 186–87; official report, 224
Stanton, Capt. W. S.: 9, 16
Stevens, Dr. C. R.: 27, 60, 158
Strahorn, Carrie A.: 9n.
Strahorn, Robert A.: 9, 17–18, 40–41, 45, 53, 61, 72, 79, 83–84, 98, 113, 141, 152, 161–62, 174, 180, 184–85
Sturgis, Col.: 162
Sully, Brig. Gen. Alfred: 172
Summit Springs, Battle of: viii, 183
Swaim, Maj. David G.: 172, 183
Sweeney, Pvt. John: 220
Sykes, Col. George: 172

Tall Sioux: 129
Terry, Gen. Alfred: 8–9, 159
Teton Sioux: vii
Thayer, Gov. John M.: 7
"Thieves' Road": 3
Thompson Creek: 69–70, 74, 76, 78–79, 81, 85–87, 114, 132
Throstle, George: 22
Tillottson, E.: 23
Tongue River: x, 9, 16–17, 49, 52–53, 55–56, 126, 156, 189
Topajo: 39
Towne, Pvt. Phineas S.: 158
Townsend, Maj. Edwin F.: 167
Townsend, Lucy: 16
Twin: 126
Twin Springs: 17
Two Moon: 125, 130, 132

Index

Vane, Pvt. James: 227
Van Vliet, Col. Frederick: 15, 184
Virginia City, Mont. Terr.: 43

Wagon Box Fight: viii
Wagon Hound Creek: 17
Wallace, Frank "Pretty Boy": 22–23
Waln, Sim: 23
War Department: 3, 8, 67n., 159, 166
Warfield, Sgt. John C. A.: 86, 175, 186
Washita, Battle of the: viii, 183
Watt, Evan: 154n.
Whirlwind: 130
Whiskey Gulch: 17
White Antelope: 6

White Bull (Ice): 125, 128, 130
White River: 5–6
Wind River: 46, 157
Wolf Mountain, Battle of: ix. 123n., 189
Woodenleg: 128, 132
Woodenleg Creek: 49
Wounded Knee Creek, Battle of: 190
Wright, John: 45, 50, 155, 158

Yellow Eagle: 129
Yellowstone River: 8–9, 16–17, 55, 65, 156
Young, Mr.: 30
Young Man Afraid Of His Horses: 7

www.ingramcontent.com/pod-product-compliance
Lightning Source LLC
Chambersburg PA
CBHW020750160426
43192CB00006B/289